The Creation of Yugoslavia 1914–1918

This volume has been published with the support of the Center for Russian and East European Studies at the University of California, Los Angeles.

The Creation of Yugoslavia 1914–1918

edited by

Dimitrije Djordjevic

Clio Books

SANTA BARBARA, CALIFORNIA   OXFORD, ENGLAND

Library of Congress Cataloging in Publication Data

Main entry under title:

The Creation of Yugoslavia, 1914–1918.

   Papers presented at a conference held in Santa
Barbara, Calif., 1978, sponsored by University of
California, Santa Barbara and the Center for
Russian and East European Studies, UCLA.
   Includes index.
   1. Yugoslavia—History—Congresses.
2. European War, 1914–1918—Congresses.
I. Dordević, Dimitrije, 1922–   II. California.
University, Santa Barbara.   III. California.
University at Los Angeles. Center for Russian and
East European studies.

DR363.C7   949.7'01   79-22331
ISBN 0-87436-253-9

American Bibliographical Center—Clio Press
2040 Alameda Padre Serra, Riviera Campus
Santa Barbara, California 93103

Clio Press, Ltd.
Woodside House, Hinksey Hill
Oxford OX1 5BE, England

Manufactured in the United States of America

Contents

Preface

MORE THAN SIXTY years have passed since December 1, 1918, when the unification of Yugoslavs was proclaimed. During this period the country survived domestic shocks and European turmoils, among them the great war. The 1918 unification confirmed the interest of the Yugoslavs to live together in one state. However, this common life was stamped from the very beginning with differences resulting from the historical heritage, the situation created at the end of World War One, and domestic economic and political crises. The past was deeply rooted among the Yugoslavs and could not be easily erased. To a lesser or larger degree it is still evident in contemporary Yugoslavia. If we hope to understand the country in terms of evolution, we must turn to its source: the unification in 1918.

There is an abundance of scholarly works dealing with contemporary Yugoslavia. There is, however, no study in English dealing with the Yugoslav unification in 1918, which draws a line between the past and present, and serves as a departure line for studies of the new state. We hope that such an analysis can be found in the pages of this volume and that this analysis will be useful to students of modern nationalism, in general, of Yugoslav, Balkan, and East European affairs, in particular.

Yugoslav territorial integrity was secured by the 1918 unification. The unification also mirrored divergent national approaches to the structure and organization of the common state, stamped with heterogenous political philosophies of Yugoslavia's architects and the complex interests of the country's multinational society. It is generally agreed that the unification of Yugoslavs was a historical necessity which responded to the needs of the people. Evaluations of the various aspects and issues developed in this framework, however, differ. They are subject to national affiliations, various appraisals of factors involved in the formation of Yugoslavia, and experiences obtained *post factum* and their retrospective projections. Yugoslav historiography, domestic and foreign, is still dominated by answers to questions relating to how much the Serbian government pursued Yugoslavism during the war as an alternative to great-Serbianism, to what degree the Yugoslav Committee in London was the real representative of the Yugoslavs under the Habsburgs, to what extent the Yugoslavs themselves were ready in

1918 for unification, and whether Europe was willing to accept unification or was simply faced with the *fait accompli.*

Papers presented in this volume present the English-speaking reader with the results of modern scholarship in dealing with Yugoslavism, both domestic and foreign. They also throw more light on the major factors involved in the process of unification. The authors, distinguished experts in the field of Yugoslavism, summarize results of modern historiography and of their own research. There is, of course, some overlapping of subjects which was impossible to avoid when eleven papers deal with various aspects of a single topic. The papers also reflect controversies present in studies concerning Yugoslavism during the 1914–1918 war and its leading factors, especially the two poles: the Serbian government and the Yugoslav Committee in London. The papers were in general agreement, however, concerning the difficulties and obstacles which the process of unification encountered during the war. These problems were caused by the uncertainty of the war, by military defeats, by dependence on the Allies and their military and political strategy, and by internal frictions, misunderstandings, and confrontations among the protagonists of the unification, the Yugoslavs themselves.

The papers included in this volume were presented at a conference held in Santa Barbara, California, in 1978, on the occasion of the sixtieth anniversary of the Yugoslav state. The conference was sponsored by the University of California, Santa Barbara, the Center for Russian and East European Studies UCLA, and supported by the Council for the International Exchange of Scholars and the United Nations Association Chapter in Santa Barbara. The Center for Russian and East European Studies also offered financial support for the publication of this volume. Students at UCSB, doctoral candidates in Balkan Studies, devoted their time and enlivened the conference with their enthusiasm. Without the support of Dr. Henrik Birnbaum, Director of the UCLA center in 1978, and his successor, Dr. Bariša Krekić, and the Chairman of the History Department UCSB, Dr. Joachim Remak, the conference could not have taken place. Doctoral candidates Bernd Fischer and Steven Kaufman offered their valuable assistance in editing translations of Serbo-Croatian texts by Yugoslav authors. To all of them, the warmest gratitude from the editor.

Dimitrije Djordjevic

AUSTRIA

HUNGARY

AUSTRIA–HUNGARY

CROATIA–SLAVONIA

ROMANIA

DALMATIA

BOSNIA–
HERZEGOVINA

KINGDOM OF SERBIA

KINGDOM
OF
MONTENEGRO

BULGARIA

ALBANIA

borders
between States

post 1918 borders
of Yugoslavia

Austro-Hungarian lands

0   100   200 miles

GREECE

The Yugoslav lands immediately prior to World War 1

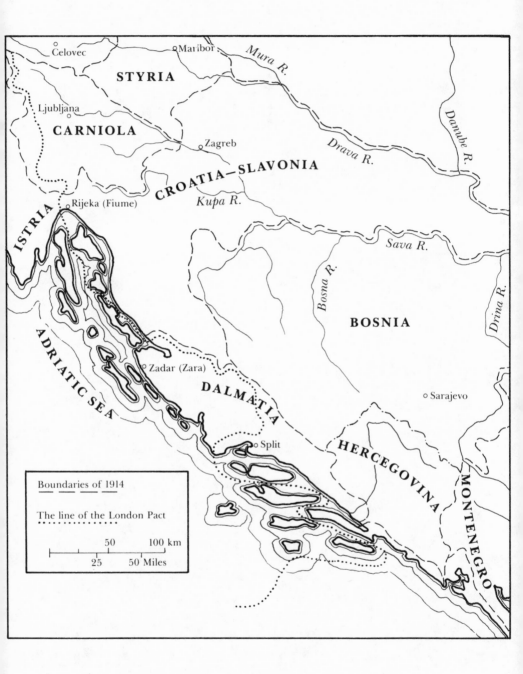

Italy's boundaries by the London Pact of April 26, 1915.

The Idea of Yugoslav Unity in the Nineteenth Century

Dimitrije Djordjevic

YUGOSLAVISM WAS AND still is a complex political and social phenomenon. Until 1918 the Yugoslavs lived divided and subjected to the rule of two empires and two independent states. They succumbed to influences coming from various civilizations, religions, alphabets and, above all, separate national renaissances. It is often told that Yugoslavism is an export commodity: if a Yugoslav is queried in Beograd or Zagreb about his nationality, he would answer that he is a Serb or a Croat; if the same man is asked the same question somewhere in Europe, his answer would be that he is a Yugoslav. However, the country has survived more than sixty years of stormy European history including a tragic fratricidal conflict during the last war.

COMPLEXITY OF YUGOSLAVISM

The complexity of Yugoslavism results from the sensitivity of nationalism, deeply rooted among the various Yugoslav peoples. Nationalism is emotional and rational; it originated from both the historical heritage and social and economic interests. In studying Yugoslavism, both past and modern, Yugoslav historians have shaded Yugoslavism with colors reflecting political trends of their epoch. Pre-war historiography emphasized the existence of one Yugoslav nation divided among three tribes, or clans (pleme).[1] Post-war historiography rejected the one-Yugoslav-nation theory, incompatible with the federal structure of modern Yugoslavia, and fostered the multinational structure of Yugoslavism. Pre-war historiography sacrificed the parts in favor of the whole; post-war historiography neglected the whole in the interest of the parts. The former produced an unreal history of Yugoslavia; the latter failed to emphasize the historical intercourse among the Yugoslavs.[2] The two volumes of the *History of Yugoslav Peoples,* published in 1953 and 1960, stopped at the threshold of nationalism in the nineteenth century.[3] Yugoslav historiansihave not agreed on what title to give to their history: *History of Yugoslavia, History of Yugoslav Peoples,* or *History of Yugoslav Nations and Nationalities.* In 1963 Soviet historians published a *History of Yugoslavia;*[4] the same title used recently by four prominent Serbian historians provoked a storm of criticism with an accent on political and national issues.[5]

Divided in the past and exposed to various foreign influences, the Yugoslavs inevitably had an uneven national development. The national emancipation moved from the periphery to the center of the Balkans and was stamped by the historical legacy of both Central European and Ottoman Balkan civilizations. The Yugoslavs clashed in the past among themselves, jeopardizing the idea of unity. Such a situation obviously created tremendous problems for the historian. It is almost impossible to register Serbo-Croatian frictions in Bosnia or Srem, Serbo-Albanian armed conflicts, Yugoslav-Hungarian confrontations, or Serbo-Macedonian disputes without hurting national sensitivities.[6]

Yugoslavism is emphasized today in the territorial framework established by the Yugoslav state in 1918. Macedonia, for example, is approached today through this framework, although the history of Macedonia belonged in the nineteenth century to the history of Bulgars and Greeks as well. For the same contemporary territorial-political criteria we include the northwestern parts of Yugoslavia in the Balkans. The Muslim nationality was only recently recognized in Yugoslavia. The question arises, however, as to its affiliation with the Islamic community in the Middle East. Practically, Yugoslavism demonstrated concentric and intermingled circles of national, social, economic and political specifics which complemented or hindered each other in the past, depending on the frame of time. The main difficulty is to find compromise between Yugoslavism and the separate developments of the Yugoslav nationalities. Related to this compromise, one must also decide whether Yugoslavism was an instrument of general Yugoslav or separate national (Serbian, Croation, Slovene, etc.) emancipation and integration. Was it a movement or a political maneuver, or was it, eventually, an expression of all these tendencies?

ORIGIN OF UNITY IDEA

Historians dealing with Yugoslavism agree that the idea of unity originated from the common ethnicity of the Yugoslavs. The development of nineteenth century linguistics, from Johan Gottfried von Herder to Frane Miklošić, found in its language the expression of the nation. The approach was supported by rationalist philosophies and romanticism in the first half of the nineteenth century. Yugoslav intellectuals espoused the theory of one Yugoslav nation, enlarging it to all the South Slavs, including the Bulgarians. Differences among them were only tribal or clannish. Some of these theories identified Serbs with Croats, but differentiated Bulgarians and Slovenians. Other distinguished Serbs as the most dynamic part of the Yugoslavs.[7]

Ethnicity supported the political necessity of the Yugoslavs to stick together in confronting obstacles which impeded their particular national emancipation on the fervent Balkan soil.[8] The ethnic mixture of Serbs and Croats in Bosnia, Hercegovina, parts of Croatia, Dalmatia and Srem made Yugoslavism even more indispensable in the era of national emancipation and frictions among developing nationalisms. Localism and regionalism had to be countered by national identity. Yugoslavism was opposed to the two multinational states which impeded the emancipation of Yugoslav nationalities. Polith Desančić, a Serbian politician in Southern Hungary, in the 1860's pointed to two processes taking place in Europe. Nations trapped in multinational states tended to break the existing framework and establish their own independent states. Nations divided among various states tended to remove political obstacles and unite. The name of the game was one nation—one state.[9] Stressing a multinational Yugoslav concept meant weakening the historical justification of the Yugoslav cause. The Yugoslav movement found supporters among intellectuals and young people. More theoreticians than practitioners, they were idealists and daydreamers. Only a daydreamer could have envisioned in the nineteenth century the dissolution of the Habsburg and Ottoman states, a precondition for the unification of the Yugoslavs. The idea of one Yugoslav nation appears in the Illyrian movement in Croatia in the 1830's, in Strossmayer's and Rački's Yugoslavism in the 1860's, as well as in the programs of the Yugoslav Youth at the beginning of the twentieth century.[10] This concept of unitarian Yugoslavism was also espoused by Serbian intellectuals at the beginning of the twentieth century.[11] The Yugoslav social-democrats in the Habsburg monarchy did the same by contrasting it with proletarian internationalism.[12] Stjepan Radić, the founder of the Croatian agrarian movement in the twentieth century, distinguished Yugoslavism in the Habsburg monarchy, based on the patriarchal rural community.[13] Unitarian Yugoslavism prevailed among intellectuals in the nineteenth century in their confrontation with the developing separate nationalisms.

Although it played a positive role in the process of Yugoslav unification, unitarian Yugoslavism proved erroneous when applied. Instead of making one nation, the Yugoslavs developed separate Yugoslav nationalities. Nationalism was essentially a democratic movement which enlarged the social basis of politics. Instead of homogenization, this enlargement introduced ethnic disunity. Problems of ethnicity and the role of a common language were familiar to the intelligentsia. The conservative, illiterate and generally xenophobic peasant, however, had no affinity for linguistic sophistication. Similar was the reaction of the growing middle class involved in a bitter competition for a limited market. Much more than to ethnicity, people responded to religious affiliations. Catholic, Orthodox and Muslim religions remained the dividing line between the Yugoslavs in the nineteenth century and stamped their separate national identifications. Milorad Ekmečić is correct in stating that applied in this patriarchal and agrarian Christian world of religious intolerance, the linguistic formula for unity, borrowed from intellectual circles in Europe, was not sufficiently realistic.[14] Instead of one Yugoslav nationalism, the Yugoslavs developed separate national renaissances which resulted, after a brief period of instinctive Slavism or South Slavism, into particular Serbian, Croatian, Slovenian, and much later, Macedonian or Montenegrin nationalisms. Although the Yugoslav idea could be temporarily and occasionally used for specific national integrations, as with the Croats, the inborn feeling of belonging to a separate nation prevailed. Social and economic developments during the century strengthened such feelings. The idea of Yugoslav unity originated among intellectuals primarily as a rational solution to specific national interests attainable through the unity of goals. Intended to symbolize a nationality, it formulated practically a national-political ideology. Ethnicity existed in this ideology, which offered a Yugoslav scope instead of some other, like Balkan or South Slav, but the separate national interest still prevailed. The difference between an inborn and emotional national feeling and a rationally acquired ideology is obvious. The inborn national affiliation is a part of human nature and cannot easily be changed. The ideology relies on the appraisal of national interests. It is flexible and subject to modifications. Both facets were present in nineteenth century Yugoslavism. The necessity for the Yugoslavs to join together in order to accomplish their separate national interests allowed Yugoslavism to survive and persist. Flexibility, characteristic for an ideology, caused ups and downs in its application and echoed in the deep and dangerous crises which often jeopardized the idea of unity.[15]

NATIONAL IDEOLOGIES

The study of the Yugoslav idea belongs to the study of national ideologies. Such movements were essentially social and political. They expressed trends created by the switch from feudal atomization to capitalistic economic integration. The integrated national society had to replace the earlier dispersed and disconnected social parts. Yugoslavism could play a double role in this process: either to support specific national integrations of various Yugoslav peoples or to appear at the end of separate national integrations, as a kind of super-national structure. According to some historians, "Yugoslavism played an integrating role only for the Croatian people. It did not influence the constitution of the Slovenian and Serbian peoples. For them Yugoslavism obtained its significance only when the process of their national integration was already over."[16]

Social structures among Yugoslavs varied greatly, thus offering a spectrum of interests expressed through their national emancipation. First of all, there were three large zones, each stamped with different social structures. These were the zones under the Habsburg monarchy, under the Ottoman empire and under the two developing independent states, Serbia and Montenegro. Under the Habsburgs there originated an aristocratic society of mostly foreign Central-European origin and based on the large landed estate, supported by the Catholic Church. The Ottoman empire throughout the century witnessed a confrontation between the Muslim landlord and the Christian serf, stamped by further deterioration of its economic and administrative system. Serbia received as a result of the 1804 revolution an agrarian society based on small peasant land ownership coupled with the emerging national middle class. Finally, Montenegro gradually introduced a state organization replacing its disintegrating tribal system. But these were only general frameworks for further distinctions which marked the development of each Yugoslav people, divided between these three zones and between themselves. The Serbian social structure encompassed the middle-class Serbian society in Southern Hungary, the patriarchal society in the Military Frontier, the serf in Bosnia and Hercegovina as well as the free peasant in Serbia. The Croatian society was even more differentiated. In Northern Croatia, a European estates-agrarian system existed, while an urban society of Italian-Mediterranean type prevailed in Dalmatia. In the Frontier (until 1883) a military organization survived, based on the enlarged family (the Zadruga). At the same time in Slovenia the growing German middle class hindered the development of the domestic bourgeoisie. The Muslim population was about fifty per cent of the Bosnian cities, while in Macedonia the old Balkan Çarsi survived, with Greeks, Vlachs, Turks, Jews and Armenians. In Montenegro the tribal cattle-breeder made up the bulk of the population. It is true that on the bottom of this social ladder stood the peasantry which comprises the overwhelming part of the Yugoslav population. It provided one common denominator in respect to the social structure. But modern nationalism and national integration did not originate among the peasantry. It resulted from the philosophy and activity of the upper social layers. These layers differed significantly among themselves in various parts of Yugoslav territories.[17]

The variety of social forms influenced not only the formation of Yugoslav ideology but national renaissances of separate Yugoslav peoples. It gave birth to localism and regionalism, and produced a spectrum of Yugoslav programs from cultural to political unification, as well as from Central European to Balkan solutions of the Yugoslav problem. This was particularly manifested among the two main factors of Yugoslavism, the Croats and the Serbs.

CROATION NATIONAL RENAISSANCE

Croatian national renaissance in the nineteenth century had to overcome regionalism manufactured by different social and political environments in Northern Croatia, Slovenia, the Frontier, Dalmatia and Bosnia and Hercegovina.[18] Influenced by the situation in the Habsburg monarchy, both Croatia and Slovenia produced a new national society which represented an amalgam of townspeople, emancipated peasants (after 1848), civil servants and the nouveaux riches which opposed the old aristocratic society of mostly German and Hungarian origin. The Dinaric Alps divided Dalmatia from Croatia, and so did political ties with Austria and Hungary, respectively. Croatian nationalism primarily emphasized a cultural renaissance which had to lay foundations for the social, economical and political unification of the Croatian people. One could establish a pattern in this evolution of national thought, starting from the use of the vernacular in literature and administration, and moving further towards cultural and territorial autonomy, in order to finally reach the goal of national independence.[19] The leadership of this movement was recruited mainly among the small nobility (in lieu of a developed middle class), townspeople and lesser clergy, but practically without the involvement of the peasantry, removed from politics by the absence of universal suffrage.[20] Faced with such socio-political divisions, the Croats delegated a threefold task to Yugoslavism: to help overcome Croatian national regionalism by offering a broad basis for national unification (The Triune Kingdom), to mobilize the process of Croatian integration into a single nation by obtaining the support of other South Slavs, and, finally, to stimulate the development of a national culture.[21] The movement was based upon Renaissance tradition, adapted to romanticism and encouraged by similar movements among the Poles and the Czechs. The Yugoslav ideology was the first expressed in the 1830's in the Illyrian movement in Croatia. The Illyrians preached the foundation of a general Yugoslav national culture, political freedom and national unification.[22] Some Croatian historians delineate "Slavic Illyrianism from political Croatism." Illyrians were Yugoslavs when preaching the cultural Yugoslavism, Croats when fostering the political unification of Croatia in the framework of the Habsburg monarchy.[23] It seems logical that Croatian interests proper would have an advantage over Yugoslavism, according to a Balkan peasant-saying that the shirt is closer to the body than is the coat. In fact, Illyrianism offered a spectrum of options to Croatian politics both in Yugoslav as well as in Croatian directions. Almost all later representatives of Croatian politics, from the Yugoslav-oriented Bishop Strossmayer to the exclusive Croatian nationalist Starčević, began their political activity among the Illyrians. One could say that the process of Croatian national integration was accomplished in the period from the 1830's to the 1860's. After reaching these primary objectives, the Croats no longer needed Yugoslavism for internal integrative purposes. It then became an instrument of "foreign relations," i.e., politics in the Zagreb-Vienna-Budapest triangle. These politics offered Croatia three possibilities: to go along with Hungary, to support Austria, or to foster domestic independent developments with two possible results, a proper Croatian solution, or a Yugoslav and larger emancipation, shouldered by all the Yugoslavs. Strossmayer's Yugoslavism in the 1860's and especially in the crisis of the reorganization of the Habsburg monarchy in 1867, was aimed at the unification of Croatian lands (The Triune Kingdom), the obtainment of support from all the Yugoslavs in confronting the Hungarians, and the placement of Croatia in the center of a presumed Yugoslav unit in a federalized Habsburg state.

SERBIAN INTEGRATION

The Serbian national integration somewhat differed from the Croatian in the sense that the Serbs did not need to use Yugoslavism in the process of their national integration. Like the Croats, they displayed a variety of social structures, although these structures were less developed and more tied to the patriarchal, rural community. Regionalism, although present, was less evident among the Serbs. This was due to specifics of the Ottoman rule which leveled the Serbian society, and to the ethnic movements of the Serbian peasant in colonizing parts of the Western and Northern Balkans. The Ottoman millet system equated ethnicity with religion. Islam never manifested proselytism in converting the infidel, which the Christians proved so often. The distinction between the ruling Muslim landlord and the subservient Christian Rayah imposed a community of goals and interest upon the subjected patriarchal village. The Serbian Church, which long survived the collapse of the Serbian medieval state, projected the idea of statehood deep into the centuries of Ottoman foreign rule.[24] The important factor in maintaining the awareness of national unity was the colonization process of the Serbs.[25] Colonists preserved ties among the dispersed Serbian settlers. Rooted in the conservative and patriarchal village, these ties worked against regionalism and helped maintain the memory of the "old country" and national-ethnic unity. Šumadia was settled by colonists coming from Hercegovina, Montenegro and Bosnia during the eighteenth century. The Serbian settlers in Southern Hungary maintained almost throughout the eighteenth century the mentality of emigrants, facing another civilization and longing to return back home. These settlers enlarged the area of the Štokavian dialect and of the popular folklore. Vuk Karadžić based the Serbian literary language on this dialect from Eastern Hercegovina. Ties were further encouraged by the geographic entity created by the Danube-Morava-Vardar valleys. Finally, the national renaissance originated from revolutionary

achievements of the Serbian peasant in Šumadija coupled with intellectual stimuli coming from the Serb town dweller in Southern Hungary.
Feelings of national integration were already manifested in the response which the 1804 Serbian uprising found among Serbs living in
Southern Hungary, Bosnia and Hercegovina and other Serbian settlements.[26] Further national integration was stimulated by the existence
of the Serbian state, developed after 1830, and performed in the
alliance between the primitive and growing middle class and the emancipated small land-holding peasantry, unique among the Yugoslavs.

In the Serbian national development there was no immediate need
for Yugoslavism. Therefore there is a tendency among modern historians to deny the existence of any Yugoslavism among the Serbs, who
from the beginning sought the accomplishment of a Pan-Serbian idea.
As all black and white approaches, such hypotheses are one sided. It is a
fact that Yugoslavism among the Serbs had a different evolution than
among the Croats which resulted from the specifics of their developments. Yugoslavism was incorporated into the Serbian political program later, after the accomplishment of Serbian national integration.
Like the Croats, the Serbs were aware of the difficulties facing their
national emancipation. Obstacles imposed the necessity to seek support. It could be best found in the ethnically similar neighborhood.
Serbian national integration could be achieved without Yugoslavism,
but Serbian political emancipation could not, due to the intermingling
of Serbs with Croats in Bosnia, Hercegovina, Dalmatia and parts of
Croatia. Yugoslavism became an instrument in gathering all the Serbs
and in confronting the legitimism of the two surrounding empires, the
Habsburg and the Ottoman. In fact it was Pan-Serbism that brought
Serbs to Yugoslavism. Contrary to Croatia, however, Yugoslavism was
not the only issue for Serbia. Parallel to it, there was a South Slav,
namely Bulgarian, issue. During the nineteenth century up to 1878,
Serbia faced two options: the Western Balkan and the Eastern Balkan
programs. The first led Serbia into conflict with the Habsburg monarchy, the second with the Ottoman empire. The former offered prospects only after the 1848 crisis exploded in Central Europe; the latter
responded to Serbian historical experiences in forming the Serbian
state to the detriment of the Ottomans. Foreign and domestic political
developments determined which option, the Western or Eastern,
commanded the most interest at any given time. The weak Serbian
state in a stage of early development expressed both defensive and
aggressive tendencies. Defensiveness resulted from the continental
isolation of Serbia, sandwiched between two great powers, both opposed to her further development. The primitive stage of Serbian
political, economic and cultural existence could but augment its fears
for continued existence. The offensiveness mirrored the aggressive
nationalism of a young society in the full process of growth. Political

realities oriented Serbia towards the Eastern Balkan Ottoman option, in breaking the surrounding chain at its weakest part. Two interests appeared: the core interest and the pan-national interest. The core interest of Serbian nationalism envisaged the unification of Serbia with Montenegro and the annexation of Bosnia and Hercegovina, thus accomplishing the unification of the majority of the Serbs. The pan-national interest went further, in attempts of Serbia to play the role of a Balkan South-Slavic Piedmont, copying the contagious Italian example. Until 1878 the main emphasis of Pan-Serbian dreams was not directed towards Yugoslavism, but towards Bulgaria and the unrealistic restoration of the medieval Balkan empire. The issues of the Eastern Crisis in 1878, the formation of the Bulgarian state and the assignment of Bosnia and Hercegovina to Austria-Hungary marked the end of such plans. Serbia was pushed deeper in the Balkans, towards the South, in the direction of Macedonia and the Aegean Sea. This directional change opened the rivalry with Bulgaria and Greece. The temporary truce between Serbia and the Habsburg monarchy at the end of the century, however, was incompatible with Serbian nationalism and only suited the Austro-Hungarian policy of status quo in the Balkans. Serbian politics had to turn towards the Western Balkans in accordance with the Serbian national self-determination process. It was then that Serbia faced Yugoslavism. This became apparent especially when the struggle on the two fronts was successfully won in the South during the Balkan wars of 1912–13. The switch resulted in the bitter worsening of relations with the Habsburg monarchy and the armed clash in 1914.

Although the Yugoslav option was finally introduced to Serbia by the development of the historical intercourse in the Balkans, the Eastern and Balkan option prevailed in Serbian politics throughout the nineteenth century. It was based on a centuries-long common life in the Ottoman empire and the resulting religious and cultural affinities. The Western, Yugoslav option was in the meantime almost neglected in Serbia. First, the Habsburg monarchy was a much stronger opponent than the Ottoman state. Second, the Western Yugoslav option meant for Serbia an encounter with an essentially Catholic-Latin and German civilization. The confrontation with a similar and developing Croatian nationalism could only but alienate Serbian nationalism and cool the fires of Yugoslavism. The Serbs were reluctant from the very beginning to replace their name with the Illyrian one suggested by the Croats. The Pan-Serbian national program from 1844 brushed aside the Western Yugoslavs and placed the accent on Balkan emancipation, including the Bulgarians.

As in Croatia, the promoters of Yugoslavism in Serbia were intellectuals, mostly university professors. At the beginning of the twentieth century they discovered Yugoslavism through their scholarly work. Geological, ethnographic, linguistic and historical studies of the Yugoslav area enlarged their political horizons.[27] In a developing country, as Serbia was in the nineteenth century, scholars enjoyed a great prestige in the public. These scholars introduced the principle of Yugoslav unification in the political program of the Independent Radical Party, the second strongest political party in Serbia. Naturally, their Yugoslavism was greatly colored by their Serbian nationalism,[28] but they did not differentiate between interests of the Serbian state and of Yugoslavs in general. According to them Serbia was called to play the leading role in the struggle for the unification as a father or older brother would do. This paternalistic role of Serbia, according to these intellectuals, originated from independent Serbian statehood achieved in the nineteenth century, and from geo-politics which set the Serbs in the middle of the Yugoslavs, placed them on the Danube-Morava-Vardar transverse line and stretched them from the Danube to the central Dinaric Alps, thus making them the bulk of the Yugoslav population. For the intellectuals, as well as for the revolutionary youth, Serbia symbolized the struggle for Yugoslav unification in the decade preceding World War One.

YUGOSLAVIAN POLITICAL OBJECTIVES

Various political frameworks to which the Yugoslavs were subjected determined their political objectives. The centralized and bureaucratized Habsburg system enabled political activity but prevented revolutionary explosions in general. The decline of the Ottoman administration in the Balkans stimulated revolutionary peasant and national outbursts. In general terms the Serbian movement was directed against a foreign state, trying to destroy the existing framework of foreign rule. The Croatian and Slovenian movement aimed at reforming the establishment in order to obtain national recognition. Further on, different situations resulted in the formation of different political philosophies. The military monarchy, which resulted from the Serbian 1804 Revolution, developed the concept of a centralized state establishment. This concept was easily applied in the ethnically homogeneous and rather uniform Serbian peasant society. It became the instrument for further accomplishments of national independence. In the multinational structure of the Habsburg monarchy, federalism was the only token which could enable national self-recognition. Croatian self-determination espoused federalism from 1848 till the end of the Habsburg monarchy as its political creed. In spite of the frictions existing in Serbia between the state and the village, and between the city and the village, the peasant faced his *own* state establishment, whatever its faults may be. In Croatia the centers of power were foreign, thus creating a tradition of resentment and rejection of imposed political and economic might. Nineteenth century political intercourse pushed the Serbian peasant towards the state, the Croatian and the Slovenian peasant away from it. Due to all these and other reasons, Pan-Serbism did not necessarily have to reject Yugoslavism for its own accom-plishments. On the contrary, it could stamp Yugoslavism with a pan-Serb preponderance. On the other hand, Pan-Croatism was essentially the rejection of Yugoslavism, and had to become a separatist move-ment.

Yugoslav political emancipation affected both the Habsburg and Ottoman empires. Thus, the Yugoslav emancipation became a Central European and a Balkan problem. Theoretically the Yugoslav unifica-tion could have been achieved either in the framework of the Habsburg monarchy (federalistic or trialistic solutions) with the accent on its Central-European component. Or it could have been accomplished around the growing Serbian and Montenegrin states, as an expression of the general Balkan national emancipation, presuming the dissolu-tion of both the Habsburg and the Ottoman states. Rivalries among European powers whose interests were intermingled in the Eastern Question could only but aggravate Yugoslav issues. To the Habsburg monarchy Yugoslavism was a threat to internal integrity and foreign stability, as a possible instrument of Russian Balkan policy. Conversely, imperial Russia never had a clear affinity for an Orthodox-Catholic, Serbo-Croatian-Slovenian combination which could involve Central Europe in Balkan affairs. It was natural to expect, under the circum-stances, that the Croatian national movement would primarily strive for the political unification of Croatian lands into one Yugoslav unit *within* the framework of the Habsburg monarchy. Bishop Strossmayer attempted to find a Yugoslav solution *inside* a federalized Habsburg monarchy. Only during a brief period after the 1866 failure of the federalistic concepts did the Bishop approach a solution of Yugo-slavism outside of the monarchy, by establishing a federal state with Serbia.[29] He was suspicious of the cultural and political capacities of the Orthodox-Ottoman Serbs in pursuing a Yugoslav program and doubted Serbia's ability to endure. The collapse of federalist concepts in Austria-Hungary caused by the switch from centralism to dualism in 1867 heavily damaged the Yugoslav cause. On the other hand, the Serbs sought a solution of the Yugoslav problem *outside* of the Habsburg monarchy. They were suspicious of everything coming from an alien Central-European civilization. Even the Serbs from the Habsburg monarchy received in Serbia the pejorative name of Swabians (*nemač-kari*). Strossmayer's Yugoslavism was accepted with reservations due to the Catholic affiliation of the Bishop. The Serbo-Croatian dispute over the question to whom Bosnia and Hercegovina belonged reflected, after their occupation by Austria-Hungary in 1878, the controversies expressed in Yugoslavism. The inclusion of the two provinces into Croatia would have strengthened the Croatian and Yugoslav situation in the Habsburg monarchy. An autonomous status for Bosnia and Hercegovina, cherished by the Serbs, would have raised hopes for an

eventual Serbian annexation of the two provinces in the future, resulting in a Serbian-Balkan solution for Yugoslavism.[30] Mutual distrust and
the lack of knowledge about each other's aspirations and mentalities
greatly affected the Yugoslav idea of unity.

Yugoslav orientation was gradually changed at the beginning of
the twentieth century. This was partially due to the further national
development of the Yugoslavs, partially to failures of their separate
endeavors. The growing Serbo-Bulgarian rivalry in Macedonia threatened to block Serbian southward expansion. The Hungarian movement for independence jeopardized the dualistic structure of the
Habsburg monarchy and stimulated similar movements among other
nationalities. A new young generation of Yugoslavs, both Serbs and
Croats and Slovenes, appeared, who introduced more tolerant attitudes in regard to the exaggerated nationalism. The 1905 Croato-
Serbian coalition fostered the idea of Yugoslav cooperation.[31] Serbia
introduced after 1903 a dynamic and aggressive national policy in
which Belgrade became the center of Yugoslav manifestations. Again,
this policy was not a straight-line development and suffered such crises
as the annexation of Bosnia and Hercegovina in 1908. But at least the
Yugoslav rapprochement attempted to pave the way and prepare the
spirits for the unification of 1918. Both movements, inside and outside
of the Habsburg monarchy, seriously jeopardized the very existence of
the Danubian state. The result of the Serbian victories in 1912–1913
Balkan Wars was the accentuation of the conflict with Austro-Hungary.
Placed in a large historical context, the small undeveloped Serbian state
could not threaten the Habsburg monarchy. The danger came from
the process of national emancipation which was gaining ground in the
Balkans and of which Serbia was one of the representatives. Both
Pan-Serbism and Yugoslavism were involved in the fatal conflict which
served as a cause for the outbreak of the war in 1914.

THE DEVELOPMENT OF the Yugoslav idea in the nineteenth century
was stamped by two factors: the unifying and the dividing one. The
unifying component resulted mainly from the fear of confronting the
obstacles which impeded national emancipation. Whenever the Yugoslavs were threatened from abroad they collaborated among themselves. Such was the situation in 1848, in the 1860's, at the beginning of
the twentieth century and during World War One. The same reaction
to external pressures is present in the most recent days. The dividing
factor was expressed in the general characteristics of modern
nationalism: in exclusive national ambitions, economic competition, in
the frictions inherent in defining what is "mine" and what is "theirs,"
with reference to the past and justifications in history.

Historians are able to study the origins and developments of

Yugoslavism through the activity of its promoters. They were either distinguished intellectuals or fervent youngsters. It is not known how deep their philosophy penetrated into the large segments of the population, especially the patriarchal village community. As a consequence, our appraisal of Yugoslavism is centered on the intellectual and social elite, which still comprised the minority of the entire population. The peasant could instinctively feel the Yugoslav ethnicity, or share common interests with other Yugoslav peasants, but he was essentially much more interested in practical and local daily issues than in remote theories of a large national unity which, to say the least, surpassed his knowledge in geography. The instinctive feeling of national unity, if there was any, cannot be defined as political program for action. Obviously Yugoslavism lacked deeper roots in the past.

The intellectuals and the social elite tried to find in Yugoslavism either an instrument of national integration or an answer to domestic localism and dispersion of national energies. But the theory was one thing, its application another. More time was necessary to find the right way in applying Yugoslavism to practice, especially in approaching the Yugoslavs among themselves, teaching them more about each other and overcoming the legacy of a divided history. Banned from diplomatic language because of the international situation, exposed to the growth of separate nationalisms reflecting the modernization of various Yugoslav national societies, Yugoslavism was restricted to private writings, individual endeavors or terrorist activity of a revolutionary youth. In such circumstances the idea of unity could not penetrate deeply into the body of the Yugoslavs. The World War suddenly brought to the surface the question of the Yugoslav unification, a question which the Yugoslavs themselves had not yet defined in practical political terms. Serbia brought to the new common state her centralistic historic experiences. Croatia fostered her decentralistic and federalistic concepts inherited in the struggle for recognition in the Habsburg monarchy. Both carried into the new state mutual distrust for a Catholic-German and Orthodox-Ottoman civilization, respectively. When the Habsburg monarchy collapsed as the consequence of the war, the unification of the Yugoslavs was suddenly presented not as an intellectual theory of a social elite, but as a fact of practical politics. Politics which did not allow any delay. There is no question that common ethnicity and language laid the foundation for the program of unification in 1918, but the question still remains: was the 1918 unification unanimous and generally accepted by all the Yugoslavs at that moment, or was it the result of the brilliant performance of Serbia and her army in the war and the war itself? Was unification prompted by the fear of the Yugoslavs that they could not safeguard their national territory from foreign aspirations (the London Pact), or endeavors to maintain the social order threatened by a developing revolution in the territories of the former Habsburg monarchy? Yugoslavia in 1918 resulted from the application of the principle of national self-determination, but also from interests expressed in the given historical moment. Interests which made up the origins and development of the Yugoslav idea in the nineteenth century.

Notes

1. See Viktor Novak, "Jugoslavenska istoriografija izmedju dva svetska rata i njeni savremeni zadaci," *Istoriski Časopis*, Beograd 1949, I, sv. 1–2, 3–21. The most characteristic for the "unitarian" approach is *Istorija Jugoslavije*, by Vladimir Ćorović (Beograd, 1933).

2. For example, *Povijest hrvatskog naroda 1860–1914*, by Jaroslav Šidak, Mirjana Gross, Igor Karaman, Dragovan Šepić (published by Školska knjiga, Zagreb 1968), neglects almost completely the existence of the Serbs in Croatia. The authors, distinguished historians, recognize the fact that "Serbian history in Croatia is not yet approached and studied." See: Introduction, p. XI.

3. Modern trends in Yugoslav historiography can be best ascertained in the three volumes published on the occasion of international congresses of historians: *Ten Years of Yugoslav Historiography 1945–1955*, Beograd 1955; *Historiographie Yugoslave 1955–1965*, Beograd 1965; *The Historiography of Yugoslavia 1965–1975*, Belgrade 1975.

4. *Istoria Jugoslavii v dvuh tomah*, Akademia Nauk SSSR, Moskva 1963.

5. Vladimir Dedijer, Ivan Božić, Sima Ćirković, Milorad Ekmečić, *History of Yugoslavia*, Belgrade 1974, p. 752. For the critics see: Milorad Ekmečić, "Odgovor na neke kritike Istorije Jugoslavije (XIX vek)," *Jugoslovenski istorijski časopis*, 1974, 1–2, 217–281.

6. On the occasion of the 50th anniversary of the formation of Yugoslavia, in 1968, long discussions took place concerning commemoration of the event. Finally a solution was found in having a symposium in Zagreb under the title: "On the Occasion of the 50-ieth Anniversary of the Collapse of the Habsburg Monarchy and the Formation of Yugoslavia."

7. Mirjana Gross, "Zur Frage der Jugoslavischen Ideologie bei den Croaten," in: *Die Donaumonarchie und die Südslawische Frage*, Hrgsb. A. Wandruszka, R. Plaschka, A. Drabek, Wien 1978, p. 34.

8. Vaso Čubrilović, "Istorijski osnovi postanku Jugoslavije 1918," in *Naučni skup u povodu 50 godišnjice raspada Austro-Ugarske monarhije i stvaranja jugoslovenske države*, Jugoslovenska akademija znanosti i umjetnosti, Zagreb 1969, p. 68.

9. Dr. Polith, *Die orientalische Frage und ihre organische Lösung*. Wien 1862. See also: Vaso Čubrilović, *Istorija političke misli u Srbiji XIX veka*, Beograd, Prosveta, 1958, p. 258.

10. In the ideas of Franjo Rački prevailed also a Christian concept of Yugoslav unity. See Mirjana Gross, "Ideja Jugoslovjenstva Franje Račkoga u razdoblje njezine formulacije 1860–1862," in: *Historijski Zbornik*, XXIX–XXX, 1976–7, 332.

11. One of them, professor and statesman Milovan Milovanović, wrote in 1895: "The Serbs and Croats are . . . one and the same nation" (*Srbi i Hrvati*, Beograd 1895, 3). Jovan Skerlić suggested the acceptance of Latin alphabet in Serbia and of the ekavian dialect in Croatia. Jovan Cvijić saw the unity in the common language and the patriarchal culture (Vaso Čubrilović, "Jovan Cvijić i stvaranje Jugoslavije," in: *Jugoslovenski narodi pred Prvi svetski rat*, Srpska akadamija nauka i umetnosti, Beograd 1967, 990).

12. The social-democratic conference in Ljubljana in 1909 concluded that "the Serbs, Croats, Slovenes and Bulgarians are not separate nations, but only elements of one unique nation whose unification can be achieved only through the cultural and political activity of the social-democrats," Vlado Strugar, "Jugoslovenska Socijaldemokratija o ujedinjenju svojih naroda," in: *Naučni skup u povodu 50-godišnjice raspada Austro-Ugarske monarhije i stvaranja jugoslovenske drzave*, Zagreb 1969, 231.

13. Mirjana Gross, "Zur Frage der jugoslavischen Ideologie bei den Croaten," 35–6.

14. *History of Yugoslavia* (ed. by Vl. Dedijer *et al.*), 294–5, 306–307.

15. Dimitrije Djordjevic, "Yugoslavism: Some Aspects and Comments," in: *South Eastern Europe*, 1, 2, 1972, 192–3.

16. Mirjana Gross, "Ideja Jugoslovjenstva Franje Račkoga," 331. See also Jaroslav Šidak, "Studije iz hrvatske povijesti XIX stoljeća," Ed. Institut za hrvatsku povijest Sveučilišta u Zagrebu, *Rasprave i članci* 2, Zagreb 1973.

17. See: *History of Yugoslavia*, Chapter 27: "Profiles of Societies in the Second Half of the Nineteenth Century," 357–367, also: Mirjana Gross, "Social Structure and National Movements Among the Yugoslav Peoples on the Eve of the First World War," in: *Slavic Review*, December 1977, 628–643.

18. Most historians agree upon this. See: Mirjana Gross, "Social Structure and National Movements," 628–629, *History of Yugoslavia*, 300; Vaso Čubrilović, "Istorijski osnovi postanku Jugoslavije," 89.

19. See: Charles Jelavich, "The Croatian Problem in the Habsburg Empire in the Nineteenth Century," *Austrian History Yearbook* III, 2, 1967, 83–115; Bogdan Krizman, "The Croatians in the Habsburg Monarchy in the Nineteenth Century," *same revue*, 116–158. For the Slovenians see Fran Zwitter, "The Slovenes and the Habsburg Monarchy," *same revue*, 159–188.

20. Universal male suffrage was introduced only in Austria in 1907.

21. Mirjana Gross, "Zur Frage der Yugoslawischen Ideologie bei den Croaten," 22–23.

22. The best studies of the Illyrian movement are: Ellinor Murray Despalatović, *Ljudevit Gaj and the Illyrian Movement*, East European Monographs, 12, New York-London, 1975; Wayne Vucinich, "Croatian Illyrism: Its Background and Genesis," in: Stanley B. Winters and Joseph Held eds., *Intellectual and Social Developments in the Habsburg Empire from Maria Theresa to World War I*, Boulder 1975, 55–113; Jaroslav Šidak,

"Hrvatski narodni preporod—Ideje i Problemi," *Zbornik Studije iz hrvatske povijesti XIX stoljeća,* Zagreb 1973.

23. Jaroslav Šidak, "Jugoslovenski ideja u hrvatskoj politici do prvog svjetskog rata," *Enciklopedija Moderna,* 3–4, 1967, 10. Some historians, like Milorad Ekmečić, see in this dualism only the difference between the closest and more remote goals which responded to the realistic approach to the situation in Croatia, Ekemečić, "Odgovor na neke kritike," 237.

24. Čubrilović, *Istorija političke misli u Srbiji XIX veka,* Prosveta, Beograd 1958, 23–28.

25. The first to point to the importance of migrations for the national unity of the Serbs was the geographer Jovan Cvijić in *Balkansko Poluostrvo i južnoslovenske zemlje,* Zavod za izdavanje udžbenika SR Srbije, Beograd 1966, 189. V. Čubrilović developed this theory further: "The awareness about the ethnic and cultural connection of the country with the neighboring Yugoslav lands and peoples which remained in the memory of the colonists, developed into the general consciousness of the people," creating the consciousness of the Serbian state. V. Čubrilović, "Jovan Cvijić i stvaranje Jugoslavije," 980.

26. Dimitrije Djordjevic, *Revolutions nationales des peuples balkaniques 1804–1914,* Ed. Institut d'Histoire, Beograd 1965, 28–31.

27. In this period Serbia produced such first-rate scholars as the geologist Jovan Žujović, the botanist Nedeljko Kašanin, the linguists Ljuba Stojanović and Aleksandar Belić, the lawyer Slobodan Jovanović, the historian Stojan Novaković, the literary critics Bogdan and Pavle Popović and Jovan Skerlić as well as the geographer Jovan Cvijić. About their role in Serbian political life see Vaso Čubrilović, "Jovan Cvijić i stvaranje Jugoslavije," p. 967 and "Stojan Novaković," *Spomenica posvećena 50-godišnjici smrti Stojana Novakovića,* SANU, Beograd 1967, 11–22. Also: Slobodan Javanović, *Jedan prilog za proučavanje srpskog nacionalnog karaktera,* Vinzor, Kanada 1964.

28. Upon Serbia's procurement in 1912 of an outlet to the Adriatic Sea, Jovan Cvijić justified the annexation of a part of Albania as an "anti-ethnographic necessity," Joven Cvijić, "Izlazak Srbije na Jadransko more," in: *Glasnik Srpskog geografskog društva,* God, 2, sv. 2, Beograd 1913.

29. Vasilije Krestić, "Jugoslovenski politika Josipa Jurja Strosmajera," *Istorijski Glasnik,* I, 1969, 9–28; see also: *ibid, Hrvatsko-ugarska Nagodba 1868 godine,* SANU, Posebna izdanja, Beograd 1969, 344–366. The project for a joint federal Yugoslav state is published in Vojislav Vučković, *Politička akcija Srbije u južnoslovenskim zemljama Habsburške monarhije 1859–1874,* Beograd 1965, Doc. 144, p. 237–281.

30. Dimitrije Djordjević, "The Serbs as an Integrating and Disintegrating Factor," *Austrian History Yearbook,* III, 2, 1967, 71; Wayne Vucinich, "The Serbs in Austria-Hungary," *same review,* 27–34.

31. Mirjana Gross, *Vladavina hrvatsko-srpske koalicije 1906–1917,* ed. by Institut društvenih nauka, Beograd 1960; Dimitrije Djordjević, "Tentatives de collaboration serbo-hongroise en 1906," *Acta Iugoslaviae historica,* 1, 1970, 117–143.

Serbian War Aims

Milorad Ekmečić

IT HAS BECOME a rule in studies concerning World War One to emphasize "war aims as weapons of war."[1] During the war, weaponry was adapted to new needs, but the fact remained that among all the applied instruments of war, war aims changed the least of all. Only in moments when victory seemed blurred did Serbia's war aims differ from trends extolled at the beginning of the conflict. In these moments ideals gave way to routine politics, in order to save what could be saved. Thus, these two phenomena cannot be identified. War aims, and the politics connected with them, resulted from a continuity originating from a national ideology formed before 1914 and have a clear, evolving continuity. Routine politics had no continuity at all and was adapted to the outcome of military and political conflicts during the war itself. This occurred with Serbia during the critical period on the front in November 1914 when the Austro-Hungarian military offensive antici-pated a Serbian defeat and when Serbian headquarters asked the government to seek peace[2] by initiating a policy of compromise with Austria-Hungary. Still, one must be careful in deriving conclusions, due to the two factors involved: 1. The possibility of the army creating its own war aims, and 2. that a radical swing from previously established principles could also figure as a policy of blackmail towards the Allies and their demands for territorial concessions to the Bulgarians in Macedonia.

Manifold factors enter into the research of the policy of war aims: the general historical interest and the direct interest of ruling groups in one state; the continuation of a natural process in the development of politics and the level of development of national ideology, as well as the possibility of realizing the anticipated political concepts. The final picture of war aims becomes clear through the encounter with the historical evolution of national ideology and the direct interest of governing groups in a state.

The widely accepted but false assumption that the war would be short caused Serbian war aims, from the very beginning of the war in 1914, to be formulated in their final form. Serbian military science predicted that "future war will not last more than 2–3 months."[3] Due to

this conviction the formulation of Serbian war aims had a declarative
character. The battle of Kolubara in December 1914, where a Serbian
victory was anticipated, was emphasized as *the* decisive battle of the
entire war. The Niš Declaration issued on December 7, 1914, in which
the world was informed of Serbia's determination to fight for the
creation of a unified Yugoslav State, coincided with the offensive
undertaken in the Kolubara battle. The anticipation of an early victory
by the Allies and their pressure to yield to the demands of Bulgaria and
Italy determined the attitude of Serbian diplomacy. A search for the
moment to declare war aims characterized in its entirety Serbian diplomatic activity at that time. Very little was done to materialize or
organize such activity. It is also characteristic that the movement towards the formation of a Yugoslav Committee and the organization of
groups of intellectuals to be sent abroad did not start during the initial
months of the war, but only after the strategic concepts of a "short war"
proved erroneous. The estimates in Russian military circles about
Russia's incapacity to wage a war on two fronts and the idea that the
only promising attack was to be in the direction of Berlin[4] also had
major political consequences in Serbia. These considerations influenced Serbia more than any other country in the war, because they
presumed that Serbia would yield to the demands of Italy in Dalmatia
and Albania, and of Bulgaria in Macedonia. Serbia in 1914 was not
diplomatically prepared for such realities.

ATTEMPT TO FORMULATE NATURAL TRENDS

One of the basic characteristics of the policy of war aims was the
conspicuous attempt to formulate natural trends of the Serbian and
Yugoslav people expressed through a long historical process originating in the national renaissance at the end of the 18th and the beginning
of the 19th century. The fundamental consideration is that these
processes were not yet accomplished and that they disposed, in the
Yugoslav area, with remarkable political forces. The day following the
outbreak of the war, the Regent Alexander proclaimed that the major
goal of the war was to be a final settlement with Austria-Hungary, due
to her historical incapacity to solve the Yugoslav question.[5] At the same
time the Serbian prime minister Nikola Pašić drew the frontiers of the
future state on the Segedin-Maribor-Klagenfurt line.[6] At the end of
August 1914, when a study group of scholars was formed to determine
war aims, their program encompassed a Yugoslav State with Croatia,
Slovenia, Bosnia and Hercegovina, Vojvodina and Dalmatia, and later
Bulgaria as well.[7] The opening line of the circular-note of September 4,
1914,[8] stressed that such a state was "one, ethnic and economic, region
with a compact mass of one (*jednoplemeni*) people." On more than one
occasion the Serbian government acknowledged to the Allies its goal to
form a unique Yugoslav State.

In an effort to formulate war aims, and obviously afraid that the army might do so without its control, the government assembled a group of scholars in Nish with the task of elaborating and documenting the idea of a future, common state. Death prevented Jovan Skerlić, the leading intellectual of his time, from participating in this activity, although his ideas were constantly present and in many respects remained leading ideas throughout the war. At the beginning, the task of this group was to write scholarly and popular treatises about the Yugoslav question. Only later were its members divided and sent on political missions to various European countries and the United States. Ivan Meštrović, the Croatian sculptor, who traveled first to Italy and then London, was close to this group. Of all Yugoslav intellectuals he undoubtedly was the best known.

The main figure in coordinating the activity of this group in Nish was the geographer and anthropologist Jovan Cvijić. Others in the group included the doyen of Yugoslav historians Stojan Novaković and the linguist Aleksandar Belić. Jovan Cvijić first published the brochure "Unity and psychological types of the Dinaric South Slav,"[9] which he wrote at Pašić's request in November 1914. His thesis was that "due to its geographical position, as well as ethnic composition, Serbia was predestined to bind or link Western and Eastern Yugoslav lands and tribes." Serbians inhabited a part of the mountainous Dinaric zone which spreads from Stiria to the Albanian range (Prokletije). Being a geographer, Cvijić placed the accent on the geograpic unity of Yugoslav territories, stressing that the zone "had through geological times the same historical development, being morphologically unique." Here he presented basic ideas elaborated later in his large study *The Balkan Peninsula*. This work was at first published in French,[10] based upon a series of lectures Cvijić gave at the Paris Sorbonne. In this book Cvijić explained the concept of South Slav ethnic unity in which, despite cultural differences, an ethnic entity exists. The transition from Slovenes to Croats, from Croats to Serbs, as well as from Serbs to Bulgars, is smooth. From village to village the transition is not even conspicuous. Taken as a whole, however, one can realize new and different qualities.

Cvijić based his ideas about the ethnic unity of the South Slavs on years of researching the origins of the population in the Eastern and Central parts of contemporary Yugoslavia. The research was done by a group of scholars from the Serbian Academy of Sciences. Cvijić contended that the population in the *stokavian* region was formed by migrations originating in Hercegovina, Montenegro, Kosovo and Northern Albania, ultimately resulting in the formation of the Serbian medieval state, which was subsequently crushed by the Ottoman invasion. Later shepherd migrations, following herds, which Cvijić calls methanastazic movements, changed settlements and created a new ethnic picture in this region, totally different from that which had existed before the Ottoman intrusion into Yugoslav lands. This area is the main connecting link which binds together the Western and Eastern parts of the South Slavs from the center. Historically, it was predestined to make up the central and fundamental cornerstone of the future state.

Cvijić's ideas were complemented by the linguistic and literary aspects of Aleksandar Belić's study "Serbia and the South Slav question."[11] In early history all Serbo-Croatian dialects, including Slovenian, were united linguistically. They were separated later but still represent a mutually dependent entity.

The weak point in Cvijić's and Belić's thinking was not the presentation of ethnic unity between Serbs and Croats. An inquiry which the Srpski Književni Glasnik undertook before the 1914 war showed that most of the leading Serbo-Croatian intellectuals saw the necessity of creating a unified Serbo-Croatian literary language, based on the ekavian dialect. The difficulty appeared in explaining the Macedonian problem and the affiliation of Macedonia to the Serbo-Croatian and not the Bulgarian center. Cvijić began with the philosophy of Otto Bauer,[12] one of the ideological leaders of Austro-Marxism, that Macedonia represents the strategic center of influences in the Balkans. Whoever holds Macedonia holds the main keys for hegemony in the Balkans. In Macedonia proper Skoplje is the central point. In 1906 Cvijić published a study on the ethnic composition of Macedonia.[13] The thesis was that Macedonian-Slavs are, in regard to their nationality, an undefined ethnic group, placed between Serbs and Bulgars. It was presumed that they would accept the nationality of that state which could absorb them for the longest period of time. Belić spoke about "Serbo-Macedonian" and "Bulgar-Macedonian" dialects.

Aside from the two above-mentioned scholars, Stojan Novaković published a study in French called "The Yugoslav Problems" just before his death.[14] He stated that the Yugoslavs are one nation, divided by religion into two essential parts. One was attracted by Constantinople, the other by Rome. Different centers initiated different national cultures, and "both of the centers joined their political affiliations to Christianity." The historian Stanoje Stanojević expressed the same concept in his study *What Serbia Wants*. In order to strengthen Croatian resistance to the Hungarians, studies by the Croatian historian Ferdo Šišić were published in Serbia, although the author lived in Zagreb at the time.

The activities of this group of scholars and intellectuals had a more significant cultural than political effect. The Yugoslav idea in 1914 was overloaded with historicism. Its main weakness therefore was that it was perceived more as a historical fact than a realistic disposition of living people. A political organization of any kind, regardless of how minor in structure and composition it might be, would have had a much greater impact on the world's public opinion than all these books written in order to justify a program. The Yugoslav population was considered as "an appearing nation." The term comes from articles and papers written in 1912 by the Croatian writer and scholar Milan Marjanović, and published in a separate book entitled *The Appearing Nation*.[15] This idea had already overwhelmed Yugoslav intellectuals before 1914 and the ideas expressed by Cvijić and Belić were by this time integrated into existing research concerning the history and language of Serbs and Croats. It was thought that the idea of their national unity had already won and that the opposition to the finalization of the process of unification was directed against history and, thus, condemned to failure. Most young people, moreover, expressed the same idea.

FORMATION OF "YUGOSLAV COMMITTEE"

After the first few months of the war it became clear that the conflict would not end as quickly as expected, and that decisive battles would not occur at the very beginning of the war. The Serbian government adapted its war aims to these new circumstances. Resulting from the crisis connected with Italian neutrality, a Yugoslav Committee was formed in Nish in 1914. The committee was formed because of the fears that the future Yugoslav community might be destroyed in its initial phase, through the policy of preservation and reformation of the Habsburg empire, as well as Croatian and Slovenian separatism, which could obtain international support. Hints in this direction were obtained from diverse sources. The great powers, including Russia, considered the possibility of the reformation and democratization of Austria-Hungary, transforming it into a confederation of sovereign nations. In most cases this was discussed in the secluded circles of the European chancelleries, but there were people openly acting on behalf of such a solution. There was a good number of rather influential politicians in Great Britain, like Noel Buxton, as well as intellectuals with influence in public life, who thought that the unification of Yugoslavia was an impossibility. Such a democratic state was thought to be an ideal in the framework of which the reality of national conflicts would create "several Ulsters" in Europe without being able to level the existing misunderstandings. Those in Great Britain who favored the dissolution of the Habsburg Monarchy—like Seton-Watson—thought a federative Yugoslavia could offer leadership in the future state to the more developed Catholic West.[16] A defined interest lay behind such concepts, Catholicism being closer to Western Europe than Yugoslav Orthodoxy. Seton-Watson suggested that the future capital city be located in Sarajevo, or move from place to place. Both Catholic groups in France and the Italian government were opposed to a unified Yugoslav State.

The traditional separatism in Croatia, with the support of the great powers, forced the Serbian government to push for the formation of the "Yugoslav Committee." On October 27, 1914, Nicola Pašić issued final instructions in his Nish apartment concerning the formation of the Committee: "Objectives: formation of a unified Yugoslav, eventually a Serbo-Croatian, State. Without a specific state organization to safeguard the national characteristics of each group (pleme). *Way to proceed:* As negotiations with Montenegro for a real union (army, foreign policy, trade and communications, finances) are already going on, the unity of the Serbs is secured. One could offer concessions to Croats, without undermining state unity and burdening the process of crystallization of one nation, i.e., a) to mention the name of Croatia in the name of the State, if necessary a coronation with one Croatian crown; b) the historical individuality of Croatia to be represented in State emblems, armors and standards; c) equality of religious rights, expressed if necessary in ranking the high Church prelates; d) equality in the use of alphabets; e) complete civil equality. The Constitution must be extended immediately to all parts of the State. If necessary, moreover, one could also talk about a particular regional Croatian Diet (Sabor). One could offer similar concessions to the Slovenians, with a special guarantee for the use of their vernacular."[17]

The historical meaning of creating the Yugoslav Committee was based on the assigned task of rendering Croatian separatism impossible, specifically the organization of Croatian nationalists. Its realistic goal was to achieve the political foundation of a State in which the new Yugoslav nation would be integrated. The roots of the Committee went back to 1913, when it was decided at a meeting in Split (Stojanović, Trumbić, Smodlaka) that prominent Croatian politicians of Yugoslav orientation must escape to Italy in case of war. Pašić gave the same advice to Meštrović before the outbreak of the war. Trumbić, Supilo and Meštrović followed this plan in 1914.

London was chosen for the center of the Yugoslav Committee's activity because it was here that the negotiations to attract Italy on the side of the Allies were conducted. Since the establishment of Greek independence in 1830 London was the center where Balkan questions were resolved. There had been attempts in Britain to form such a committee with the concurrence of the British government.[18] Also it was from London that the public opinion in the United States could be most easily influenced.

ACCOMPLISHMENTS OF THE COMMITTEE

The Committee worked harmoniously and efficiently throughout the war. It successfully accomplished its historical task of preventing an international affirmation of Croatian separatism and of declaring to the world the wish of the Yugoslav people to live together in a unified State. It failed to accomplish its second task, i.e., to elaborate plans concerning the form and structure of the future State. In reference to this, Supilo took a separate course, suspecting the intentions of the Serbian government. His attitude and position were not quite clear. He was in favor of a unified and centralized State in the future, but he asked for the preservation of autonomy. Other members of the Committee separated themselves from him because of allegations that Supilo, as a "British emissary"[19] went to Rome in August 1916 to seek an agreement with Italy in favor of the formation of an independent Croatian State. Such an act was contradictory to the spirit of the policy of war aims conducted by Serbia, which would not yield to the negotiations of great powers except in the case of a definite defeat.

Misunderstandings between official Serbian policy and the Yugoslav Committee were of minor significance compared with the historical unpreparedness of the Yugoslav area to form a united State. Some Croatian political parties represented in the Diet in Zagreb in 1914 had their representatives in Switzerland. One such representative was Ivan Krajač,[20] who worked on behalf of a plan by Dr. Lorković to form an independent Croatian State with an English Prince as ruler. Krajač was not a man of political significance, and little is known about the steps he undertook during his activity abroad.

A significant embarrassment for the Yugoslav cause was the fact that the politicians in most cases talked in general terms and each specific orientation was justified as the wish of the entire population. This methodology was later repeated by scholars who did not make efforts to establish what percentage in each particular nation wished the creation of a common State. This relates specifically to Croatia proper (uža Hrvatska) where even Croatian politicians, from Supilo on, criticized those not strongly engaged in the struggle for the creation of a common State. No Moslem politicians or public figures of distinction participated in this struggle. Modern scholarship has failed to consider the attitudes of the common man in the 1914–1918 war and his view of the future State. Some Austrian officials estimated that on the eve of the 1914 war Dalmatia was lost for Austria. Indeed, at the beginning of the war political terror was introduced in Dalmatia. An investigation of the number of those arrested could serve as a model for such research. A second element might be found in individual declarations.

Supilo declared in 1915 that for Croatia proper (Banska Hrvatska) "the majority of the population" was not in favor of the formation of a common Yugoslav State and that the Yugoslav idea was represented only among young people.[21] This analysis was probably correct for that time, although it has to be questioned in consideration of the growing number of supporters of the future State at the end of the war, ex-

pressed in official estimates. In August 1918 General Sarkotić estimated
that the Yugoslav idea embraced all of Dalmatia while in Croatia and
Slavonia only 60% of the population.[22] The same official estimated in
May of the same year that in Bosnia and Hercegovina 50% of the
population was "infected by the Yugoslav idea" and that in Croatia the
majority of the population stayed faithful to the Emperor.[23] If this data
can be accepted seriously, it would lead to the conclusion that the
majority of the population in Croatia proper (60%) was inclined towards the formation of a common State only during the critical months
of June–August 1918, in the period during which the activity of political
parties was in full swing. Such a majority would not have been sufficient
for a constitutional *referendum*. Lacking the two-thirds majority, it is
likely that every realistic policy had to orient itself towards a federative
State structure in which each area would crystalize in a clearer fashion.
The elaboration of statistical parameters was not even approached in
this regard, thus making any final conclusion difficult.

Many factors prevented the common citizen from expressing his
political beliefs. The war itself destroyed the roots of existing democratic institutions. In addition the prospects of victory were uncertain.
The passive part of the population turned towards existing leaders.
Also important was the religious characteristic of the 1914 war in the
Balkans. Each of the basic churches (Orthodox, Catholic and Moslem)
was more a political than a religious institution. The war broke the
established harmony among them and offered them new challenges.
The policy of the Serbian Orthodox Church was directed towards
squeezing the Bulgarian Exerchate out of Macedonia and supporting
the development of the Serbian national church in that region. She
fought in Macedonia, according to a British diplomat, more for the
Kingdom of Serbia than for the Kingdom of God.[24] In Montenegro,
Moslems and Catholics were systematically converted into Orthodoxy.[25] The Ottoman proclamation of a Moslem Holy war in 1914
deeply affected the behavior of the Moslem population in Macedonia,
Albania and even to a certain extent in Bosnia. There were attempts in
Macedonia and Albania to organize Moslem guerrilla units against
Serbia.

IMPACT OF RELIGIOUS AFFILIATIONS

The policy of the Catholic Church in 1914 had the greatest impact
on the formation and final success of Serbian war aims although the
Concordat which was concluded between the Serbian government and
the Vatican in 1914, had no positive effect on the war itself.[26] Although
some intellectuals saw the necessity of joining the two Christian
churches together, the common believer upon whom the final decision
depended knew little about it. The idea remained, therefore, a political
concept with no roots. In spite of the Vatican's endeavors to remain as

an international force for whose benevolence all the states were struggling (from Turkey and Serbia to England, as typically non-Catholic
communities) the church practically supported the preservation of a
Habsburg federalized state.[27] Influential church prelates were most
suspicious of the formation of a Yugoslav state.[28]

It became clear at the beginning of the war that religious feelings
were in contradiction with Skerlić's formula about the stability of the
future state based on parallel weakening of religious affiliations in
favor of a growing atmosphere of religious tolerance.[29] Both official
policy and all the political parties were in favor of an undisturbed
growth of churches and their unrestricted influence on the population.
Instead of a growing religious indifference, the war witnessed an
intensive rise to religious feelings. In some areas, as in Hungary,[30] the
Catholic renaissance of before the war continued.

The analysis of religious feelings and affiliations is important for a
rational approach to the attitudes of the populations. This is not in
respect to the high clergy, but to the common believer who made up the
majority and was in the long run the one to determine historical issues.
As a rule, the dispositions of a village priest in 1914 were of a much
greater importance for the mood of the common people than were
declarations made in London by Supilo, or in Niš by Pašić. The common people were not even aware of these declarations. In any case they
were so remote that they could express only aspects of the future.

OBSTACLES TO SERBIAN WAR AIMS

The immediate obstacle to the formation of Serbian war aims in
1914 was the policy of the great powers to which Serbia had to adapt its
behavior. There was not only a conflict with the hostile great powers,
with which Serbia waged war, but there was also a political conflict with
the allied great powers, whose required conditions were detrimental to
the Serbian war program. In spite of the fact that two hostile blocks of
great powers were at war with each other, there was among them an
interdependent relationship which influenced all of them. This is best
seen in the problem of Macedonia, as well as indirectly in some other
questions.

The main conflict in the Balkans among the Allies and their
associates was the friction between Russia and Great Britain.[31] Although Russia was the first to negotiate with Italy hoping to convince
her to give up her neutrality, it was Great Britain which assumed the
major role. In negotiations with Bulgaria the initiative went to Russia.[32]
Neither from the British nor from the Russian side was there efficient
support for the formation of a future Yugoslav State, in spite of some
declarative announcements given to Serbian diplomats. Their entire
efforts were directed towards concluding the 1915 London Pact. Serbia
was not involved in these negotiations and no one ever asked for her

approval. It was emphasized in London that Serbia would obtain Bosnia and Hercegovina and "a broad outlet on the Adriatic in Dalmatia."[33] The Croats themselves would decide about their federation with Serbia, as one could not extend the principle of nationality to the point of risking the outcome of the war.

A real union was negotiated between Serbia and Montenegro.[34] Serbia also asked for a rectification of Albanian frontiers to Serbia's benefit, in order to prevent incursions by Albanian bands into the Kosovo region. Serbian ambitions would probably have been much greater in regard to Albania if it had not been feared in Niš that they could have been considered as territorial concessions for Italian gains in Dalmatia and Istria. For that reason these ambitions were strictly concealed by the Serbian government. The result was Pašić's instruction to Serbian diplomatic agents on October 1, 1914 to ask for Dalmatia:

> Dalmatia wants unification with Serbia—it is its ideal, a requirement of its national interests, finally, the ultimate wish of the entire Serbo-Croatian people. It will suffice Italy to obtain Trentino, Trieste and half of Istria, with Pola. To ask for more would provoke a reaction and would be of profit to Austria.[35]

Serbia had fewer difficulties in justifying its policy in Dalmatia, Croatia and Slovenia than it did in Macedonia. In Macedonia, Serbia lacked the support of prominent personalities unlike the case with Croats and Slovenes. Additionally, in Macedonia the policies of the two belligerent blocks were inter-related. Basically, both sides promised Bulgaria almost the same territories in Macedonia. A segment of the Macedonian emigrants in Bulgaria, who belonged to the former "Supreme Committee," had already during the Balkan wars assembled a new "Macedonian Committee" with a strict pro-Austro-Hungarian orientation. At the same time an Albanian Committee had been founded in Constantinople, under Young-Turk leadership. The very day of the Austro-Hungarian declaration of war on Serbia, July 28, 1914, the Austro-Hungarian ambassador in Sofia reached an agreement with the Bulgarian prime minister to smuggle Bulgarian bands into the Serbian part of Macedonia.[36] Plans concerning this activity were elaborated in Austro-Hungarian military headquarters prior to 1914. Giraldi was the agent to whom this task was assigned. He was previously engaged in struggling against the Italian influence in Albania.

MACEDONIAN PROBLEM

Due to all these factors, the Macedonian problem received a much larger consideration and was connected with the causes for the outbreak of World War One. Plans for an Austro-Hungarian economic mobilization, conceived of between October 1913 and May 1914, dealt with an eventual war envisaged for the fall of 1914.[37] According to these plans, herds of cattle were to be transferred to Adriatic harbors. Obviously, the future battlefield was assumed to be in Albania and Macedonia, as a part of a new Balkan war. The Sarajevo assassination resulted in changes; the war was transformed into a direct encounter with Serbia. The Austro-Hungarian Council of Ministers had established its war aims by July 19, 1914. Serbia was not to be annexed, but was to be territorially reduced to the benefit of the neighboring states.[38] Until December 1914 it was decided that Macedonia would be given to Bulgaria, while Austria would procure a territorial connection with Bulgaria, via Beograd and Šabac. A similar connection with Albania was to be realized through the Mount Lovćen and the Montenegrin Littoral. Austro-Hungarian war aims surrendered all of Serbia to future Bulgarian intentions.

Such a situation indirectly influenced the policy of the Allies towards Bulgaria to a much larger degree than was the case with their policy towards Italy. The Allies disagreed in regard to the extent of the territory to be conceded to Bulgaria as well as in regard to the state which had to make these concessions. They only agreed upon what had to be taken from Turkey. The French and the British tried to spare the Greeks, and the Russians the Serbs—at least at particular moments and in a cautious manner. Serbia had the most difficulties in dealing with the British. Besides a traditional distrust in the Serbian monarchy which originated in the 1903 regicide, the British cherished a rather undefined Mediterranean policy. In Serbia, British attitudes were motivated by her fears of Russia in the future. The intellectuals on both sides caused great difficulty. The approach of the British intellectuals towards Serbia was imbued with a kind of "Lawrence of Arabia" complex. British intellectuals were not only in the habit of offering advice on how to follow the policy of the Allies, but of participating in the decision-making process, even to the extent of dominating it. Becoming a hero in the history of a foreign people was usually a painful experience. Serbian politicians, moreover, had more contacts with British intellectuals than with British official policy officials.

Not until the secret treaty between Austria-Hungary, Germany and Bulgaria was signed on September 6, 1915, did Serbia begin yielding concessions to Bulgaria. It was on September 13, 1915, that the powers of the Entente finally guaranteed Macedonia to Bulgaria, regardless of the final destiny of Serbia and the concessions assigned to her.[39] But it was too late and this activity did not greatly influence the formulation of Serbian war aims in the spring and summer of 1915. Serbia was protected by the fact that Bulgaria was basically an Austro-Hungarian ally and that they together had been preparing a new Balkan war even before the outbreak of the 1914 world conflagration. Consequently, Serbia was not pushed into taking the initiative and had only to wait for her opponent to make a mistake. This happened when Bulgaria joined the war in 1915.

The Bulgarian irredentist policy towards Macedonia was carried out with such intensity and irritation that all the tactics of concessions and attempts to reach an agreement came under suspicion. Bulgarian national public opinion could be satisfied and appeased only by total satisfaction of its desires—not a part of but the entire territory of Macedonia. The British representative in Sofia came to the conclusion that

> . . . even a period of a millennium of Serbian rule in Macedonia would not reconcile Bulgaria with the loss of her irredenta. This factor would probably determine the attitude of the coming generation, not only in regard to Serbia but to Bulgarian foreign policy in general.[40]

The Allies attempted to restore the Balkan block and to join it to Bulgaria, and eventually Turkey. A pre-condition was that Serbia concede a part of Macedonia to Bulgaria. Russia seconded this idea. It was not quite clear what Serbia had to give up. The diagonal line going from the northeastern Serbo-Bulgarian frontier to Lake Ohrid with Skoplje and the so-called "pending zone" under the arbitration of the Russian Tzar and established in the 1912 Balkan Alliance Treaty, was subject to discussion.[41] Even before the 1912 agreement, the Bulgarians were more inclined to concede Skoplje to Serbia than to accept Russian arbitration. The Serbian government was of the opinion that the line suggested by Russia went horizontally from Kriva Palanka to the Korab mountain, south of Skoplje and Tetovo, which would remain Serbian.[42] The Serbian government seldom yielded to the demands forwarded by her allies. It disagreed with the Russian division line and offered only the small portion of Southeast Macedonia, with Štip and Radović to Bulgaria, where it was estimated that the local populations tended more towards Bulgaria than Serbia. In the center of Macedonia, in Skoplje, a pro-Bulgarian opposition to Serbia had not developed. In principle, the Serbian government refused to allow the Bulgarians access to the Vardar Valley. This decision was presumably dictated by the fear that Bulgaria would jeopardize Serbian communication lines in the Vardar Valley towards Thessaloniki. It was believed that this city would eventually be allotted to Serbia.

REOPENING OF BALKAN PROBLEMS

The Serbo-Bulgarian situation reopened the Greek problem. At the beginning of the war Greek diplomats tried to mediate between the Serbs and Bulgars, but quickly withdrew, fearing that a renewed Balkan Pact would impose upon Greece concessions to Bulgaria around Kavala. The French approach to Bulgaria as "the political pivot of the Balkans"[43] pushed the Greeks away from negotiations with Sofia. The essential motive in Greek politics during the first war years was the fear of a Slavic threat on the northern frontiers in the future. As one British diplomat wrote,

> I often experienced in Athens, in conversations with Mr. Venizelos and regardless of his loyalty to the alliance with Serbia, a constant fear of the Slavic danger, of the same kind expressed by the late King George.[44]

The Serbian government had fewer difficulties in formulating its war aims with regard to Rumania. The government demanded the maximum territorial gains expressed in the May 20, 1915, memorandum.[45] Serbia claimed the entire Banat to just east of Arad. These claims were justified by the need to protect the capital city and to enable the colonization of poor peasants from the Dinaric Alps, who usually moved to the United States. On their side, the Rumanians also announced intentions to obtain from the Allies the entire Banat, to the Tisza confluence with the Danube. Due to military setbacks at the beginning of July 1915, Russia opened negotiations with Rumania, promising maximum gains.[46] Approximately at the same time on April 15, 1915, the London Pact was signed. This promised Italy a part of the Dalmation littoral. It was a temporary defeat for Serbian war aims.

These were the historical circumstances under which the Serbian War Program was formed. During the first phase the war aims were shaped by the confrontation between the tendency of the Allies to revise the clauses of the peace treaty ending the 1913 Balkan war, and the tendency of the Serbian government to realize the Serbo-Croatian unification in the framework of a future state, regardless of pressures coming from the side of the Allies. The first factor demanded that Serbia behave as an object of the activity of the great powers, who attempted to force Serbia to relinguish a part or all of Macedonia in order to attract Italy, Bulgaria, Rumania and Greece. Prospects offered to Serbia included aggrandizement in the West, by obtaining all of Bosnia and Hercegovina, with wide access to the Adriatic littoral through a part of Dalmatia. The second factor in this conflict required that Serbia theoretically determine her future in accordance with the democratic legacies of European civilization and in the framework of the national unification with Croats and Slovenes. This second factor was ultimately realized. It was made public during the first days of the war and was finally formulated in the Declaration of the Serbian Skupština in Niš on December 7, 1914. The public declaration of the Serbian government concerning the goal to unite Serbs, Croats and Slovenes in a common Yugoslav State represented the final range and the focal point of the Serbian policy in formulating war aims in 1914. It became the historical framework for the safeguard of the democratic future based on historical legacy. It became the main political base on which the unification of 1918 was finally achieved. The historical mission of the new state was considered to be the fulfillment of a century-old struggle to reach this goal; a state resulting from the legacy of European civilization, pitted against German tendencies for world hegemony in the war.

Notes

1. A. J. P. Taylor, "The War Aims of the Allies in the First World War," in: *Essays Presented to Sir Lewis Namier*, ed. by Richard Pares and A. J. P. Taylor, London 1956, p. 776.

2. Milorad Ekmečić, *Ratni Ciljevi Srbije 1914* (Serbian War Aims), Beograd 1973, p. 89–91.

3. D. M., "Perspektiva rata u Evropi" (War Prospects in Europe), in: *Ratnik, Mesečni vojni list*, LXXVI, Vol. 4, April 1914, p. 1–3.

4. B. A. Emec, *Očerki vnešnei politiki Rossii 1914–1917*, Moskva 1977, p. 150.

5. Manifesto of Regent Alexander, Niš July 16/29, 1914, in: Ferdo Šišić, *Dokumenti o postanku kraljevine Srba, Hrvata i Slovenaca 1914–1919*, Zagreb 1920, p. 2; "Naredba br. 1 Vrhovnog Komandanta za svu srpsku vojsku" (Order Number 1 to the Entire Serbian Army from the Commander in Chief) August 4, 1914, in Kragujevac, in: *Veliki rat Srbije za oslobodjenje i ujedinjenje Srba, Hrvata i Slovenaca* (The Great War of Serbia for the Liberation and Unification of Serbs, Croats and Slovenes), Beograd 1924, I, p. 17.

6. Memoirs of General Panta Draškić, manuscript in the Archives of the Serbian Academy of Sciences and Arts, Beograd, no. 14211.

7. Dragovan Šepić, "Srpska vlada i počeci Jugoslovenskog Odbora" (The Serbian Government and the Origins of the Yugoslav Committee), in: *Historijski Zbornik*, Zagreb 1960, no. XIII, p. 1–45, citation from the notes of J. M. Jovanović.

8. Circular of the Ministry of Foreign Affairs to legations abroad, 22 August/4 September 1914, State Archives of Yugoslavia, Str. Pov. no. 4600.

9. Published in Niš under the pseudonym "Dinaricus." Later reprinted in *Govori i Rasprave*, Beograd 1924, II.

10. Jovan Cvijić, *La Peninsule balkaniques: geographie humaine*, Paris 1918.

11. Published in Niš in 1915 with a remark "published as manuscript."

12. Enver Redžić, *Austromarksizam i jugoslavensko pitanje* (Austro-Marxism and the Yugoslav Question), Beograd 1977, p. 134. It is a question of who originated the slogan that the struggle for Macedonia is the struggle for the hegemony over the Balkans. This slogan was stressed by many other ideologues and politicians of the time.

13. Jovan Cvijić, *Remarks on the Ethnography of the Macedo-Slavs*, London 1906.

14. Stoyan Novakovitch, "Problèmes Yougo-Slaves," in: *La Revue de Paris*, 1 September 1915.

15. Milan Marjanović, *Narod koji nastaje. Zašto nastaje i kako se formira jedinstveni srpsko-hrvatski narod.* (The Originating Nation: Why It Appears and How the Unique Serbo-Croatian Nation Is to Be Formed), Rijeka 1913.

16. "Scotus Viator," Memorandum (without title and address), 1 October 1914, Public Record Office, London, F. O. 371/1905, no. 55136 (later in text P.R.O.). The memorandum was recently published in: R. W. Seton-Watson i Jugosloveni Korespondencija 1906–1941, I, 1906–1918, Zagreb-London 1976, pp. 180–186. In his writings R. W. Seton-Watson did not openly expose these ideas, although one could assume that he subconsciously doubted that the religious split in Yugoslavia was deeper than one usually thought it to be. It is true that in his lecture "The Role of Bosnia in International Politics 1875–1914" (in: Proceedings of the British Academy, XVII, 1931, p. 36) he called those who spoke about the impossibility of overcoming the religious gap in Yugoslavia "the foolish propagandists."

17. Dr. Nikola Stojanović, *Jugoslovenski Odbor* (The Yugoslav Committee), Zagreb 1927, pp. 10–11.

18. Milorad Ekmečić, Ratni ciljevi Srbije 1914, p. 346.

19. *Ibid.*, p. 370. There are not enough sources to establish with whom he was in contact in England. In his letter to R. W. Seton-Watson (London, July 1916) he said, "this day I will go a little about—you know where" (Correspondence, I, p. 269) but this does not constitute proof. Through his letter to R. W. Seton-Watson one could see that the latter did not approve of his "Croatism."

20. *Ibid.*, p. 327.

21. Dragovan Šepić, "Svjedočanstva suvremenika o radu Frana Supilo 1914–1917" (Testimonies of Contemporaries about the Activity of Frano Supilo 1914–1917), in: *Historijski Pregled*, 4, 1963, p. 307.

22. Dr. Milada Paulova, *Tajna diplomatická hra o Jihoslovany za svetové války*. Praha 1923, pp. 157–158.

23. Milorad Ekmečić, "General Sarkotić i planovi spasa manarhije 1918," (General Sarkotić and Plans to Save the Monarchy in 1918), in: *Zbornik radova posvećen uspomeni S. Nazečića*, Sarajevo 1972, p. 441.

24. Cracanthorpe to Gray, Beograd 26 May 1914, P.R.O. F.O. 421/290, no. 90, p. 86.

25. More detailed in the unpublished manuscript from Branko Babić, *Politika crnogorske vlade u novim krajevima dobijenim u Balkanskom ratu. Od kraja 1912 do sredine 1914.* (Politics of the Montenegrin Government in the newly acquired regions during the Balkan War. From the End of 1912 till the middle of 1914.) Doctoral dissertation presented in December 1977 at the Sarajevo University.

26. Milorad Ekmečić, Ratni ciljevi Srbije, p. 124.

27. Dr. George Pfeilschifter, *Religion und Religionen im Weltkrieg.* Freiburg, 1915, pp. 77–81. The Belgian government accused the Vatican of having friendly relations with Germany. Similar voices were also heard in France.

28. J. de Salis to Balfour, Rome 18 May 1918, P.R.O. F.O. 371/3134, no. 92288. He quotes the conversation with Cardinal Gaspari.

29. Jovan Skerlić, "Slobodna misao u Srbiji" (1911). In: *Sabrana dela*, VII, Beograd 1964, p. 267.

30. Dr. Georg Pfeilschifter, o.c. p. 29.

31. In his extensive review of my book *Ratni ciljevi Srbije* (in: *Jugoslovenski istorijski časopis*, 3–4, 1976) Nikola Popović criticized this statement. Until the eve of the 1917 February Revolution, France was unanimous with Russia in breaking Germany as a state, but the only real partner in projecting the future of the continent was Great Britain.

32. Milorad Ekmečić, o.c. p. 281–283.

33. Edward Grey personally minuted the report of his minister from Niš (P.R.O. F.O. 371/2257, no. 53757, from 3 May 1915): "Serbian apprehensions are not warranted. The victory of Allies will secure for Serbia *at least* (inserted by pencil) the liberation of the whole of Bosnia and Hercegovina, their union with Serbia, and wide access to the Adriatic in Dalmatia. Whether the Federation with further [sic] will naturally be a matter to be decided by Croats themselves."

34. Milorad Ekmečić, o.c. p. 414.

35. Pašić to legations in London, Bordeaux, Petrograd and Rome, in Niš 17 September, 1 October 1914, State Archives of Yugoslavia Pov. br. 5533.

36. Milčo Lalkov, "Iz Deinostte na avstro-ungarskata diplomacia na Balkanite v načaloto po prvata svetovna voina" (About the activity of Austro-Hungarian diplomacy in the Balkans at the beginning of the First World War) in: *Bulgaria i evropskite strani prez XIX-XX vek*, Sofia 1975, p. 185.

37. The Ministry of Interior to the Joint Ministry of Finances, Vienna 27 May 1914, Archives of Bosnia and Hercegovina, Präs, no. 640.

38. Wolfdieter Bihl, "Zu den österreichisch-ungarischen Kriegszielen 1914," in: *Jahrbücher für Geschichte Osteuropas*, Band 16, 1968, 4, pp. 505–509.

39. V. A. Emec, *Očerki vnešnei politiki Rossii 1914–1917*, p. 151.

40. O'Rayly to Sir Edward Grey, Sofia 13 January 1914, P.R.O. F.O. 421/289, no. 50.

41. This transpired from the notes of Milovan Milovanović "*Istorik pregovora za zaključenje srpsko-bugarskog ugovora od 29 februara 1912*" from 31 March 1912, in: Savo Skoko, *Drugi Balkanski rat. Knjiga Prva. Uzroci i pripreme rata*, Beograd 1968, p. 398. During the negotiations the Serbs suggested the arbitrage of the Russian Tzar, while the Bulgarians accepted it only at the beginning but rejected it later. They "accepted our line of delineation completely. Consequent to their behavior during the negotiations the Bulgarians preferred to accept our askings than to leave the question open, to be submitted to Russian arbitrage." Thus the entire "contested zone" was in fact allotted to the Serbs by the treaty.

42. The map of the division in 1914 can be found in my book *Ratni ciljevi Srbije*, p. 546.

43. George B. Leon, *Greece and the Great Powers 1914–1917*, Thessaloniki 1974, p. 79.

44. Sir Francis Elliot to James Rennel Rodd, Athens 19 October 1914, P.R.O. F.O. 371/2009, no. 66643.

45. Aide Memoire of the Serbian Legation in London to Foreign Office, London 7/20 May 1915, P.R.O. F.O. 371/2257, no. 63945.

46. V. A. Emec, *Očerki vnešnei politiki Rossii 1914–1917*, p. 212.

The Serbian Government, the Army, and the Unification of Yugoslavs

Alex N. Dragnich

SERBIAN GOVERNMENTS WERE from an early period concerned with unification with their "brothers" outside Serbia. This was even before Serbia had an army, which, as it was created and strengthened, served the state and the people loyally. There was a period, however, when its enthusiasm for unification drove it to actions which were designed to support the government's program, but which resulted in a conflict with state power.

While my subject is limited largely to the years immediately preceding the First World War and the war years themselves, a few paragraphs on earlier years are necessary to give the presentation a better perspective.

As Serbia began to gain some autonomy in the early part of the 19th century, her leaders demonstrated their awareness that "out there" were "brothers" that needed to be liberated. The concept of brother was, however, in some respects exceedingly vague. The leaders knew that there were Serbs in the adjoining territories—people who spoke their language and seemed to possess a common heritage. They did not know the extent of these territories, or the number of people involved. They knew, however, that some Serbs in Dalmatia had gone over to Roman Catholicism and that many in Bosnia-Hercegovina and "Old Serbia" (Macedonia)) had converted to Islam. Hence Njegoš's well-known saying, "Brat je mio koje vjere bio" (A brother is dear whatever his religion be). But uniting with one's brothers would remain for decades but a dream.

The first formal and systematic statement about the goals for unification is to be found in the *Načertanije*, prepared in 1844 by the eminently talented Serbian leader, Ilija Garašanin.[1] He hoped that his statement would constitute for Prince Alexander Karadjordjević and his governments a program for Serbia's foreign and national policy. He foresaw that the Turkish empire in Europe would be falling apart, and from this basic assumption he, as a responsible political leader, sought to chart the best possible course for Serbia. Although the text of the

Načertanije was not known to the Serbian public until 1906, the Austrians had secretly obtained a copy as early as 1883.

Some historians have argued that the *Načertanije* was a blueprint for a Great Serbia, while others have maintained that it was a design for a South Slav (Yugoslav) state. Such arguments are futile, it seems to me, unless we are willing to attribute to Garašanin an ability to visualize precisely future events, which he never assumed.

More important is his assessment that the Ottoman empire in Europe would disintegrate, and his realization that Russia and Austria would seek to fill the vacuum which would be left as that empire crumbled. Such moves by Austria and Russia, he believed, would be to the detriment of the Serbs and other South Slavs. A farsighted realist, Garašanin knew that it would not be easy to prevent such penetration by these two great powers. Nevertheless, he believed that the only promising way of attempting it would be through the creation of a large, strong, and independent state composed of South Slavs. And, in his view, the leadership to this end could come only from the newly emerging Serbian state; no other South Slav state even existed except for tiny Montenegro. There is reason to believe that he saw in France a western power that might be sympathetic to his projected program.

IMPLEMENTATION OF THE NAČERTANIJE

The first concrete steps toward implementing the *Načertanije* were not taken until the regime of Prince Mihailo Obrenović in the 1860s. Garašanin's work was set back during the years of the oligarchical rule of the Defenders of the Constitution, but he survived to serve Mihailo as prime minister between 1861 and 1867. Mihailo knew that Serbia was helpless without an army and without allies in the Balkans. Mihailo was a shrewd leader, but the domestic problems he faced were critical, troublesome, and unyielding. However, he did create a national army and made alliances with other Balkan peoples. And in 1867, he forced the Turks out of garrisons that they had maintained in Serbian cities, but he did not believe that Serbia was yet ready for a general campaign to drive them out of Europe.

Mihailo's untimely death in 1868, and the coming to the throne of his fourteen-year-old cousin, Milan, put an end for a time to Mihailo's dream of a war against Turkey. Milan soon learned how weak Serbia was when it confronted the Turks in the wars of 1876 and 1877. Soon after that, however, Serbia had a standing army, but in the ill-fated war with Bulgaria in 1885, Serbian arms were not impressive. It was not until the Balkan wars that Serbian military strength was demonstrated in battle.

Lack of success on the battlefield, however, did not destroy the dream of unification. In the late 1870s a new Serbian leader was coming on the scene. He was Nikola Pašić, who founded the Serbian Radical party in 1880, and who more than any other single person engineered the creation of Yugoslovia in 1918.

In the original program of the Radical party, published in January 1881, there was an expression of concern for South Slav areas not yet united with Serbia. Initially this was viewed as a desire to unite Serbian lands, but after 1903 there was more of a tendency to think in broader Yugoslav terms, predominantly espoused by intellectuals and youth. And all Serbian political parties began to view this type of manifestation—inside and outside Serbia—with a certain sympathy. Moreover, the leaders of these parties began after 1905 to establish contacts with some Serbian and Croatian politicians from Croatia.

Following the success of the first Balkan war in 1912, the idea of broadening the state to include the South Slav lands of Austro-Hungary, and not just Bosnia-Hercegovina, began little by little to penetrate the leading circles of all Serbian political parties. In June 1913, for example, there was discussion in the Radical party caucus about Serbian tasks after the accounting with the Turks. The Radical leaders, Nikola Pašić, Stojan Protić, and Lazar Paču, arguing in favor of arbitration of the Russian tsar in Serbia's conflict with Bulgaria, spoke of Serbia's other tasks, including work on liberation and unification with Croatians and Slovenes.[2]

SURFACING OF THE YUGOSLAV QUESTION

With the outbreak of war in 1914 between Austro-Hungary and Serbia, the Yugoslav question came to the surface and, in fact, became a matter on the agenda of Serbia's foreign policy. As R. W. Seton-Watson observed, it was obvious that in case the Central Powers won the war both Serbian kingdoms (Serbia and Montenegro) would cease to be independent and become vassals, but in the contrary event, Serbia would easily win a position similar to that of Piedmont, and would unite the Yugoslavs under its banner. Dr. Ivan Hribar, a resident of Austro-Hungary and a supporter of Yugoslav unification, after talks with Serbia's prime minister (Pašić) in 1913 and early 1914, became convinced that Pašić was the Yugoslav Cavour who would unite the South Slavs.[3]

The Serbian government lost no time in moving in this direction. Even before the outbreak of the war, Prime Minister Pašić, in a memorandum of a conversation with the Russian tsar in January 1914, when Pašić was hoping to find a Russian princess for the heir to the Serbian throne, observed that if circumstances permitted she might become princess of the "Serbo-Croatian Yugoslav people."[4] And Prince Regent Alexander in his order to the army of August 4, 1914, mentions "Serbian Bosnia-Hercegovina," and the "millions of our brothers . . .

from Bosnia-Hercegovina, from Banat and Bačka, from Croatia, Slavonija and Srem, and from our seacoast of rocky Dalmatia," to whose screams Serbia was for years compelled to listen.[5]

Before discussing the Serbian government's concrete steps toward unification during the war years, it needs to be noted at the outset that these met obstacles all along the way, placed there by Serbia's great allies, and this was to continue to a greater or lesser degree well into 1918, when France and Britian finally recognized that the Austro-Hungarian empire could not survive. In a diary note of August 25, 1914, Serbia's assistant foreign minister recorded that he had told a Russian representative that Serbia's war aim was the solution of the whole Yugoslav question through unification of all Serbs, Croats, and Slovenes, but got a negative response.[6] The Russian realized, as did Britain and France subsequently, that such a solution meant the destruction of Austria-Hungary, an outcome they were not willing to recognize until the spring of 1918.

Efforts to Save the Habsburg Monarchy

The Entente powers favored saving the Habsburg monarchy for different reasons. Britain did not wish to see Serbia expand because she looked upon Serbia as Russia's vassal, and she did not want the spread of Russian influence in the Balkans. France viewed Germany as the main enemy and not Austria-Hungary. Russia was opposed, among other things, for dynastic reasons, to the destruction of the Austro-Hungarian empire. Moreover, she was fearful that Orthodoxy in Serbia would suffer through union with Catholic Croats and Slovenes, and that a Yugoslav state might come under the influence of the Vatican and Italy. In addition, Russia had interests which could be satisfied only by having good relations with France and Great Britain. Finally, all of the Entente powers questioned whether the Croats and Slovenes wanted to unite with Serbia, because they had seen no evidence that they were making any difficulties for the Austro-Hungarian authorities.

Of more immediate importance than any of these reasons was the desperate desire in 1914 and early 1915 of the Entente powers to get Italy, Bulgaria, and Rumania into the war on the allied side. This meant concessions to Italy in Dalmatia and Istria, to Bulgaria in Macedonia, and to Rumania in the Banat, the latter two at the expense of Serbia, while the concessions to Italy were at the expense of Croats and Slovenes especially and hence an obstacle to the formation of a Yugoslav state.

The Entente powers offered to compensate Serbia by promising that after the war she could get Bosnia-Hercegovina, most of Dalmatia, and part of Albania. But the Serbian government, while reluctantly going along with some concessions to Bulgaria, kept its eye on the larger goal, and made its stand known. Although it seemingly could do little to influence its great allies, it nevertheless proceeded to work energetically on its plans, and never ceased trying to persuade its allies that they should support these plans.

PUBLIC DECLARATION OF SERBIA'S WAR AIMS

The first formal public declaration of Serbia's war aims is to be found in the Niš Declaration, approved by the Serbian cabinet on December 7, 1914.[7] This declaration was approved immediately after formation of a coalition cabinet, to include not only Pašić's Radicals, but also representatives of the Independent Radicals and the Progressives. It stated clearly that Serbia's main war aim, next to victory, was the liberation and unification of all Serbs, Croats, and Slovenes. This position was approved by the Serbian Skupština. The great allies did not, however, accept the Yugoslav program as put forth in the Niš Declaration.

Prior to this formal declaration, however, Prime Minister Pašić had been at work within his own government and through diplomatic channels to prepare the way. Within a month of the outbreak of hostilities in the summer of 1914, he had his ministry of foreign affairs preparing formulations and explanations of the Yugoslav program. Moreover, he assembled a group of outstanding ethnologists, geographers, historians, economists, and international lawyers whose task was to prepare studies that would justify the goal of a common South Slav state. In September he had sent instructions to his ministers in allied capitals, setting forth in fairly precise form the projected territorial boundaries of the new Yugoslav state after the defeat of Austria-Hungary.

In order to assure peace in the Balkans, Pašić asserted that this could be done most effectively by the creation of "one national state, geographically sufficiently large, ethnographically compact, politically strong, economically independent so that she could live and develop independently and in harmony with European culture and progress." Such a state, he said, would have a population of about twelve million "Serbs, Croats, and Slovenes," and a territory of some two hundred and thirty thousand square kilometers. Interestingly enough, this would constitute a territory larger than the one Yugoslavia was to get at the end of the Second World War.

Pašić had also perceived the need for propaganda work in the main allied nations. Aside from the desirability of having articles written about Serbia—her brave army, her democratic society, her sacrifices, and her aspirations—it was necessary to have organization and spokesmen. To the latter end, Pašić sent to Rome, in early November, 1914, Nikola Stojanović and Dušan Vasiljević, two Serbs from Bosnia, whose task was to establish the Yugoslav Committee.[8] Before long they were joined by important Croatian voices in the names of Ante Trumbić, Franjo Supilo, Ivan Meštrović, Hinko Hinković, and others (including Serbs and Slovenes) from Austro-Hungarian territory. Initially, the role of the Committee was to inform the allies concerning the plight of the South Slavs in Austria-Hungary, and to win them over to the idea of destroying the dual monarchy and the creation of a South Slav state. Subsequently, when the Serbian government learned of the secret Treaty of London (1915), which made important concessions to Italy at the expense of Yugoslav lands, the Committee was asked to toil energetically to nullify that treaty.

ROLES OF THE YUGOSLAV COMMITTEE

The Yugoslav Committee saw itself in different roles, among them as a representative of Serbs, Croats, and Slovenes in the dual monarchy, and thereby a negotiator with the Serbian government with respect to the nature of the future state. Because of evidence of separatist tendencies, particularly in certain Croatian Catholic circles, one of the most important roles that the Committee was to play in the course of the war was to incapacitate Croatian separatism in allied states.[9]

The Serbian government, acting largely through Prime Minister Pašić, even during the terrible defeats in 1915 and the Golgotha that was the retreat through the Albanian mountains in winter, never lost sight of the major goal. Once on the Greek island of Corfu, he worked with his allies to rehabilitate the remnants of the Serbian forces so that they could return to battle, as they did in 1916. But he also pressed his political program. The latter became more difficult as the Yugoslav Committee, emboldened by Serbia's weakened position, sought a more decisive voice in shaping the future. It began presenting memoranda to allied governments, purporting to represent the South Slavs in the dual monarchy. And it sought to organize and influence South Slavs in North and South America.

Pašić was soon discovering that among his other problems was the evolving situation wherein the South Slavs could not speak with one voice. The Yugoslav Committee, encouraged by certain influential voices of British public opinion, was asking no less than to share power with the Serbian government. Yet Pašić, as the prime minister of an allied state, could not constitutionally share his or his cabinet's power even if he wished to, which he did not, because he was convinced that in dealing with his allies one voice—a united front—would be more effective. After the Russian Revolution in March 1917, however, it was painfully obvious to Pašić that Serbia had lost her most loyal supporter in the person of Tsar Nicholas II.

THE CORFU DECLARATION

Under these circumstances, Pašić was left no choice but to seek an understanding with representatives of the Yugoslav Committee. In July 1917, they met on Corfu, and out of these meetings came the Corfu

Declaration, signed on July 20th. Full of sentiments of unity, brotherhood, and common interests, the Declaration consisted of 14 specific
points concerning the organization of their common future state, a
state that the great allied powers were still unwilling to list as one of
their war aims. The Declaration was in part designed to force the allies
to accept the dissolution of Austria-Hungary. It was also an answer to
the South Slav deputies in the Austro-Hungarian parliament, who in
May 1917 had issued a declaration urging the union of the provinces of
the monarchy where Slovenes, Croats, and Serbs lived into one state
under the scepter of the Habsburg dynasty.[10]

The first point of the Corfu Declaration says that a state of Serbs,
Croats, and Slovenes will be a "constitutional, democratic, and parliamentary monarchy with the Karadjordjević dynasty at the head."
Aside from this, Serbia did not ask for any privileged status or any veto
power, as had Prussia, for example, when she was unifying Germany.
Moreover, Serbia was ready to give up her democratic constitution,
convinced that a constituent assembly would produce one for the
common state. In addition, Serbia indicated a willingness to give up her
flag and other national symbols.

Pašić and his colleagues, as well as a majority of the representatives
of the Yugoslav Committee, agreed that the future state should be a
unitary one, with certain rights of local self-government.[11] The final
point of the Declaration stated that a constituent assembly would adopt
a constitution "by a numerically qualified majority," a vague and imprecise provision nowhere defined, which was to cause trouble before,
during, and after the deliberations of the constituent assembly in 1921.

When the Bolshevik Revolution of November 7, 1917, knocked
Russia out of the war, Pašić saw his and Serbia's position weakened. At
the same time, new hopes sprouted in the Yugoslav Committee that it
could now get more than the Corfu Declaration offered.

At the beginning of 1918, Pašić realized that the hour may be late.
The military situation looked grim. Russia was out of the war and Italy
was badly hurt. American forces were on the way but progress was slow.
Austria-Hungary had earlier indicated a willingness to sign a separate
peace, and the Western allies had been receptive. Who was to say that
there would not be a compromise end to the war? Lloyd George and
President Wilson had both indicated that they favored autonomy for
the oppressed nationalities in the Habsburg monarchy. And the latter's
preservation would make it easier for the Western allies to live up to the
promises made to Italy in the Treaty of London.

In these circumstances Pašić sought, in the latter half of January
1918, to determine from his great allies what their intentions were. He
had noted that in statements by Lloyd George and President Wilson
there were demands for liberation of Italians and Rumanians but not
for the liberation of South Slavs. Moreover, they had demanded the

revision of the treaty that gave Alsace-Lorraine to Germany, but had not asked for a revision of the Treaty of Berlin which had in effect turned Bosnia-Hercegovina over to Austria-Hungary. Therefore, Pašić asked his ministers in London and Washington to find out if these incongruities were accidental or intentional.

When news leaked out concerning Pašić's directives, his action was interpreted as perhaps a reluctant willingness to abandon the Yugoslav solution to the South Slav question, and to settle for the territorial acquisitions that were promised to Serbia earlier. This seeming wavering by Pašić was the first since the beginning of the war, but it was brief and he soon returned to the program of the Niš Declaration.[12]

Nevertheless, Pašić's attempt to ascertain allied intentions, as well as the allied policies themselves, made for serious and difficult disagreements between the Yugoslav Committee and the Serbian government in the months ahead. Following the recognition by allied governments, in June 1918, of the right to independence for the Polish and Czech peoples, the Yugoslav Committee openly demanded that it be internationally recognized as the representative of the Austro-Hungarian Yugoslavs. Pašić opposed this demand, because he realized that the Western allies would thereby be provided an opportunity to play one group of South Slav representatives off against the other, to the detriment of the common cause. He did offer to include in the Serbian cabinet three representatives of Serbs, Croats, and Slovenes from Austria-Hungary, but this offer was rejected by the president of the Yugoslav Committee, Trumbić.[13]

While Yugoslav developments seemed to be moving slowly in the first part of 1918, they came with such rapidity toward the end of the year that events tended to overtake all South Slav political leaders. In the early part of the year Pašić continued to make pro-Yugoslav statements, but these did not seem to make any particular impact on anyone. On the contrary, an ill-concealed campaign seemed to be building so as to undermine Pašić, a campaign which some British publicists engaged in actively. At the same time, German and Austro-Hungarian forces were collapsing, and in their wake new events were taking place. Perhaps the most important of these was the proclamation in Zagreb in October of the formation of a new state of Slovenes, Croats, and Serbs, and the creation of the National Council as its governing body.[14]

THE NATIONAL COUNCIL

The establishment of the National Council was at once welcomed by the Yugoslav Committee and yet regretted because the Council seemed to be replacing the Committee as the voice of the South Slavs in the disintegrating dual monarchy. Nevertheless, Trumbić and his friends valiantly sought international recognition for the National

Council. To them this seemed to be a propitious moment to extract concessions from Pašić, who realized that they were being aided by some of Pašić's political opponents from Serbia. In the hope of minimizing the impact of discordant voices, he asked Prince Regent Alexander's permission to undertake talks that could lead to a coalition cabinet, and received Alexander's approval. Before these talks could be concluded, Pašić found himself at Geneva in much more far-flung discussions, which included representatives of the Yugoslav Committee and the National Council.

At the Geneva meeting Pašić found himself alone in representing the Serbian government. Lined up against him were three representatives from the National Council, three from the Yugoslav Committee, and three of his political opponents from Serbia. He was outnumbered nine to one, but in the interests of national unity he went along to conclude an agreement, which he knew would not be legally binding. The agreement provided that, pending the constituent assembly, the Serbian government and the National Council would constitute a type of dual authority, the former in Serbia proper and the latter in the newly constituted South Slav state outside Serbia. At the same time a type of joint cabinet would be formed in Paris (6 to be named by the Serbian government and 6 by the National Council). The Geneva Declaration, as the agreement was called, was destined to remain a dead letter. It was rejected by the Serbian cabinet sitting on Corfu, and also by the National Council in Zagreb even before the latter heard of the action of the Serbian cabinet.[15]

Meanwhile, South Slav politicians were being overtaken by other events. Before further negotiations between the Serbian government and the National Council could take place, some of the lands for which the Council sought to speak were deciding in favor of union with Serbia (Vojvodina, Montenegro, and 42 out of 52 districts of Bosnia-Hercegovina), while another part was beset by a rebellion led by demobilized Croats who had fought in the Austro-Hungarian army, and still another part was being occupied by Italian troops who sought to assure Italy the promises of the Treaty of London.

In the light of these developments, representatives of the National Council rushed to Belgrade in an effort to reach agreement with the Serbian government. They carried with them certain conditions, which were really contrary to the Corfu Declaration. These were apparently rejected in Belgrade, because none of them appeared in the acts of union of December 1, 1918, either in the statement by the delegates to Alexander or in his response. Following the proclamation of union and the creation of the Kingdom of the Serbs, Croats, and Slovenes, the Serbian parliament and the National Council declared their respective missions concluded, and voted themselves out of existence.

It needs to be emphasized, however, that in the process of pursuing South Slav unification, the Serbian government was confronted with other problems of major importance. Uppermost was Serbia's continued participation in the war, which her leaders believed would shape the outcome of all major political questions. Following some brilliant military victories in 1914, Serbian forces had been compelled in late 1915 to retreat across the Albanian mountains to the Greek island of Corfu. Consequently, it was imperative for Serbia to return to the military front—the only logical one being the Salonika Front.

While on Corfu, the Serbian government was almost totally dependent upon her great allies, mainly France and Great Britain. Although the latter would have preferred a "holding action" on the Salonika Front, the Serbian government believed imperative that Serbia participate actively in the war operations, and thereby demonstrate her standing as an important ally. In this the Serbian leaders were no doubt influenced by the fact that they had not been asked to participate in the allied conferences held in 1916 and 1917 in Rome, Paris, Petrograd and Saint Jean de Maurienne.[16] In the end, of the total of allied forces on the Salonika Front (482,246), Serbian soldiers accounted for 102,500. Moreover, on that front Serbian forces bore some of the heaviest fighting and achieved some of the most significant victories.

The Serbian government also faced perilous internal problems in 1916 and 1917, involving the cabinet, political opposition in the Skupština, disaffected elements in the army, and Prince Regent Alexander.[17] One of the critical questions was the responsibility for the military disasters of 1915. Pašić, who held the posts of prime minister and minister of foreign affairs, managed to hold together an uneasy coalition cabinet which was created after the outbreak of the war in 1914. But the members (a majority) of the Skupština who had fled with the Serbian army in late 1915 wanted to have their say, and Pašić was forced to permit sessions on Corfu in the autumn of 1916. Moreover, Alexander was unhappy with Pašić, but the latter's high standing with the Allied Powers prevented his dismissal. More serious for Pašić, but also for Alexander, was the conflict that surfaced between the civil and military authority, which led to the trial and conviction by a Serbian military tribunal in 1917 of several army officers.

"UNION OR DEATH" ORGANIZATION

The civil-military conflict in Serbia, whose history cannot be traced here,[18] took on a concrete form with the creation in 1911 of the secret revolutionary organization called Union or Death (*Ujedinjenje ili Smrt*). The primary base of the organization was the army, although initially important political and intellectual leaders were also members. The aim of the Union or Death organization was unification, and in this they viewed Serbs and Croats as one people, although not the Slovenes, who were not mentioned. Article 7 of their constitution mentions Bosnia-Hercegovina, Montenegro, Old Serbia, Macedonia, Croatia, Slavonija and Srem and Vojvodina, and Dalmatia. While the organization's constitution was secret, its official publication, *Pijemont*, made it evident that the organization was conceiving South Slav unification more narrowly than was the Serbian government, especially after the Niš Declaration in December 1914.

The goal of Union or Death and the professed patriotism of the organization's founders could not, however, mask the fact that the existence of such an organization was contrary to the elemental principles of a constitutional state, to say nothing of its being in conflict with military regulations. The organization was in effect arrogating to itself certain attributes of state power, which led to a conflict between the civil and the military authority. The conflict came to a head in 1917, as Serbian troops were fighting their way back to the homeland on the Salonika front. At that time several army officers were arrested and brought to trial at Salonika. They were convicted and three of the organization's leaders were executed, while others were imprisoned or pensioned.[19] Interestingly enough, the head of the organization, Colonel Dragutin Dimitrijević (Apis), before being shot shouted: "Long Live Great Serbia! Long Live Yugoslavia!"

As the Serbian army returned victorious to the homeland, its Yugoslav mission became increasingly important, and certain of its regiments and divisions even took on the name "Yugoslav" (e.g., Yugoslav Division instead of Vardar Division). The fact that Lloyd George had told Pašić as late as October 15, 1918, that the nature of Yugoslavia would depend on whether the Serbian army reached certain regions made it imperative that the army move into the Banat, Bosnia-Hercegovina, Croatia, and other regions which were inclined toward the Yugoslav movement.[20] And it was necessary for the army to move with all deliberate speed, because Italian troops were already occupying certain parts of Dalmatia and laying claim to them on the basis of the Treaty of London. In this mission, the Serbian army acquitted itself well, particularly in view of the many shortages in men and materiel.

In various discussions about the Serbian government and the unification of the Yugoslavs, attention always centers on one personality—Nikola Pašić—while another personality—Prince Regent Alexander—is almost totally ignored. Yet a pro-Yugoslav Serbian politician who had no love for Alexander, Dragoljub Jovanović, more than once told me that in the Serbian government the only important figure who was really for Yugoslavia was Alexander. Pašić and others, he said, had reservations, but not Alexander, who was clear, explicit, and decisive.[21] In Jovanović's opinion, Pašić was for Yugoslavia because he knew that Alexander was. Moreover, he said, high Serbian military officers who were for Yugoslavia held such positions in large measure because of the influence of Alexander.

EVALUATION OF NIKOLA PAŠIĆ

A final word needs to be said about Nikola Pašić, who had to navigate a number of treacherous political waters. He had a number of opportunities and pretexts (e.g., the Treaty of London) to settle for a Large Serbia, but he did not. As Professor Ekmečić has written, "In his conceptions of the future state as a European state, Pašić was unambiguous and clear to the end."[22] At times he could not seem to win in political discussion. If, for example, he spoke of the right to self-determination of the Croats and Slovenes, and that he would not insist on unification, he 'was accused of betraying the Yugoslav ideal and wanting a Large Serbia. When he defended the Corfu Declaration, and urged all South Slavs to abide by it, he was said to want Serbian hegemony. Serbian nationalists, on the other hand, have often condemned him for passing up the opportunity to create a Large Serbia. In much Yugoslav and other scholarly literature, Pašić is treated too simplistically. More recent Yugoslav scholarship has, however, tended to treat Pašić much more objectively, and to put in truer perspective the role of the Serbian government generally in Yugoslav unification. Much earlier Lloyd George put it very well when he wrote that Pašić was "one of the craftiest and most tenacious statesmen in South-Eastern Europe.... The foundation of the Yugoslav Kingdom was largely his doing.... He took care that this extended realm was an accomplished fact before the Peace Conference had time to approach the problem of adjusting boundaries."[23]

One cannot escape the general conclusion that the Serbian government—its political and military leaders—followed a pro-Yugoslav policy with great consistency. Individual leaders may from time to time have had private doubts and reservations, but these did not prevent them from making pro-Yugoslav decisions at all critical points along the way. With the benefit of hindsight, we might wish that at times they could have sought to avoid lack of clarity, but their general decisions were unmistakably in favor of unification of the Yugoslavs.

Notes

1. See Dragoslav Stranjaković, *Vlada Ustavobranitelja, 1842–1853* (Belgrade, 1932), pp. 268–274, and Vasa Čubrilović, *Istorija političke misli u Srbiji XIX veka* (Belgrade, 1958), pp. 159–195.

2. Dragoslav Janković, quoting Pašić's close collaborator, Lazar Marković, in *Naučni skup u povodu 50-godišnjice raspada Austro-Ugarske monarhije i stvaranja Jugoslavenske države* (Zagreb, 1969), pp. 132–33.

3. *Spomenica Nikole P. Pašića* (Belgrade, 1926), p. 60.

4. Anniversary volume, *Nikola P. Pašić* (Belgrade, 1937), p. 186.

5. Cited in Janković, *ibid.*, p. 133.

6. *Ibid.*, p. 133–34.

7. The most thorough study of Serbia's war aims, particularly in relation to her great allies, is Milorad Ekmečić, *Ratni ciljevi Srbije 1914* (Belgrade, 1973). See also Dragoslav Janković, "Niška deklaracija," *Istorija XX veka: Zbornik radova, X* (Belgrade, 1969). See also Janković's paper in *Naučni skup,* cited above.

8. Ekmečić, *ibid.*, p. 310ff. Also, see the chapter that follows in this work, by Gale Stokes.

9. Ekmečić, *ibid.*, pp. 324ff, and 370.

10. Ferdo Šišić, *Dokumenti o postanku Kraljevine Srba, Hrvata, i Slovenaca, 1914–1919* (Zagreb, 1920), p. 94. Italics mine.

11. See *Politički život Jugoslavije, 1914–1945: Zbornik radova* (Belgrade, 1973), pp. 65–66.

12. *Ibid.*, p. 67. See also my discussion of the creation of Yugoslavia in *Serbia, Nikola Pašić, and Yugoslavia* (New Brunswick, N.J., 1974), pp. 111–33.

13. *Politički život Jugoslavije,* p. 69.

14. Šišić, *Dokumenti*, pp. 189ff.

15. See my discussion of the Geneva Declaration, in *Serbia, Nikola Pašić, and Yugoslavia,* pp. 122–24.

16. Dragoslav Janković, *Jugoslovensko pitanje i krfska deklaracija 1917 godine* (Belgrade, 1967), pp. 33–39.

17. Vojislav J. Vučković, "Unutrašnje krize Srbije i prvi svetski rat," *Istoriski Časopis*, XIV–XV (1963–1965), pp. 173–229. Also see Slobodan Jovanović, *Moji savremenici: Uroš Petrović, Jovan Skerlić, Apis* (Windsor, Canada, 1962).

18. See my *The Development of Parliamentary Government in Serbia* (Boulder, Colo., 1978), pp. 107–114.

19. See Ekmečić, *Ratni ciljevi Srbije 1914*, pp. 108–112. Also my *Serbia, Nikola Pašić, and Yugoslavia*, p. 77ff.

20. See my *Serbia, Nikola Pašić, and Yugoslavia*, pp. 131–32. Also, see Bogdan Krizman in Vasa Čubrilović, et al. (eds.), *Naučni skup u povodu 50-godišnjice raspada Austro-Ugarske monarhije i stvaranja Jugoslavenske države* (Zagreb, 1969), p. 200.

21. Conversation with Jovanović, June 1976.

22. *Ratni ciljevi Srbije 1914*, p. 435.

23. *Memoirs of the Peace Conference* (New Haven, 1939), Vol. II, p. 525.

The Role of the Yugoslav Committee in the Formation of Yugoslavia

Gale Stokes

THE BREAKUP OF Austria-Hungary in the name of national self-determination brought about the creation of an equally multi-national new state, Yugoslavia.[1] It is paradoxical that the idea of Yugoslavism, emphasizing as it did the subordination of historical peoples to an ideal of brotherly unity, should have triumphed at a moment of nationalist exaltation, especially since Yugoslavism was popular only among the youth and a few intellectuals at the outbreak of World War I. This outcome may be attributed, in part at least, to the activities of a group of politicians and intellectuals from the Habsburg lands who escaped into Western Europe at the beginning of the war and organized themselves into a political action group called the Yugoslav Committee. By 1917 this committee had become a quasi-independent body with a head-quarters in London and private financial support. Members of the committee had close connections with the French and British governments, and emigrants who supported the committee in the United States even had some influence on American policy.[2] In 1917 the committee reached an agreement with the Serbian government that a new Yugoslav state would be founded after the war, so that when separate peace talks with Austria-Hungary failed for the last time in 1918 the committee was in position to push for the complete dismemberment of that ancient state. When the war ended, the committee's efforts had helped create an atmosphere in which the establishment of a Yugoslav state became not only an acceptable policy for the allies, but a desirable post-war goal.

The Yugoslav Committee, therefore, has with justice been considered an important element in the history of the formation of Yugoslavia.[3] It would perhaps be an exaggeration to say that without this committee no Yugoslavia would have emerged, but its significance is unquestionable. And yet, there is another side to the story, a more ominous side whose history is still being written, because the Kingdom of the Serbs, Croats and Slovenes did not turn out to be the sort of state the Yugoslav Committee had hoped.

Frustrated by German and Hungarian domination in the Habsburg Monarchy, the Croatian and Slovenian members of the Yugoslav Committee had sought to create a state in which no people would dominate or feel dominated. Aware of the dangers of imbalance in a multi-national state, Croatian and Slovenian émigrés insisted throughout World War I that post-war Yugoslavia would have to be a fusion of peoples, an equal partnership or organic union, not a Slavic Habsburg Empire in which certain national groups were favored. Despite their understanding of this danger, their insistence that it must not happen, and their work to avoid it, committee members could not prevent the creation of a Yugoslavia that was dominated by Serbs. The costs of this failure were incalculable. Politics in interwar Yugoslavia never functioned normally, because the only real issue was the national one. Hitler's easy success in 1941 was partially attributable to widespread disaffection with Belgrade, and the victory of Tito's Partisans during World War II was in important measure the result of the promise to put into practice the ideal of equality among the Yugoslav peoples.

PROBLEMS OF THE YUGOSLAV COMMITTEE

The history of the Yugoslav Committee, then, is one of many important successes, and one fundamental failure. The purpose of this article is not to enumerate or praise the successes, which has been done often enough, but to analyze the failure. The basic reason the Yugoslav Committee did not find it possible to create the state of equal peoples it sought was that the committee only worked within the limitations of its situation and never transcended them, so that in the end its success was limited as well. To achieve the equitable Yugoslavia it desired, the committee would have had to overcome four liabilities: its émigré nature; its vulnerability to Serbian initiatives; the incompatibility of its territorial aims with Italian aspirations; and its Croatian, even Dalmatian, composition.

The émigré nature of the committee was its most obvious and problematical feature. Just before and just after the beginning of actual warfare in 1914, several prominent Croatian politicians from Dalmatia succeeded either in leaving the Habsburg lands or in not returning. Ante Trumbić, Frano Supilo and Ivan Meštrović established a nucleus around which later émigrés could gather. But no matter how well balanced this nucleus strove to become by additions from inside Croatia and Slovenia, no matter how much support it could generate among South Slavic immigrants in the new world, and no matter how favorably inclined friendly individuals close to allied governments became, the committee remained an émigré organization, unrecognized by the law of any state, and without official sanction to represent the people for whom it claimed to speak. In the early stages of the war this did not matter. The committee could conduct its propaganda easily enough as a private interest group. But later, its only hope of influencing the character of the new Yugoslav state was to be formally recognized by the Great Powers as the legal representative of an allied people. To achieve diplomatic recognition, however, the Yugoslav Committee needed the acquiescence of the two allied powers already interested in South Slavic lands, Serbia and Italy.

The small likelihood that Serbia would permit the Yugoslav Committee to achieve legal status was implicit in the assumptions under which its Premier, Nikola Pašić, helped the committee form itself in 1914 and 1915. Serbia's immediate fear in 1914, besides collapse, was that an early peace would be signed before she could formulate comprehensive war aims.[4] Very early, therefore, the Serbs laid out a maximum program calling for the creation of a large South Slavic state. On September 21, 1914, Pašić formally suggested borders for a postwar state that stretched well into Habsburg lands, split Istria with Italy, and claimed all of Dalmatia. These proposed borders conflicted with Italian ambitions in the Adriatic and would necessitate the destruction of the Habsburg Empire.[5]

THE ESTABLISHMENT OF THE YUGOSLAV COMMITTEE

At the same time, the Dalmation émigrés in Italy had begun to discuss their situation. They concluded that the best hope for the future of Croatia and Slovenia lay in the creation of a new Slavic state on the Adriatic. This state would have to include Serbia, so that it could act as a Slavic barrier to German penetration into the Balkans, but more importantly it would provide a chance for Croatia and Slovenia to become independent of Austrian and Hungarian domination. These conclusions led to specific goals that were remarkably similar to those of Pašić: dismemberment of the Habsburg Empire, and acquisition of lands on the Adriatic. Already in October Frano Supilo was in France trying to interest French politicians in adopting the destruction of Austria-Hungary as a war aim.

When Pašić heard of Supilo's campaign in France and realized that Serbian and Croatian goals coincided, he quickly grasped that the Croatian émigrés, who had excellent contacts, could be helpful in popularizing Serbian war aims in Western Europe. Accordingly, he sent two special emissaries to Italy to offer the émigrés financial support in their common effort. On November 22, 1914, these representatives concluded an agreement with Ante Trumbić in Florence to establish a Yugoslav Committee consisting of leading émigré politicians of the three major South Slavic peoples. The purpose of the committee would be "to assist in the creation of a united Yugoslav (possibly Serbo-Croatian) state by informing leading circles and by publicity activity."[6] As this wording indicated, the committee was to assist Serbia through a propaganda effort. As far as Pašić was concerned, this was the extent of its purpose and authority.[7]

Pašić unquestionably sought the creation of a Yugoslav state.[8] The position papers worked out for him in the fall of 1914 demonstrate this, as does the Niš Declaration of December 7, 1914, by which the wartime Serbian government committed itself to a Yugoslav goal.[9] But quite naturally, Pašić did not think of Serbia as merely a partner of the other South Slavs in the struggle to create this new state. He thought of Serbia as a liberator. Since he considered the Macedonians and Montenegrins as Serbs that should be united with the motherland, he had no thought of allowing them any special status. The Croats and Slovenes were clearly not Serbs, so he was willing to allow them their national symbols, alphabet, religion, and even their traditional political organs. But the new Yugoslavia was not going to be an amalgam of these peoples. It was going to be a state in which the victorious Serbs would grant their new acquisitions equal rights as Serbs or as associated peoples. Pašić's supporters found this prospect emotionally satisfying, but they also had a good legal argument, since Serbia was recognized as an independent state and therefore could expand legitimately without a revolutionary European settlement.[10]

WORRIES OF CROATS AND SLOVENES

The Croats and Slovenes did not find the idea of liberation by the Serbs a congenial prospect. The example of Macedonia worried them. When Serbia seized Macedonia from Turkey and Bulgaria in the two Balkan wars, she did not extend normal constitutional rights to the newly acquired territory, even though she insisted that the Macedonians fulfill the regular obligations of citizens, including taxation and conscription. The Croatian émigrés in Italy who agreed to propagandize for a Yugoslav state had no desire for Croatia to become another Macedonia.[11] They were willing to begin cooperating, even if at first the Yugoslav Committee was subordinate to the Serbian government, because they believed there could be no Yugoslavia without Serbia. But they firmly believed that the logic of events would eventually transform the Yugoslav Committee into an equal partner.

Doubtful of Serbian intentions but assured of Serbian financial support, the committee members began to work. They laid plans for Yugoslav legions composed of volunteers from allied prisoner of war camps, invited politicians from Croatia proper and from Slovenia to join the emigration, and sent their representative to America, where he met with an enthusiastic welcome. But fearing that their interest in the Adriatic would spark a reaction from Italian nationalists, they did not make the committee's work public.

As one of the primary organizers and most prominent figures of the Yugoslav Committee, Frano Supilo spent the early months of 1915 attempting to work out a clearer understanding with Serbia and the Allies of what Croatia's future might be.[12] In the early spring this effort took him to Niš, the wartime capital of Serbia, where he found it very difficult to discover from Pašić what sort of terms the Croats could expect if they were to unite with Serbia. From Aleksandar Belić's semi-official *Srbija i južnoslovensko pitanje* [*Serbia and the South Slav Question*], he learned that the Serbs believed no special compact was needed. Belić claimed that Serbs and Croats were simply the same people with two names, so that any sort of autonomy that divided them would go against the national consciousness.[13] The dangers for the less numerous Croats of uniting with the Serbs before achieving agreement on the terms of unification were obvious to Supilo, but he was not able to find much sympathy for his point of view.

REACTION TO TREATY OF LONDON

Unsuccessful in Niš, Supilo travelled on to Petersburg to seek assurances from the Tsarist government. Instead of assurances he found disaster. Late in March, Sergei Sazonov, Russian Foreign Minister, let slip to Supilo that the Allies were about to promise Italy Dalmatia in return for her declaration of war. Supilo immediately informed both Pašić and Trumbić of this finding, but despite a month of frenzied activity by all three men, they were not able to head off the debacle. On April 26, 1915, Italy and the Allies signed the Treaty of London, by which lands claimed by the Yugoslavs on the Adriatic were assigned to Italy.[14] Stunned by this provocation, on April 30 Trumbić hastily assembled Croatian and Slovenian émigrés in Paris and brought the Yugoslav Committee out into the open. Designating London as its headquarters and electing Trumbić president, the now public committee sent a delegation the very next day to Delcassé to complain about the concessions to Italy, and within a few days it produced a policy memorandum setting out aims that directly conflicted with Italian goals.

Territorially, the committee's memorandum of May 1915 went beyond Pašić's memo of September 21.[15] Besides Dalmatia, it claimed for the Yugoslavs all of Istria, Gorica and Koruška, allowing to the Italians less territorial gain in the case of victory over Austria than Austria herself had offered as a reward for staying neutral. This emphasis on Slovenian and Croatian claims in the Adriatic was only natural for the Yugoslav Committee, since its composition was heavily Croatian, and its leadership Dalmatian. Just as the Serbs considered Macedonia inviolate, and the Italians came to see the Treaty of London as unchangeable, so the committee became intransigent concerning lands to which it was emotionally attached.

The committee's obduracy cannot be considered solely a matter of principle, such as self-determination, or nationality, although this is no

doubt how many saw it. On occasion, for example, members of the
Yugoslav Committee suggested that Serbia give up part of Macedonia
and concentrate on creating an outlet to the sea. This position was fully
comparable to the Serbian view that Macedonia was untouchable, but
compromises on the Adriatic might be possible. And, just as Serbia
gave up too little too late in Macedonia to prevent Bulgaria from
attacking her, so eventually Trumbić conceded too little too late on the
Adriatic to obtain Italian support. From the first moments of the
committee's public existence this strong Adriatic orientation hindered
the evolution of a realistic policy.

YUGOSLAV COMMITTEE'S RESTRAINTS

By the time the Yugoslav Committee began the public phase of its
work in May 1915, then, the restraints within which it worked for the
rest of the war were established. It was an émigré committee with a
special interest in the Adriatic question and Dalmatia, it was an uneasy
junior partner of Serbia, and it was in conflict with Italy. Its goal,
beyond the day-to-day demands and programs, was the creation, with
Serbia, of an equitable Yugoslav state on the ruins of the Habsburg
Empire.

This requirement that a Yugoslavia could exist only if Austria-
Hungary ceased to exist had an important effect on the work of the
committee. Until the spring of 1918 the likelihood that the Allies would
seek the breakup of Austria-Hungary was small. The remoteness of the
possibility of a Yugoslav state meant that committee members felt only
the relatively light pressure of working out ideal plans, not the inexor-
able urgency associated with immediate and actual possibilities. With so
much else uncertain, there seemed to be no compelling reason to break
with Serbia even though the committee was not achieving equality, or
to accommodate Italian wishes in the Adriatic, even though Italy continued to oppose Yugoslav aspirations there. In 1916 and 1917, therefore, the committee took two crucial steps that confirmed its original
relationship to Serbia, thereby helping to ensure that the committee
would not achieve its ultimate goal.

By 1916 relations between the Serbian government and the Yugoslav Committee had become strained. In trying to convince Bulgaria to
enter the war against the Central Powers, the Allies had made Serbia
several territorial offers. Quite naturally, when rumors of these possibilities leaked out the Croats and Slovenes felt that they were being
callously parcelled out as compensations, not treated as peoples with
their own aspirations. At one point, in an effort to work out a solution,
Supilo endorsed a compromise suggestion made by Sir Edward Grey
that Bosnia and Hercegovina, Southern Dalmatia, Slavonia, and
Croatia be allowed to choose their future by plebiscite after the war.
This formula only worsened the situation. The Serbian government

interpreted it to mean that Supilo was preparing the ground for the creation of an independent Croatia, while members of the Yugoslav Committee objected that Supilo had made this important compromise without consulting them. Supilo responded vigorously.[16] He hoped, he said, that successful prosecution of the war would produce a state that would be the "harmonious product of all our national strengths, a fusion of spirits, traditions, and hopes." But for this to happen, Serbia would have to accomplish fundamental political, constitutional, and cultural reforms that would prevent what he called a serbo-orthodox exclusivism from destroying Yugoslav unity. If Serbia did not change, Supilo warned, unification would have to await a more opportune moment. In the meantime, in the absence of reform, all those Yugoslav lands in which a majority of people wanted to be united with Croatia should be granted that desire.

Supilo's outright threat to seek a separate Croatian state did not achieve the support of the Yugoslav Committee. Naturally, the Serbian members of the committee, as informal representatives of Pašić's government, opposed it, but so did the Slovenes. One of Supilo's blind spots was that he thought of Slovenes much in the same way that he complained Serbs thought of Croats. He considered Zagreb the center of Croatian-Slovenian activity, and did not understand that the Slovenes found this offensive. Naturally, therefore, he could not count on their support of his Croatian-centered idea. Even some Croats opposed Supilo. Still, at a plenary meeting of the committee in February 1916, the crisis was patched over. The committee formally reaffirmed its commitment to a broad unification, but placed many of Supilo's views in a policy memorandum to the French government on March 13. This was only a temporary solution, however.

WORSENING OF SERBIAN SITUATION

The situation of the Serbian government had changed dramatically for the worse by 1916. Thoroughly defeated by the Austrians under German leadership and hounded by the Bulgarians from the south, the Serbian army had conducted a heroic but costly retreat through the winter of 1915–16 that took it finally to the island of Corfu. In the spring of 1916 Pašić was bearing the political consequences of this defeat, threatened on the one side by the machinations of Regent Alexander Karadjordević, and on the other by disloyalty of an important segment of the military under the leadership of Colonel Dimitrijević-Apis.[17] In an effort to improve his fortunes at home by success abroad, Pašić travelled to Paris, London, and Petrograd in May 1916. Under great pressure, not certain of the outcome of the war, and none too confident of the purposes of the Croatian emigration, Pašić stated in an interview to the Russian press that he was ready to recognize Italy's predominant interest in the Adriatic.

Pašić's statement outraged the Yugoslav Committee, particularly Supilo, for whom it simply demonstrated the impossibility of trusting the Serbs to protect Croatian and Slovenian interests.[18] Supilo demanded the Yugoslav Committee break its relations with Serbia. But, once again, an emergency session of the full committee did not agree.[19] Harmony with Serbia was considered so vital that the committee simply asked its president, Trumbić, to speak privately with Pašić. To restrain Supilo from using his great personal influence to promote a break with Serbia, the committee prohibited any member from making personal contacts and statements without approval from Trumbić. Supilo responded to this gag rule by resigning from the committee, leaving it firmly under Trumbić's leadership until the end of the war.[20]

Supilo had accurately assessed the underlying attitude of Pašić and his government. Not only was Pašić a superb politician, a magician of appearance and nuance, and a dogged pursuer of personal power, he also was a true representative of the faith of all Serbian politicians in Serbia's destiny as the liberator of the Balkans. Supilo grasped that in something as basic as the structure of a future Yugoslavia, Pašić could never yield, either politically or temperamentally. Some others saw this, but none were hard-headed enough to follow the logic of the realization to its unpalatable conclusion: a break with Serbia. So Supilo was isolated, and despite its doubts, the committee tied itself even closer to Serbia.

CORFU AGREEMENT

A year later, conclusion of the Corfu Agreement seemed to indicate that the decision of 1916 had been correct. This agreement, which was achieved by lengthy and difficult negotiations between the representatives of the Yugoslav Committee and the Serbian government, was signed by Pašić and Trumbić July 20, 1917.[21] It called for the creation of a democratic, constitutional Kingdom of Serbs, Croats, and Slovenes under the Karadjordjević dynasty in which the cultural and religious rights of all three peoples would be preserved. A constitutional assembly to be held after liberation would determine the internal organization of the state.

The two signatories interpreted the Corfu Declaration quite differently. The Yugoslav Committee believed it had achieved basic agreement with Serbia. Even Supilo's pessimism was momentarily overcome. Despite the failure of the conferees to agree on the organization of the new state, it seemed that a great step forward for Yugoslavism had been achieved, and many still hold that this was the case.

Today, however, one may doubt that this positive interpretation is the whole truth. Pašić did not come to the negotiations because of any desire to plan for the future Yugoslav state. He called for discussions only under severe pressure, and after the agreement had been signed he ignored it except as a device for silencing those who accused him of ignoring the committee. Internally, Pašić's government was under attack for accepting Regent Alexander's scheme to rid the army of disloyal elements. By this plan Colonel Dimitrijević-Apis and his closest collaborators had been condemned to death for treason and attempted assassination. There is considerable doubt that these charges could have been sustained in a fair trial, but no doubt whatsoever that Apis and his organization, "Union or Death," were a center of independent power that had disrupted Serbian public life for years. "Union or Death" had been involved in the assassination of Franz Ferdinand and its machinations had resulted in the fall of Pašić's government in June 1914. The basic question was who would be the final authority in Serbia, the Prince, the army, or the government. Because of his opposition to Pašić, Apis had close links with the opposition parties. Therefore, when Pašić decided to go along with the Regent's plan to remove Apis he lost the support of these parties, with whom he had been allied in a coalition government since 1914.[22] Apis's trial also hurt Serbian regard abroad, since it was represented by Pašić's enemies not as an effort to establish the authority of the civilian government but as an act of political revenge.

Pašić faced other uncertainties. In May 1917, the South Slavic political parties remaining inside Austria-Hungary proclaimed their desire for unification "under the sceptre of the Habsburg-Lorraine dynasty."[23] It appeared possible that the new Emperor Charles might be on the verge of forestalling Serbian gains by granting the Croats and Slovenes some sort of autonomy within the empire. Rumors of peace feelers further indicated that Serbian war aims might be in danger. Furthermore, Pašić was worried that the Yugoslav Committee, which he still considered simply an arm of Serbian propaganda, was slipping away from him. Not only did the committee constantly have its own views on affairs, but by 1917 it had become financially independent due to the generous support of the emigrant community in South America.

Rapprochement with the Yugoslav Committee would have a positive effect on all these problems. It would provide an antidote to the bad press Pašić was receiving abroad over the Apis case by pleasing the foreign supporters of the committee; it would mollify the opposition, which tended to favor accommodation; it would reaffirm Serbian claims to represent the Habsburg South Slavs in spite of the May Declaration; and it would draw the committee into closer cooperation with Serbia.

Having called for the meeting to serve these clear short-term ends, Pašić almost ignored the agreement after it was made. Before the ink on his signature was dry, he left Corfu to attend the conference on Balkan problems being held at Versailles. Rather than present the agreement officially to the Powers, as the Yugoslav Committee hoped, he contented himself with belatedly and reluctantly making it known to them only orally.

In a way, of course, the standard interpretation of the Corfu Agreement as a positive step for Yugoslavism is correct. The agreement put both the Serbian government and the Yugoslav Committee on record as pursuing the same broad goal. But unfortunately for the Yugoslav Committee, it was not realized at the time, nor has it been clearly seen since, that the agreement was also a masterful diplomatic success for Pašić.[24] In return for acceptance of the Karadjordjević dynasty, with its clear implication of Serbian continuity, Pašić agreed to the principles of democracy, civil rights, and constitutionalism. This was not any sort of concession for him, since all of these were features of pre-war Serbia and matched well the policy he had enunciated in 1914. Beyond that, however, Pašić conceded nothing. He did not change his view that Serbia should be the liberating power, nor did he make any agreement that would hinder his ability to organize the state after the war. In a typically brilliant maneuver, he achieved several short-term goals while putting the committee in his debt by giving it something it wanted, all the time retaining full initiative for himself in those things he considered most important. Without giving up anything fundamental, he severely limited the Yugoslav Committee's freedom of action by linking it more closely to Serbia than it had ever been before.

ITALIAN-YUGOSLAV DIFFERENCES

Committed now to cooperating with Serbia in the creation of a new state rather than going it alone, as Supilo had suggested, Trumbić had reason to hope in 1918 that progress in modifying Italian policy might also be possible. The solid rock of that policy was foreign minister Sidney Sonnino.[25] Sonnino had negotiated Italy's entrance into the Great War in return for South Tirol, Trentino, Istria, and central Dalmatia with its islands. Sonnino considered the acquisitions in the north the final stage of Italian unification, and those on the Adriatic necessary for Italian security. Since the treaty also provided that the Great Powers could eventually assign some of the Adriatic lands to Slavic states, he believed that the treaty was a "working formula" from which all could profit.[26] He was wrong. The Slavs saw the treaty only as a threat to their unification, not as a starting point for negotiations. Nonetheless, from the moment Sonnino secretly negotiated the treaty until his death in 1922 he resolutely held out for every last inch of territory promised him. As a result, even though some influential Italians favored a modified policy of cooperation with the South Slavs, Italian foreign policy remained until the end of the war extremely hostile to both Serbia and the Yugoslav Committee.

Late in 1917 English supporters of the Yugoslav cause began trying to do something about the deep differences between the Italians and the Yugoslavs.[27] Several meetings ensued, including one between Trumbić and the head of the Italian government, Vittorio Orlando. The eventual outcome was the Torre-Trumbić agreement of March 1918.[28] Andrea Torre was the chairman of an *ad hoc* committee of the Italian parliament that was trying to organize a public meeting of the leaders of the Habsburg nationalities in exile for propaganda purposes. He had come to London to get the agreement of the Yugoslav Committee that was needed if the meeting was to be held. Trumbić was not enthusiastic. He refused to discuss border issues with Torre, and by insisting that the Italians renounce the Treaty of London he pushed their discussions to an impasse. Only when Henry Wickham Steed, foreign editor of *The Times* and a staunch supporter of Yugoslavism, frankly told Trumbić that his attitude would forfeit the support of Steed and his friends did Trumbić consent at the last minute to a statement of rather general principles. The Yugoslavs recognized the legitimacy of Italy's policy of national unity and the Italians recognized the Yugoslav goals of unification and independence. No specific territories were mentioned because "national unity" for the Italians included the same lands the Yugoslavs meant when they used the term "independence." Accordingly, and just as impossibly, it was agreed that territorial disputes would be decided after the war on the basis of the principle of nationality but in a way that would not injure the vital interests of either people. Rather than deciding anything, the Torre-Trumbić agreement simply recognized the two parties had incompatible goals: "nationality" for the Yugoslavs, and "vital interests" for the Italians.

But this was enough, and the Congress of Oppressed Nationalities was duly held in Rome in April 1918, bringing together not only the Yugoslavs, but Poles, Czechs, and Rumanians as well. Orlando, along with other Italians more or less sympathetic to the South Slavs, attended the two-day meeting, but the intense feelings and rivalries precluded meaningful negotiations. The only communiqué adopted by the congress was simply a verbatim rendering of the Torre-Trumbić agreement.

Despite the superficial nature of this accomplishment, it appeared to many that the Pact of Rome, as it was called, implied that the Italians were willing to renounce Dalmatia and the Yugoslavs Trieste and Istria. For this reason it created considerable enthusiasm among the subject nationalities and was a great propaganda success. Leo Valiani has even gone so far as to say that the congress "represented a mortal blow to Austria-Hungary."[29] But for the Yugoslav Committee the ratification of the Pact of Rome was the Italian counterpart of the Corfu Declaration, with Sonnino playing the part of Pašić. Just as Pašić had drawn the committee more closely to Serbia by concessions that did not forfeit his own initiative, so Sonnino allowed the Pact of Rome to achieve a propaganda success for the Italians without budging an inch on the Treaty of London. Sonnino did not approve of Torre's initiatives except in so far as they might help an Italian propaganda effort, did not attend the Rome Congress, and did not turn away from his obsession with the Treaty of London. Having committed himself to cooperation with the obdurate Pašić in 1916 and 1917, Trumbić committed himself to finding a compromise with the unyielding Sonnino in 1918.

These commitments proved to be the committee's downfall. When the war began to draw to a close, Trumbić realized ever more clearly that unless the committee could achieve formal recognition as the representative of the Habsburg South Slavs it would not be able to influence the shape of the post-war state. The last few months of the war were taken up with this fruitless task. None of the Powers would recognize the committee, even though they recognized the Czechoslovak National Committee and expressed increasing sympathy with the Yugoslav aims, unless Serbia and Italy also agreed. Agreement with Italy meant agreement with Sonnino, who continued to ignore the South Slavs and to consider the Treaty of London inviolate. The last possibility of a modification of his position occurred in August 1918, when Leonida Bissolati, the socialist Minister without portfolio, convinced Orlando to call the first full meeting of the Italian cabinet in two years to discuss foreign policy. One of his main motives was to achieve a more balanced Italian policy toward the Yugoslavs. The importance of this opportunity was so obvious that for the first time Trumbić was moved to modify the committee's maximum territorial claims, originally established in reaction to the London Treaty in 1915. But when his compromise offer fell far short of total acceptance of the London Treaty, Bissolati could only get the cabinet to agree to an official statement recognizing the existence of "the movement of the Yugoslav peoples."[30]

This result was not encouraging, but it was enough to make it seem that progress was being made. It was not. The Italian government did not publish its mild statement, which fell far short of recognition, until September 25, and more importantly, Sonnino did not change. He intended to occupy the Yugoslav lands promised Italy by the Treaty of London as enemy territory. Recognition of the Yugoslav Committee would make those lands friendly territory, preventing their occupation. The futility of the committee's campaign received its final confirmation at the meeting of the Supreme Allied War Council at Versailles on November 1, at which time the Italians easily brushed aside the Yugoslav demands for recognition and received permission to occupy territory up to the line of the 1915 agreement.

Pašić's Strength and Intransigence

Pašić too was intransigent. Responding to a request from Trumbić that Serbia support formal recognition of the committee, he claimed that the Serbs, Croats, and Slovenes were already adequately represented by the Serbian government, and that it would be a mistake to have two centers of power. This policy took enormous personal strength on Pašić's part. He was ruling without a majority in a rump parliament. An intense opposition criticized his every move, and most of this opposition favored an accommodation with the Yugoslav Committee. His potential friends in the West, both in France and England, were becoming estranged by his unwillingness to negotiate. Robert W. Seton-Watson, England's foremost authority on Eastern Europe, publicly attacked him, and when he visited London in early October 1918, British Foreign Minister Balfour warned him in person that no positive outcome for the Yugoslavs could be expected if he continued his adamant attitude.[31] And yet he stood firm against recognition.

By the end of October, as the Central Powers neared collapse, a new element entered the picture. Throughout the war the politicians who had remained in Austria-Hungary had been constrained to follow policies that were more or less loyal to the crown. But this did not prevent some of them from expressing their desire for unification and recognition, as the May Declaration demonstrated. In the difficult year of 1918, those parties that were inclined toward the creation of a larger Yugoslavia gained in strength. When it was obvious that the days of the monarchy were numbered, intense activity by these parties led to the creation in Zagreb of a government of the Serbs, Croats, and Slovenes in the Habsburg lands on October 29, 1918. With the formal approval of the Croatian Sabor and shortly of Emperor Charles himself, the *narodno vijeće,* as this government was styled, proclaimed itself sovereign. Immediately its president, the Slovenian Anton Korošec, set off to Geneva to seek recognition from the Allies and to establish relations with the Serbian government and Yugoslav Committee. Korošec immediately contacted both Pašić and Trumbić, and when he learned that the Allies were meeting in Versailles during the first few days of November to discuss armistice terms for Austria, he designated the Yugoslav Committee in the person of Trumbić as the official representative there of the *narodno vijeće*.

The Yugoslavs were not able to influence the Versailles meetings, but the allied powers did recognize that something had to be done about the existence of two, now three, groups that claimed to represent portions of the Yugoslav peoples. The French government in particular summarily directed Pašić to meet with Trumbić and settle their differences. Accordingly, these two met in Paris on November 4. On

Korošec's invitation, however, they immediately adjourned to Geneva to attempt to achieve agreement on the composition of a joint government, as demanded by the Allies. The Serbian opposition was also represented at this meeting, which took place from November 6 to November 9.[32]

GENEVA AGREEMENT CREATES DUAL GOVERNMENT

Trumbić appeared to have the strongest hand at Geneva, since the Serbian opposition parties opposed Pašić's intransigence, as did Korošec. Pašić realized that he would have to come to a distasteful compromise, and on November 9, 1918, he signed the Geneva Agreement, even though it did not accord with his views. By this compromise, put forward by Trumbić, a dual government reminiscent of the Dual Monarchy it was in part replacing would be formed. This new government would regulate the joint activities of the South Slavs, but the *narodno vijeće* and the Serbian government each would retain sovereignty over their own local affairs. The members of the joint government would take their oaths to their own sovereigns, Alexander Karadjordjević in the case of the Serbs, and the *narodno vijeće* in the case of the Habsburg Slavs. A more lasting constitutional arrangement would be worked out later.

This agreement, had it lasted, meant unification on the equal basis the Yugoslav Committee had sought. It appeared that Trumbić and the Yugoslav Committee had succeeded. But once again, and for the last time, appearances were deceiving. When Pašić first notified his government on Corfu of his signature, Stojan Protić, his closest political associate, accepted the decision. But the next day, November 10, Pašić sent a telegram to Protić in which he broadly hinted that if the Regent wished another sort of arrangement he could accept the government's resignation. On November 11, Protić changed his mind and repudiated the Geneva Agreement. The government resigned. Within a few days Pašić destroyed the support of the Yugoslav Committee among Serbs by asking the political parties that had opposed him for so long to join in a coalition government. Accepting the opportunity to participate in the making of a new Serbia, these parties lost much of their interest in the Yugoslav Committee, and the Geneva Agreement was forgotten.

Meanwhile, support of the committee was being undermined in Zagreb as well. Prince Alexander did not favor the Geneva Agreement since it did not require all of the persons in the new state to take an oath of allegiance to him. This obviously influenced Protić's rejection. But another important reason for Protić's step was that he discovered on November 10 that the balance of forces in the *narodno vijeće* was shifting away from the Yugoslav Committee. The main South Slavic political force in the Habsburg Monarchy for the decade preceding 1918 had been the Serbo-Croatian Coalition. Although originally founded by men such as Supilo and Trumbić, during World War I it had remained passive toward the efforts of others to bring forth a new Yugoslav state. Only with difficulty and at the last minute was the Coalition enticed into the *narodno vijeće*. Its acceptance of the national program was considered the final step that would insure the creation of a new Yugoslavia. However, when the Coalition entered the *narodno vijeće* it immediately became the dominant force and its leader, Svetozar Pribićević, the strongest figure. Pribićević was a Serb who favored unification along the lines suggested by Pašić and Protić, not those favored by Korošec and Trumbić. Fortuitously, Protić had received word on this favorable situation on November 10 from Prince Alexander, who was not in Corfu, but in Belgrade, having entered the Serbian capital only the day before with his victorious army. Protić was able to repudiate the Geneva Agreement in the knowledge that the *narodno vijeće* was likely to do so also eventually under Pribićević's leadership. In fact, on November 25, this is just what happened.

In November the rapidly changing course of events moved completely out of the control of the Yugoslav Committee. The Serbian army occupied Belgrade on November 1. By November 13 a military representative of the high command was in Zagreb, encouraging Pribićević. By the end of the month the *narodno vijeće*, without consulting Trumbić or Korošec, decided to join Serbia immediately and without conditions. On December 1, 1918, Alexander received the petitioners of the *narodno vijeće*, as well as representatives of other bodies from Montenegro, Bosnia and Hercegovina, and the Vojvodina, and announced the formation of the new Kingdom of the Serbs, Croats, and Slovenes.[33] The Croats and Slovenes had done just what Supilo had feared in 1915 and what Pašić all alone had hoped they would do: they had agreed to unification with Serbia without first working out the terms.

EVALUATION OF YUGOSLAV COMMITTEE'S ROLE

There is probably only one way the Yugoslav Committee could have improved upon this result. If the Yugoslav Committee had understood how accurately Pašić represented the deep feeling of most Serbs that Serbia should be the liberator of the South Slavs, its only course of action would have been to break with Serbia. If the committee had appreciated the impossibility of agreeing with Sonnino on any terms less than full acceptance of the Treaty of London, its only solution would have been to accept that treaty. But these were impossible choices. Not only did the Serbian government have its representatives on the Yugoslav Committee, but even among the Croats there was no agreement that Pašić's way was wrong. The Slovenes could not accept Supilo's proposal to break with Serbia because Supilo treated the Slovenes as merely adjuncts to Croatia. Furthermore, none of them would have agreed to give up the Adriatic lands Italy craved. The Yugoslav Committee was in a similar position to that of the Polish government in exile during World War II. The only way the Poles could have reached an accommodation with Stalin would have been to recognize the 1941 borders. But the very reason the Poles went into exile in the first place was to protect 1939 Poland. For both the Poles and the Yugoslavs, the one thing they most needed to do was the one thing to which they would never consent.[34]

Politics may be the art of the possible, but in this case the only way the Yugoslav Committee could have succeeded would have been to practice the art of the impossible. The committee needed to accept the Treaty of London and break with the Serbs. Had the Yugoslavs accepted the Italian claims they would not have lost much more territory than they did anyway, but they would have opened up enormous positive possibilities. One of the constant and unsuccessful struggles of the committee, for example, was to create a Yugoslav Legion from Habsburg prisoners of war in Italy.[35] The experience of the Czech Committee in exile showed how important it was to have such a force in being. In the spring of 1918, when the manpower shortage was critical on the western front, the Czechs had been able to extract concessions from the Allies because they controlled Czech legions that could be assigned to the front. Sonnino did not want the Yugoslavs to have such legions because he feared they would be used on behalf of the South Slavs in the lands Italy had been promised in 1915. But if the committee had accepted the Treaty of London, this fear would have been allayed and perhaps Sonnino would have let the Yugoslavs form their legions. With these forces at their back, the committee might have been recognized in mid-1918 at the same time the Czechs were.

This is all the more likely because of a second result acceptance of the London Treaty would have produced. From the beginning, the fact that many Slavs lived in the territories the Italians claimed by the Treaty of London threatened the Italian aims. They needed some group that spoke for these Slavs to agree to Italian rule. The Yugoslav Committee was such a group. But acceptance of the Italian territorial demands by the committee would gain legal significance only if it were a legal entity, not just an émigré group. It is almost certain, therefore, that if the committee had accepted the London Treaty the Italians would have favored recognition, because in that way any possible ethnic stain on the Italian claims would have been wiped clean.

Naturally, acceptance of the Treaty of London would have meant breaking with Serbia, as Supilo suggested. Difficult though this would have been, it too would have had positive effects. For example, Pašić's opposition to recognition would have been much less effective if the committee was not seen as subordinate to the Serbian government. As the war drew to a close and the *narodno vijeće* came into being, the

Yugoslav Committee could have offered the new state its assets: military forces and formal recognition, a combination that would have been hard to resist. Two possibilities would have opened up. Either two South Slavic states would have been established at the end of the war, or Serbia would have had to meet the Yugoslav Committee and *narodno vijeće* on equal terms and work out a mutually satisfactory agreement. In either case, the chances that Serbia could dominate Croatia and Slovenia in a post-war state would have been greatly lessened, and the goal of the Yugoslav Committee would have come much closer to realization.

In fact, of course, none of this happened. Frano Supilo was willing to break with Serbia and even to make concessions to Italy, but most of his colleagues, including Ante Trumbić, were not. Trumbić believed that the exclusion of Serbia from a South Slavic movement would eviscerate the entire idea of Yugoslavism. Therefore, he was always willing to make one more effort to work out an agreement with Pašić. The irony of this position was that precisely his belief that Serbia was necessary to a new Yugoslavia made it impossible for Trumbić to make the cold-blooded decision that could have made an equal partnership possible. This, coupled with his inability to negotiate realistically with Italy, prevented the committee from transcending its émigré status and reduced its historical role to that of a propaganda agent for Yugoslavism.

In this capacity, the Yugoslav Committee was extremely successful. But in its political goal, it was not. One's evaluation of this outcome depends a good deal on whether one is a pessimist or an optimist. The pessimists will say that Trumbić failed because he did not have the greatness to correctly evaluate the situation and lead his committee to the extremely difficult decisions that hindsight shows were necessary. The optimists will point out that Trumbić always kept before his eyes the ultimate goal of a unified Yugoslavia, successfully created a climate of opinion in Europe favorable to that idea, and had the charity and vision to refuse to consider a new Yugoslavia without Serbia. Both evaluations are correct, but in either case, the result did not turn out as Trumbić had hoped.

Notes

1. Some of the research for this article was done at the Illinois Summer Research Laboratory for 1978. I would like to thank both the Russian Center at the University of Illinois and Rice University for making my stay at the Laboratory possible.

2. The extensive efforts on behalf of the Yugoslav movement by South Slavic emigrants in North and South America will not be discussed in this article. For their influence on American policy see Victor S. Mamatey, *The United States and East Central Europe, 1914–1918: A Study in Wilsonian Diplomacy and Propaganda* (Princeton: Princeton University Press, 1957) and George J. Prpić, "The South Slavs," in Joseph P. O'Grady, *The Immigrants' Influence on Wilson's Peace Policies* (Lexington: University of Kentucky Press, 1967). I am not aware of similarly extensive treatments of the strong Yugoslav movement in South America, although Paulová discusses it briefly (pp. 226–35).

3. The first major interpretation of the Yugoslav Committee was Milada Paulová, *Jugoslavenski odbor* [*The Yugoslav Committee*] (Zagreb: Prosvjetna nakladna zadruga, 1925). It remains important, even though it is an *apologia* for Trumbić and the committee. A basic bibliography may be found in the superb study, which is now the standard interpretation of the period, Dragovan Šepić, *Italija, saveznici i Jugoslavensko pitanje, 1914–1918* [*Italy, the Allies, and the Yugoslav Question, 1914–1918*] (Zagreb: Školska knjiga, 1970). The two standard studies in English are Michael B. Petrovich, *A History of Modern Serbia, 1804–1918* (New York: Harcourt, Brace, Jovanovich, 1976), Volume II, pp. 621–82, and Ivo J. Lederer, *Yugoslavia at the Paris Peace Conference: A Study in Frontiermaking* (New Haven: Yale University Press, 1963), pp. 3–78. Two collections of documents are Ferdo Šišić, *Dokumenti o postanku Kraljevine Srba, Hrvata i Slovenaca 1914–1919* [*Documents on the Creation of the Kingdom of the Serbs, Croats and Slovenes, 1914–1918*] (Zagreb, 1920), and Dragoslav Janković and Bodgan Krizman, eds., *Gradja o stvaranju jugoslovenske države* [*Materials on the Creation of the Yugoslav State*] (Belgrade, 1964). Neither collection was available to me during the preparation of this article. See also Vaso Bogdanov, *et al.*, eds., *Jugoslovenski odbor u Londonu* [*The Yugoslav Committee in London*] (Zagreb: The Yugoslav Academy, 1966).

4. Milorad Ekmečić, *Ratni ciljevi Srbije 1914* [*Serbian War Aims in 1914*] (Belgrade: Srpska kniževna zadruga, 1973), pp. 208–14. See also the solid study by Dragoslav Janković, *Srbija i jugoslovensko pitanje, 1914–1915* [*Serbia and the Yugoslav Question, 1914–1915*] (Belgrade: Institut zu savremenu istoriju, 1973).

5. Šepić, *Italija, saveznici i jugoslavensko pitanje*, pp. 12–13 (map). Pašić's memorandum had been preceded by a note to the allied governments on September 4 in which he had said that the best way to assure the allied war aim, the containment of Germany,

was to create a strong national state in the Balkans that would consist of all Serbs, Croats, and Slovenes (Ekmečić, pp. 88–9).

6. Šepić, *Italija, saveznici i jugoslavensko pitanje,* p. 32.

7. As late as October 1918, Pašić said that he had created the Yugoslav Committee and given it money "for propaganda and nothing more" (Šepić, *Italija, saveznici i jugoslavensko pitanje,* p. 358).

8. This is one of Ekmečić's main points. As he puts it, "In the war smoke of 1914, it was seen clearly in Serbia that her five minutes of history had come . . . " (p. 84). For a supportive biography of Pašić, see Alex Dragnich, *Serbia, Nikola Pašić, and Yugoslavia* (New Brunswick, N.J.: Rutgers University Press, 1974).

9. The key statement of the declaration was that Serbia's war aim was "the liberation and unification of all our unliberated brothers: Serbs, Croats, and Slovenes." The Bulgarophile Noel Buxton, who was present, describes the event as follows: "The skupshtina met in a concert hall attached to a cafe. The deputies sat close together on rows of small wicker chairs facing the president. On his right along the wall sat the eight members of the new Cabinet which had just been formed, with a green baize table before them lit by two candles. . . . M. Pasich . . . then rose. . . . His long grey beard and somewhat threadbare frock coat made him a striking figure as he stood and read by the dim candle light his momentous declaration" (Noel and Charles Roden Buxton, *The War and the Balkans* [London: Allen and Unwin, 1915], pp. 41–2). The basic work on the Declaration is Dragoslav Janković, "Niška deklaracija" ["The Niš Declaration"], *Istorija dvadesetog veka,* X (1969), pp. 7–111.

10. Ekmečić, *Ratni ciljevi,* pp. 214–18.

11. The committee made this fear public at the very end of the war, when Trumbić had lost hope that Serbia would allow the committee to be recognized (Šepić, *Italija, saveznici i jugoslavensko pitanje,* p. 357).

12. Of the two main leaders of the Yugoslav Committee, Frano Supilo and Ante Trumbić, Supilo has occasioned the most interest among historians. Dragovan Šepić published his letters and memoranda from the war period in *Pisma i memorandumi Frana Supila (1914–1917)* (Belgrade: Serbian Academy of Arts and Sciences, 1967) and some further items in *Politički spisi* [*Political Writings*] (Zagreb: Znanje, 1970). The latter contains an extended biographical introduction on Supilo's life until 1914. See too Šepić, "Hrvatska u koncepcijama Frana Supila o ujedinjenju" ["Croatia in Fran Supilo's Conceptions of Unification"], *Forum,* 7 (1968), pp. 342–81, and Tereza Ganza-Aras, "Frano Supilo u svjetlu najnovijih istraživanja" ["Fran Supilo in the Light of the Latest Research"], *Historijski zbornik,* XXV–XXVI (1972–3), pp. 387–406.

13. Šepić, "Hrvatska u koncepcijama Supila," pp. 355–6; Šepić, *Italija, saveznici i jugoslavensko pitanje,* pp. 43–4; Ekmečić, *Ratni ciljevi Srbije,* pp. 101–3; Paulová, *Jugoslavenski odbor,* pp. 26–34.

14. The provisions of the treaty did not become public until they were published by the Bolsheviks in 1917, but the main provisions were surmised almost immediately by the interested parties.

15. Šepić, *Italija, saveznici i jugoslavenski pitanje,* pp. 89–92.

16. *Ibid.*, pp. 140–46; Šepić, "Hrvatska u koncepcijama Supila," pp. 357–65.

17. For an excellent review of the problems faced by Pašić see Vojislav J. Vučković, "Unutrašnje krize Srbije i prvi svetski rat" ["Serbia's Internal Crises and the First World War"], *Istorijski časopis*, XIV–XV (1963–65), pp. 173–229.

18. Within a short while, however, Supilo realized that if the Habsburg South Slavs were to accomplish their goal of independence, accommodation with Italy was necessary. "I believe," he said, "that the Serbo-Croat-Slovene state, which has more need of Italian support than any other European power, must compensate for this collaboration with adequate concessions" (Leo Valiani, *The End of Austria-Hungary* [New York: Knopf, 1973], p. 418). Valiani believes that by 1917 Supilo would have conceded Italy dominance of the Adriatic, if not Dalmatia.

19. Supilo read his earlier memorandum of seven points to the committee, but the committee soundly rejected any idea of a separate Croatia as damaging to the ideal of Yugoslavism. For the texts of their statements, see *Nova Evropa* [*New Europe*], 13 (1926), pp. 85–6.

20. For Supilo's resignation statement, in which he accuses the Serbian government of supporting the committee with "pretty words" while thwarting it politically, see Paulová, *Jugoslavenski odbor*, pp. 211–14. Supilo's premature death a year later removed him from Yugoslav politics entirely.

21. The basic work is Dragoslav Janković, *Jugoslovensko pitanje i krfska deklaracija 1917. godine* [*The Yugoslav Question and the Corfu Declaration, 1917*] (Belgrade: Savremena administracija, 1967). For the text of the agreement see Petrovich, *History of Serbia*, pp. 644–45.

22. Vučković, "Unutrašnje krize Srbije," pp. 203–23.

23. Šepić, *Italija, saveznici i jugoslavensko pitanje*, pp. 197–205.

24. Petrovich recognizes this: "Trumbić and others may have regarded it as the Magna Charta of Yugoslav unification. For Pašić it was a tactical move in response to a given political situation" (*History of Serbia*, p. 649).

25. For a succinct review of Sonnino's career, see Salvatore Saladino, "In Search of Sidney Sonnino," *Reviews in European History*, 2 (1976), pp. 621–33.

26. Christopher Seton-Watson, *Italy from Liberalism to Fascism, 1870–1925* (London: Methuen and Company, 1967), p. 432.

27. English Yugoslavophiles such as R.W. Seton-Watson and Henry Wickham Steed are not discussed in this article, but they had a great impact on the success of the Yugoslav Committee in bringing its ideas before Europe. They founded a Serbian Society of Great Britain, established a journal to forward the cause of East European nationalism (*The New Europe*), and through official propaganda efforts in 1918 popularized the idea of destruction of Austria-Hungary (for the last, see Kenneth J. Calder, *Britain and the Origins of the New Europe, 1914–1918* [Cambridge: Cambridge University Press, 1976]). The fundamental narrative of this activity is Steed, *Through Thirty Years* (New York: Doubleday, Page and Company, 1925). Recently Hugh Seton-Watson has been investigating his father's role in Yugoslav affairs (e.g.,

"Robert William Seton-Watson i jugoslavensko pitanje" ["Robert William Seton-Watson and the Yugoslav Question"], *Časopis za suvremenu povijest*, II [1970], pp. 75–96. In cooperation with the Seton-Watson family, the British Academy and the Institute of Croatian History of Zagreb University has published *R.W. Seton-Watson i Jugoslaveni: Korespondencija 1906–1941* [*R.W. Seton-Watson and the Yugoslavs: Correspondence, 1906–1941*] (Zagreb-London, 1976), 2 vols.

28. For the following see Valiani, *The End of Austria-Hungary,* pp. 199–256; Christopher Seton-Watson, *Italy from Liberalism to Fascism*, pp. 492–97; Steed, *Through Thirty Years*, II, pp. 183–85; Šepić, *Italija, saveznici i jugoslavensko pitanje*, pp. 289–96; and Paulová, *Jugoslavenski odbor,* pp. 417–43.

29. Valiani, *The End of Austria-Hungary*, p. 240. Paulová's analysis (p. 442) is a good example of how even later supporters of the Yugoslav Committee overestimated its potential positive effect on Italian public opinion and policy.

30. Šepić, *Italija, saveznici i jugoslavensko pitanje,* pp. 337–44.

31. *Ibid.,* p. 358. Seton-Watson became so irritated with Pašić's unwillingness to recognize the Yugoslav Committee that he attacked him in a famous article, "Serbia's Choice," in *The New Europe,* 22 August 1918. "Any Serbian statesman who failed to perceive this truth [that the Austrian Slavs should be treated as an equal factor] would deserve to be regarded . . . as a traitor to the best interest of his race. In Serbia . . . our sympathy and support must be given, not to the old Oriental tendencies, now tottering to their fall, but to those new and democratic elements in whose hands the future of Jugoslavia lies." This was not an entirely fair criticism, since the Radical Party had long stood for constitutionalism and civilian government in Serbia, but when Stojan Protić responded that in his opinion "there is more reason to fear that we may encounter semi-Turkish [he is referring to Bosnia and Hercegovina] and semi-Austrian traditions nearer to you in the West," the justice of his reply was drowned out by cries of outrage, and Pašić's reputation was further weakened (*The New Europe,* 26 September 1918). The strong anti-Pašić feeling of the British Yugoslavophiles is obvious in Steed's description of his conversation with Pašić on October 8, 1918 (Steed, *Through Thirty Years,* II, 233–39).

32. For the following see Bogdan Krizman, "Ženevska konferencija o ujedinjenju 1918. godine" ["The Geneva Conference of Unification, 1918"], *Istorijski glasnik*, 1958, no. 1–2, pp. 3–32, and Dragoslav Janković, "Ženevska konferencija o stvaranju jugoslovenske zajednice 1918. godine" ["The Geneva Conference on the Creation of a Yugoslav Union, 1918"], *Istorija XX veka, Zbornik radova*, V (1963), pp. 225–63.

33. Petrovich, *A History of Modern Serbia,* pp. 663–82.

34. Compare the realistic and successful policy that Lenin forced on his unwilling comrades when he cajoled and bullied them into accepting severe losses at Brest-Litovsk, but in the process saved the Bolshevik Revolution.

35. Some Yugoslav legions were actually formed in Odessa, seeing action in the Dobrudja in 1916, but Sonnino consistently blocked the formation of such units in Italy (Paulová, *Jugoslavenski odbor, passim.*). In English see Margot Lawrence, "The Serbian Divisions in Russia, 1916–1917," *Journal of Contemporary History*, 6 (1971), pp. 183–92.

Russia's Role in the Creation of the Yugoslav State, 1914–1918

Michael B. Petrovich

OPINIONS ON RUSSIA'S role in the creation of a Yugoslav state can differ greatly, depending on one's perspective. From one vantage point one can conclude, particularly if one relies largely on the diplomatic correspondence of the day, that Russia's role was minimal and even negative. Yet it is frequently asserted, especially by more recent Yugoslav and Soviet scholars, and again with some basis, that Russia's role was enormous and even decisive. It is our aim to examine briefly this seeming discrepancy in the light of the available literature, both primary and secondary. This literature has grown substantially in the last three decades and presents not only new materials but new outlooks.

What complicates the entire subject is the involvement of not one Russia but three during the First World War: Imperial Russia, the Russia of the Provisional Government, and Soviet Russia. Moreover, there were four centers of Yugoslav activity: the governments of Serbia and Montenegro, the Yugoslav Committee in exile, and the Yugoslav leaders in Austria-Hungary, notably in the Croatian Diet in Zagreb and in the Imperial Reichsrat in Vienna. Each of these Russian and Yugoslav political entities had policies, programs and perspectives of their own. We shall deal with them in the periods of the three Russian regimes: (1) the Tsarist, from 1914 to March 1917; (2) the Provisional Government, March to November 8, 1917; and (3) the Soviet Government, from November 8, 1917, to the formation of the Kingdom of the Serbs, Croats, and Slovenes on December 1, 1918.

When the First World War broke out and embroiled Russia, in early August 1914, the idea of a Yugoslav state had not yet become an issue in international diplomacy. It was Serbia and not the Yugoslav peoples to which both unofficial and official Russia were committed. Significant segments of Russian society, under the influence of a revived Panslavism, felt strong ties of Slavic kinship and Orthodox intercommunion with the Serbs. Official Russia found reason to favor Serbia over its erstwhile protégé, Bulgaria, as an obstacle to Austro-

Hungarian economic and political expansion in the Balkans.[1]

Both this unofficial Russian Neo-Slavism and official Russian preference for Serbia found many highly placed champions in the Russian Imperial Court, the government, and particularly the Foreign Ministry. Notable among them was the Foreign Minister himself, Sergei Dmitrievich Sazonov. It was he who, at the cabinet meeting which met to consider Austria-Hungary's ultimatum of July 23 to Serbia, declared in the presence of Tsar Nicholas II that Russia could not forsake Serbia, and that Russian refusal to support Serbia would provoke such indignation inside Russia that the dynasty itself would be endangered.[2] It was also Sazonov who talked the vacillating Tsar into ordering full mobilization on July 30, as a result of which Germany declared war on Russia.[3] It was inevitable that however the Russian government approached the Yugoslav Question after the start of the war, it was always led by its pro-Serbian policy and traditional disposition.

Similarly it should be borne in mind that Premier Nikola Pašić, the chief architect of Serbia's policy in this period, was always, and understandably so, a Serb first and a Yugoslav second. In his case, too, disposition and strategy prompted him to pursue two programs simultaneously and as it seemed best to him according to the exigencies of the momentary international situation—that of a Greater Serbia and of a Yugoslav state, or his "little program" and "big program."[4] Pašić's primary aim was to unite Montenegro and as many Serb-inhabited areas of Austria-Hungary to Serbia as possible. He also accepted and supported the larger aim of the political unification of all the Serbs, Croats and Slovenes; however, whether out of opportunism or practicality, Pašić saw this unification less as the creation of a totally new political organism than an extension of an already existing and internationally recognized Serbian state. It is not easy to know, even today after so many years, just when this shrewd politician was pushing the one program or the other, and how sincerely.

It was in early October 1914 that Pašić first informed Sazonov of Serbia's postwar territorial aspirations; these included not only Serbian-populated areas but also Croatian and Slovenian territories.[5] However, it was on December 7, 1914, that the Serbian government publicly proclaimed its Yugoslav program, before the Serbian National Assembly in Niš. It referred to the cause of the "Serbo-Croatian [sic] and Slovenian people" and to "the struggle for the liberation of all our unliberated brother Serbs, Croats and Slovenes."[6]

At first it seemed that the Russian Foreign Ministry was all for this program. The new Russian minister to Serbia, Prince Grigorii Nikolaevich Trubetskoi, approved of it, while the Serbian minister to Russia, Miroslav Spalajković, was assured by the Russian Foreign Ministry that even though they had received various proposals for a Greater Croatia, they were supporting only Serbia's aims.[7] Russian

Ambassador Count Alexander Petrovich Izvol'skii in Paris wrote enthusiastically to Sazonov, "I venture to suggest here the idea that a strong and unified Serbo-Croatian Kingdom which included Istria and Dalmatia would constitute the necessary counterweight to Italy, Hungary, and Romania."[8]

ITALY'S DEMANDS

No issue affected the Tsarist government's attitude toward the Yugoslav Question as much as Italy's demands for Yugoslav-inhabited territories along the eastern Adriatic coast as its price for entering the war on the side of the Entente. It was initially Russia, more than any of its allies, that was most energetic in securing Italy's aid, even if at the expense of some Yugoslavs. Devastating losses on the Eastern Front forced Russia to seek Italy's military assistance to deflect the pressure of Austria-Hungary's armies.[9] Petrograd hoped to hurry Italy into selling its aid at a minimum price. Even Pašić, in beleaguered Serbia, was willing to have Italy take not only Trieste but a part of the Istrian Peninsula, if only Italy entered the war immediately.[10]

More than the Serbian government, it was the exiled Yugoslav leaders from Austria-Hungary, many of them Dalmatians, who were most perturbed by rumors of Allied negotiations with Italy. Having formed a Yugoslav Committee in London, they decided to send one of their number, Frano Supilo, to Petrograd, by way of Niš. Supilo arrived in Petrograd on February 22, 1915. His talks with Sazonov confirmed his worst fears. Sazonov himself made the following note on March 25, 1915, of a meeting of theirs, which recorded his saying to Supilo that the Powers would probably have to sacrifice the hopes of the Slavic population along the Adriatic to Italian demands. "These words produced a shocking effect on Supilo," Sazonov noted.[11] Supilo conveyed some of his shock in a message to Pašić. "Russian official policy," he concluded, "being concerned with a solution to the Straits Question, is wavering under pressure. The Adriatic and the Yugoslav Question are being abandoned. . . ."[12] When Supilo went the next day to Baron Maurice Schilling to express his dismay, the Russian Deputy Foreign Minister assured him that Russia did not lack sympathy for the "southwestern Slavs," but that the international situation required certain sacrifices. Supilo was advised to hasten to Paris and London to defend his cause.[13] At first Supilo resisted this advice and remained in Russia for a while hoping to persuade the Tsar and his government as well as Russian high society, but he soon saw the hopelessness of the situation and left Russia in mid-April, 1915.[14]

Meanwhile Spalajković was also reporting to Pašić Sazonov's lack of enthusiasm for Yugoslav unification. The Serbian Minister to Russia advised Pašić to make clear to the Russians that Serbia's program was not one of a takeover of the South Slavs but the realization of a common

ideal and joint interests which could not allow a part of the Croats and
Slovenes to remain under foreign rule.[15] Spalajković also reported
Sazonov's expression of disinterest in the Catholic Western Slavs who,
he said, were alien to Russia, who had done nothing for Russia in the
war, and whose territory was in any event too rocky to be of much use to
Serbia.[16] It could well seem that the Russian Foreign Minister was
seeking to justify what he was secretly doing at that very time—making
one concession after another to Italy's demands.

Although at no time was the Serbian government informed by the
Allies of their negotiations with Italy, Pašić had every reason to be
alarmed at the messages he was getting, both from his own envoys and
from the Yugoslav Committee. Accordingly he sent a note to the Allied
governments on April 5, 1915, warning them of an inevitable conflict
between the Yugoslavs and the Italians over an unjust border settlement.[17] He also sent a special mission to Petrograd consisting of two
eminent Serbian scholars, both philologists, Aleksandar Belić and
Ljubomir Stojanović. Both had been to Russia before on a diplomatic
mission during a time of crisis—in 1908 after the Austrian annexation
of Bosnia-Hercegovina. The Russian government did all it could to
keep them from coming, but Pašić was adamant, and they arrived in
Petrograd on April 28, 1915. They did not know that they had arrived
too late: the Allied Secret Treaty of London with Italy had been signed
two days before.

Though this Serbian mission was a failure before it ever began, it
provides additional insights into official Russia's attitude toward the
Yugoslav Question. In this respect the first meeting of Stojanović and
Belić with Foreign Minister Sazonov, that of May 9, is extraordinarily
revealing. The Russian treated his guests with exaggerated cordiality
and assured them how close Serbia's interests were to Russian hearts;
he promised that Serbia would be several times larger after the war,
with the inclusion of Montenegro and Bosnia-Hercegovina. When the
two Serbs assured him that the Serbs would not be satisfied until all the
Serbs, Croats and Slovenes were united, Sazonov balked. Serbia's ambitions, he remarked, could not be accomplished all at once. He said that
he was not at all sure that Austria-Hungary would dissolve after the
war. Also, he did not wish to "irritate" the Italians. Sazonov also expressed doubt that the Catholic Croats, with all their aristocratic traditions, wished to unite with the Orthodox Serbs. As for the Slovenes, he
declared, "If Russia had to wage war a single day more for the sake of
Carinthia, it would forego its liberation." (Eight years later, in an article
in Belgrade's *Novi List*, Belić reported Sazonov's statement as follows: "I
can tell you nothing about the Croats and the Slovenes. They are
fighting against us, and I declare to you: if it were necessary for the
Russian people to fight with weapons just half a day in order to free the
Slovenes, I would not agree to it."[18]) As for concessions to Italy,

Sazonov did not, of course, let Stojanović and Belić know that anything had already been promised to Italy. He professed to be surprised at his guests' refusal to recognize that Italy had any right to the Dalmatian coast, especially the cities. He irritated them by using the Italian names of Dalmatian cities—Sebenico, Zara, Fiume—as though to stress their Italian character.[19] In their report to Pašić of their conversation with Sazonov, Stojanović and Belić concluded that as far as the Russian government was concerned, the future of Yugoslav unification de- pended on several factors, most particularly on the fate of the Austro-Hungarian Empire: if the latter sued for a separate peace, then Russia and its allies would keep the Dual Monarchy intact except for concessions to Italy.[20]

RUSSIA'S MULTIPLE NEGOTIATIONS

Tsarist Russia was involved in negotiations not only with Italy but with Romania and Bulgaria that potentially affected the borders of Serbia.[21] The Serbian minister in Petrograd kept sending Pašić reports of Russia's willingness to award Romania a large part of the Banat, and Bulgaria a large part of Macedonia, in exchange for their military assistance. Indeed, Sazonov even indirectly suggested to Spalajković that it would be well to prepare Serbian public opinion for the territo- rial sacrifices that Serbia might have to make as the result of Allied negotiation with Romania and Bulgaria. All of this had to do with Serbia, as far as the Russian government was concerned. Yet it had a curious connection with the larger Yugoslav Question, even apart from the matter of future boundaries: Sazonov attempted to placate Premier Pašić by assuring him that, as compensations, Russia would support the future unification of the Serbs, Croats, and Slovenes in a single state, and that it would not conclude a treaty with Romania if Serbia were not assured that part of the Banat was inhabited by a Serbian majority.[22] Far from being placated, Pašić threatened to resign.[23]

Tsarist Russia's involvement in this phase of the Yugoslav Question lends sharper definition to a basic difference between the approaches of the Serbian government and of the Yugoslav Committee in London. The Yugoslav Committee based its efforts on the right of the Slovenes, Croats and Serbs of Austria-Hungary to national self-determination and to the establishment of a Yugoslav state that would be, in essence, a new political entity. The Serbian government, on the other hand, saw the future Yugoslavia as an extension of an already existing political entity, Serbia. How much this was simply practical Realpolitik and how much it was Serbian hegemonism is a long debated question. However, there is no doubt that the official Russian view of a future Yugoslavia was closer to that of the Serbian government than to the view of the Yugoslav Committee. Similarly, just as the future of Yugoslav unifica- tion was less important to Pašić than the salvation and aggrandizement

of Serbia and of the Serbian people, so the future of Yugoslav unification was less important to the Tsarist Russian government than the
welfare of Serbia itself, and both were less important to the Tsarist
Russian government than a Russian victory, Germany's defeat, and
certain postwar gains for Russia, notably the Straits.

This official Russian ambivalence was evident in several different
connections after the secret Treaty of London on April 26, 1915. The
question of Yugoslav Austro-Hungarian prisoners of war in Russia
provides a case in point. Many thousands of these men, mostly Serbs
but also Croats and Slovenes, appealed to the Serbian Legation in
Petrograd to be taken into the Serbian army as volunteers. The Russian
government was very reticent about allowing this, on the grounds that
it was not proper to encourage Austro-Hungarian soldiers to fight
against their own emperor to whom they had taken an oath; besides,
the Austro-Hungarian government might retaliate by using Russian
prisoners of war in the same way.[24] At first, the Russian government
allowed small groups of only Serbs to be sent to the Serbian army via
Romania and the Danube. When that route was cut off, it allowed the
formation of small units supposedly to guard Serbia's warehouses in
Odessa. Finally, the local Serbian consul, Marko Cemović, wangled an
audience with Nicholas II at the Odessa railroad station and got the
Tsar's permission to establish a Serbian Volunteer Division. At a time
when many of these volunteers wished to call themselves a *Yugoslav*
division, Russian officials fanned a conflict between the Serbs on the
one hand and the Croats and Slovenes on the other by encouraging
that element among them that favored a Slavic component within a
liberalized Austro-Hungarian federation. Ante Mandić, a representative of the Yugoslav Committee who was actively engaged in organizing
these volunteers in Russia at the time, was convinced that official Russia
preferred to keep the Catholic Slovenes and Croats in such a Danubian
federation rather than to contaminate Orthodox Serbia in a Yugoslav
state.[25] In any event, even without Russian interference, there were
enough troubles between these Yugoslav volunteers and the often
crude and chauvinistic Serbian officers which Pašić's government sent
to command them. These troubles grew to such an extent that by the
time the February Revolution broke out in Petrograd (on March 8,
1917, New Style), discipline within the volunteer division was in a
shambles.

Among the lesser officials of the Russian Foreign Ministry there
were some who supported the Yugoslav cause, men such as A. M.
Petraev and V. I. Nekrasov, but their views did not have significance
until Pavel Nikolaevich Miliukov became foreign minister in the Provisional Government. However, in 1916 it was Mikhail Grigorevich Prik-
lonskii, Director of the Foreign Ministry's Statistical Department, who
served as the expert on the Slavs of Austria-Hungary. Reactionary in

outlook, pro-Hungarian and pro-Habsburg, he belonged to that whole group of Russian bureaucrats including Boris Stürmer, I. L. Goremy-kin's successor as premier in mid-February 1916, who believed it was against Russian interests to promote the unification of the Orthodox and Catholic Slavs of the Balkans.[26]

As for the Yugoslav Question in Russian society during the Tsarist period, the only real interest at first was shown by the neo-Slavists of the conservative and even reactionary right, and that was an embarrass-ment, especially to the Yugoslav Committee, for several reasons. First, the Russian liberals and radicals tended to oppose anything that the right supported. Second, particularly after the fall of Serbia in 1915, the neo-Slavists with their Russian Big Brother complex and Orthodox outlook, clung to the idea that it was Serbia that had to be resurrected with Russian help, and that only with their inclusion in a Slavic federa-tion under the aegis of Imperial Russia could the South Slavs have any future.[27]

One segment of Russian society that especially supported the Yugoslav cause was a group of scholars in the Russian Academy of Science led by its vice-president, A. A. Shakhmatov. Encouraged and financed by the Yugoslav Committee, this group published seven books and pamphlets about the Yugoslavs.[28] Under the patronage of the Grand Duchess Maria Pavlovna, the Academy was even preparing to sponsor an exhibition of Ivan Meštrović's sculptures.[29]

As for the Russian press, the Russian government—for fear of irritating Italy—forbade newspapers from treating the Yugoslav prob-lem.[30] It was thanks to Sir Bernard Pares, noted British expert on Russia as professor at the University of Liverpool and liaison with the Russian army at the time, that Ante Mandić came into contact with the Progressive Bloc members of the Russian Duma when it met in Febru-ary 1916. His talks with them in their caucus to make them more aware of the Yugoslav cause troubled the Russian government greatly, just as did similar talks by Czechoslovak representatives. Indeed, it assigned Aleksandr Aleksandrovich Giers, lately minister to Montenegro, and Baron Boris E. Nolde, the Foreign Ministry's legal counsel, to convince the leaders of the Progressive Bloc that the whole subject of Yugoslav and Czechoslovak unification was impractical and was not really a serious question.[31]

Such, in briefest outline, were the prevailing attitudes of official Russia and of Russian society between 1914 and the February Revolu-tion in 1917.

SERBIA'S REACTION TO THE RUSSIAN FEBRUARY REVOLUTION

Though it had depended heavily on Imperial Russia, the Serbian government did not at first take the overthrow of the Tsardom as a blow. The Serbian envoy in Petrograd reported the February Revolution as something expected and natural and even as a positive change. "Even despite Miliukov," Spalajković wrote in his first report of the event, "our question can only gain from these changes, for we seek only what is founded on elementary justice and reasonable understandings of Serbian and Russian interests. Besides, now we have a guaranty in a liberal Russia in which behind-the-scenes actions are excluded. . . ."[32]

With all of royal Serbia's past ties with imperial Russia, there was no question raised over Serbia's recognition of the Provisional Government of revolutionary Russia. On March 23, 1917, Pašić, as foreign minister of Serbia, sent greetings to Russian Foreign Minister Pavel Miliukov in which he expressed "joy that the coup ended so quickly and without significant losses, and that it did not shake the might and prestige of our fraternal Russia. . . ." He reminded Miliukov that the Serbian people had always remained faithful to their blood brothers, the fraternal Russian people, "even in difficult times, even when Russian diplomacy sinned against both itself and against us, and when compromises were made at the expense of our national aspirations, . . ."[33] Serbia formally recognized the new Russian government on March 29, 1917.

The Serbian government sent no special political mission to the Provisional Government, but it did send a group of Yugoslavs who were already in Russia as "the representatives of public opinion in the Serbian Kingdom, of the Yugoslav Committee, and Serbian officers." The group included Professors Belić and Stojanović as well as Ante Mandić, representative of the Yugoslav Committee. When they visited the president of the Duma Prince Georgii E. Lvov, they found that though he called for the freedom of what he called the "Sloveno-Croatian" people, his heart was with Serbia. "We all love Serbia," Prince Lvov told them. "It has suffered more than anyone else. It must not be only restored but significantly enlarged and united into a Greater Serbia. . . . Long live Greater Serbia!"[34]

THE ROLE OF MILIUKOV

The Serbian government mistrusted Miliukov as a Bulgarophile who disliked the Serbs. Even the Croatian Supilo thought this. In March 1915 Supilo wrote to Trumbić, president of the Yugoslav Committee in London, "Even Miliukov, leader of the Kadets, has been won over to our cause. He hates the Serbs, but he likes the Croats (and Bulgars). . . ."[35] In 1913 when Miliukov had visited Belgrade as a member of an international investigatory commission organized by the Carnegie Endowment for International Peace, Pašić refused to receive the commission as long as it included Miliukov, allegedly an *ennemi déclaré* of Serbia. Indeed, as Miliukov recalled in his memoirs, he was made the object of a specially arranged hostile demonstration in his hotel on the evening of his unceremonious departure.[36] There is no doubt that Miliukov was an avowed Bulgarophile, at least until Bulgaria's entry into the war on October 14, 1915, and that he thought ill of the Serbs. In a conversation with British Foreign Minister Sir Edward Grey in spring 1916, Miliukov blurted out, by his own account, "Listen, the war occurred as a result of Serbian megalomania!"[37]

And yet when Miliukov became Russian foreign minister after the February Revolution, he came out very strongly on behalf of both Serbia and Yugoslav unification. On March 24, 1917, Miliukov issued a "Declaration of Russia's War Aims" to the French news agency "Radio" which included the statement: "We wish the creation of a Yugoslavia, solidly organized. We shall erect around glorious Serbia an impenetrable rampart against German ambitions in the Balkans."[38] It seemed as though the Provisional Government, like the Tsarist government, was seeing the Yugoslav question through the prism of its pro-Serbian policy. True, Miliukov's statement was the first public declaration by the spokesman of a Great Power that called for the establishment of a Yugoslav state, and the Yugoslav Committee in London heartily thanked Miliukov for it.[39] Nevertheless, when Miliukov received his first official visit by the envoy of the Serbian government, on April 7 (New Style), he made no mention of the creation of a Yugoslavia, but said to Spalajković, "I can assure you that Serbia will not only be returned all that belonged to it in the past, but that all of its national aspirations will be realized. For Russia this will be a debt of gratitude. The interest of Europe demands that a new Serbia emerge from this war, free, great, united, which shall serve us as a rampart against German expansion...."[40]

Instead of the Provisional Government being able to help the Yugoslavs, it asked their help in dealing with the Petrograd Soviet of Workers' and Soldiers' Deputies, which held the real power in Russia. Miliukov complained to the Yugoslavs in Petrograd that the socialists were causing him difficulties, and he begged them "to enlighten Russian public opinion" and to convince the socialists that "the partitioning of Austria-Hungary is a policy of liberation and not conquest."[41]

In her capital work on the Yugoslav Committee, the Czech historian Milada Paulová suggested that one of the main reasons why Pašić called a conference of Yugoslav leaders at Corfu in the summer of 1917 was because he feared Miliukov's republicanism and wanted to get a statement of Yugoslav support for the Karadjordjević dynasty of Serbia.[42] Ante Mandić wrote, on the other hand, that it was Pašić's fear of Miliukov's Bulgarophilism and declaration in favor of a future Yugoslav state that caused Pašić to convene the Corfu Conference in order to save what he could of Greater Serbia.[43] More recently Dragoslav Janković, the historian of that Conference, has rejected both suppositions on the grounds that Pašić knew very well at the time that the Provisional Government of Russia was very weak and that Miliukov was in fact no longer a political factor after the crisis created by his statement of May 1/April 17, 1917, concerning the alleged desire of the Russian people to fight the war until final victory. A war-weary Russian populace repudiated this statement with street demonstrations in favor of "peace without annexations and indemnities." It was not fear of Miliukov, Janković asserted, but of a Communist takeover in Russia which would lead to a separate peace by Russia that caused Pašić to confer with the Yugoslav Committee on Corfu.

Janković has offered a second modification of a view established in the literature (especially Paulová and N. Stojanović) that Britain and France, as democratic powers, from the beginning favored the Yugoslav Committee over the Serbian Government and that after the February Revolution and the entry of the United States into the war the position of the Yugoslav Committee even improved because the new bourgeois-democratic Russia, like President Wilson, stressed democratic principles, particularly the right of national self-determination. This, Janković maintained, was only partially true: The Russian Revolution raised the whole question of democratic representation and of who had the right to represent the aspirations of the Yugoslavs as a whole. Janković has suggested that Milan Marjanović was perhaps the only member of the Yugoslav Committee that understood this new populist upsurge.[44] He urged Trubić, "We must therefore establish from now on that we are the representatives and the executors of a revolution in Austria-Hungary and not just the propagators of a certain idea."[45] Janković concluded that though the general political climate which ensued after the February Revolution in Russia favored the Yugoslav Committee, its leaders did not know how to profit by it, nor could they, because of their lack of ties with the masses of their own people.[46]

Perhaps nothing illustrates better the fact that official Russia was too preoccupied with more important matters than the Yugoslav Question in mid-1917 than its lack of a reaction to the Corfu Declaration. This historic agreement between the Serbian government and the representatives of the Yugoslav Committee on July 20, 1917, was their first formal and public act calling for a united Yugoslav state and under the Karadjordjević dynasty.[47] M. I. Tereshchenko, who had succeeded Miliukov as foreign minister in the Provisional Government during the May Crisis, did send a telegram of greeting and best wishes to the Corfu Conference in which he hoped for its success "so that a close and constant unity among the Yugoslavs might be achieved in the future on the principles of self-determination, just recognition of mutual rights, and consonance of political and economic interests."[48] However, no one in Russia paid any attention to the Corfu Declaration except for a few brief notices in some newspapers. As to why there was "not even the slightest impression" made by this event in Russia, Mandić explained to the Yugoslav Committee, "the reason for this is that your telegram came just at the time the Bolsheviks came out and there was shooting in the streets, and so naturally no one was the least bit interested in such questions."[49]

Indeed, this fairly sums up the entire role of the Russian Provisional Government with respect to the Yugoslav Question after Miliukov's downfall. The one tangible contribution this government made to the Yugoslav cause was to facilitate the evacuation of Yugoslav prisoners of war, by way of Odessa, who volunteered to join the Yugoslav Legion that fought at the Salonika Front. One battalion left Russia even before the October Revolution, and the rest followed later; indeed, thanks to the ensuing disorder in Russia as a result of the October Revolution, the last unit left by way of Murmansk as late as October 1919.

THE GREAT OCTOBER REVOLUTION

Much has been written on the effects of the Great October Revolution on the Yugoslavs. Most of this literature comes from Soviet and Yugoslav Marxists who generally regard that event as a turning point in the history of all mankind, indeed, the most decisive of all. Especially during the observance of the fiftieth anniversary of the Great October Revolution in 1967, many books and articles appeared extolling the universal significance of this event. In the Yugoslav case the chief effects of the October Revolution have been treated in two related spheres: (1) the international and (2) the domestic.

One of the first acts of the Soviet regime was the declaration, on November 8, 1917, during the very first moments it came to power, of the Decree on Peace, which was passed by the Second All-Russian Congress of Soviets of Workers', Soldiers', and Peasants' Deputies.[50] This declaration proposed "to all belligerent peoples and their Governments the immediate opening of negotiations for a just and democratic peace . . . an immediate peace without annexations (i.e., without seizure of foreign territory, without the forcible incorporation of foreign nationalities), and without indemnities." The decree specifically condemned "the incorporation into a large or powerful State of a small or weak nationality, without the definitely, clearly, and voluntarily expressed consent and desire of this nationality. . . ." The Decree on Peace was followed, on November 28, by a direct appeal, by wireless, by the Council of People's Commissars to the peoples of the belligerent countries to join in the negotiations for an armistice.[51]

This proclamation had a direct effect on the Yugoslavs in the Austro-Hungarian Monarchy. In Zagreb several leaders of the Starčević Party of Rights and of the Croato-Serbian Coalition joined in making a declaration of their own, on December 3, which specifically referred to "the peace offer of the present revolutionary Russian government as issued in Tsarskoe Selo on November 28" and which announced that they, as members of the Croatian Diet, greeted this proposal. At the same time they called for "a democratic peace, a peace which shall guarantee to all nations, including the one nation of Croats, Serbs and Slovenes, complete freedom of political, cultural and economic life and progress."[52]

On January 31, 1918, the Yugoslav Caucus (Club) of deputies in the Viennese Reichsrat joined in a manifesto of their own which they sent to the Austro-Hungarian, German, Soviet Russian and Ukrainian delegations that were negotiating a peace at Brest-Litovsk. This memorandum began with a direct reference to the Decree on Peace passed by the Congress of Soviets, especially its condemnation as forcible annexation, seizure and coercion any act by a state to retain any nation against its will. On that basis the Yugoslav Caucus presented a three-point program calling for national self-determination and specifically that the Serbs, Croats and Slovenes be given all that territory on which they were compactly settled.[53] It will be noted that this declaration was considerably more radical than that which the Yugoslav Caucus had made on May 30, 1917. The May Declaration asked that all territories in the Austro-Hungarian Monarchy inhabited by Slovenes, Croats and Serbs be united "under the scepter of the Habsburg-Lorraine dynasty."[54] The memorandum of January 31, 1918, no longer assumed the existence of Austria-Hungary or its dynasty. It is noteworthy to what a degree this declaration reflected the Soviet Decree on Peace even in its phraseology.

A similar radicalization is noticeable in other resolutions of the time by various Yugoslav bodies in Austria-Hungary. Among these we may cite the resolution of the Slovenian People's Progressive Party in Ljubljana on February 2, 1918, and the joint declaration of the Croatian and Serbian deputies in the Dalmatian Diet and the Reichsrat in Vienna, which was announced in Zadar on April 14, 1918.[55]

SOVIET DECREE ON PEACE

Another early act of the new Soviet regime which gave particular joy to the Yugoslav Committee in London was the publication of the secret Treaty of London in which the Allies had promised Italy so much of the Yugoslav Adriatic Coast. Even during the Provisional Government, Premier Pašić tried in vain to get a look at the Allied treaties with both Italy and Romania, but Foreign Minister Tereshchenko refused to violate his government's obligation to maintain secrecy.[56] However, the Soviet Decree on Peace specifically declared, "the Government abolishes secret diplomacy and on its part expresses the firm intention to conduct all negotiations absolutely openly before the entire people; it will at once begin to publish in full the secret treaties concluded or confirmed by the Government of landowners and capitalists from

February to 25 October [7 November] 1917."[57] Following up on this resolution, the Soviet Commissar for Foreign Affairs Leon Trotsky issued a statement on November 22, 1917, in which he announced the forthcoming publication of secret treaties and declared all such treaties as invalid as far as the Soviet government was concerned.[58]

Though the governments of Serbia and Soviet Russia did not extend diplomatic recognition to one another, Serbian Minister in Petrograd Spalajković maintained informal relations. Just two days after the Decree on Peace was proclaimed, Spalajković sent an emissary to Trotsky to ask specifically that the Treaty of London be published as quickly as possible. Trotsky was very cooperative and even accepted the help of one of Spalajković's men to help find the treaty, which had been left buried in a pile of papers.[59] After a few days, on November 28, 1917, *Pravda* was the first to publish the treaty in its entirety.[60]

When, a month later, a delegation of military volunteers sent by the Serbian Legation visited Trotsky, he spoke to them of his friendly feelings for Serbia, which he had once visited, and told them that he had made public the Treaty of London in order to help Serbia. He even went further and pledged Soviet Russia's help to Serbia vis-à-vis Bulgaria. He once told Spalajković's agent that "revolutionary Russia would know how to punish the Bulgarian Ferdinand even worse than an offended Nicholas II might."[61] It is noteworthy that Soviet Russia no less than liberal-democratic Russia or Tsarist Russia was seeing the Yugoslav question primarily through the prism of its Serbian policy. This was altogether natural since Serbia was an established state and recognized factor in international diplomacy while the Yugoslavs of Austria-Hungary were not.

Pašić was very eager to exploit this pro-Serbian sentiment in Soviet Petrograd and repeatedly advised Spalajković to make use of Serbian socialists to propagate Serbia's program there in socialist terms. "Our national mission," the wily politician prompted Spalajković, "is not contrary to the proclaimed aims of the Russian revolution, for we desire and are fighting to free ourselves of German exploitation and to win national freedom and self-determination."[62] Again we encounter Pašić's "big program" and "little program," as when he personally instructed Milan Marinković, former socialist deputy from Pirot and his special agent in Russia, as follows: "If in Russia they do not agree that our entire people, that is, Serbs, Croats and Slovenes, be recognized the right of uniting with the Serbians through free elections, then in no case can we be denied the right to Bosnia and Hercegovina, Srem, Bačka and Banat and a part of Slavonia, where the Serbs are in the majority, as well as to Lika, Krbava with the Dalmatian Littoral. . . . We stand on the Corfu program, but if it is not possible to realize it in its entirety, then those parts which can be liberated should not be left in Austro-Hungarian slavery."[63]

SOVIET NEGOTIATIONS WITH THE CENTRAL POWERS

One other international act of the new Soviet government touched on the Yugoslav Question—the peace negotiations between itself and the Central Powers at Brest-Litovsk in December 1917. Though the resulting treaty was subsequently renounced by both sides and declared null and void, the negotiations themselves affected the Yugoslavs in several ways. They certainly energized and radicalized Yugoslav hopes and declarations within the Dual Monarchy, as we have noted in connection with the memorandum of January 31, 1918, by the Yugoslav Caucus in the Reichsrat to all the delegations at Brest-Litovsk. Similar messages came to the Soviet delegation from Yugoslav groups abroad—on January 6, 1918, from a meeting of Yugoslavs in Geneva; on January 12, 1918, from Ante Trumbić, president of the Yugoslav Committee in London.[64] Moreover, an agreement was reached at Brest-Litovsk over the exchange of prisoners of war which affected over 200,000 Yugoslavs in Russia. Now they were free either to go back home or to join the Serbian army at the Salonika Front.[65] In either case these men had a marked effect on the further development of the Yugoslav cause.

After Brest-Litovsk there were no contacts between Serbia and the Soviet government. When the Germans advanced on Petrograd during a breakdown in the negotiations, Spalajković and his staff fled to Finland, and he actually took part in various counter-revolutionary moves against the Soviet regime.[66] When Spalajković left Vologda for Archangel and the protection of Allied troops there in July 1918, this brought a *de facto* break in relations between Serbia and Soviet Russia.

However, the effects of the October Revolution and of its aftermath on Yugoslav affairs did not cease. There is a considerable body of literature on the subject whose main theme is perhaps best expressed by the Yugoslav historian Ferdo Čulinović, author of a whole book, in 1967, on "The Echoes of October in the Yugoslav Lands": "The influence of the October Revolution in the Yugoslav lands was particularly great; the further development of the national movement attests to this. . . . Without minimizing the significance of other factors, it may be boldly asserted that it was particularly the influence of the October Revolution and the right of peoples to self-determination as proclaimed by the Soviet government in the fall of 1917 that intensified the national movement in the Yugoslav lands."[67]

In late 1917 and early 1918 there were two programs of Allied war aims that affected Yugoslav destinies. The Soviet Russian Decree on Peace and subsequent Soviet Russian declarations up to and including the peace negotiations at Brest-Litovsk called for a democratic peace and the self-determination of subject nationalities, including the right of secession and independence. This was understood, quite rightly, by the Yugoslav leaders in Zagreb, Vienna and London to mean the dissolution of the Austro-Hungarian Empire and the possible creation of a Yugoslav state. The war aims proclaimed by the leaders of the Western Allies at that time fell far short of that solution. In his Trade Unions Address on January 5, 1918, Prime Minister David Lloyd George declared that the *dissolution* of Austria-Hungary was not part of Allied war aims. Three days later President Woodrow Wilson enunciated his famous Fourteen Points. While Point XI promised certain gains to Serbia, Wilson ignored the broader program of Yugoslav unification; instead, in Point X he referred to *autonomous* development for the peoples of Austria-Hungary rather than their independence. One student of the question, Ivo Lederer, has asserted that "part of the blame for this must be attributed to Milenko Vesnić, Serbian minister in Paris, who in December 1917 headed a special mission to Washington." The only non-American consulted by Wilson on Point XI, Vesnić apparently did not press hard for recognition of the Yugoslav national program. He did indicate opposition to the preservation of the Habsburg Empire and to any attempt to conclude a separate peace, which disappointed Wilson.[68] Actually the Western Allies could hardly have called for the dissolution of Austria-Hungary at the very time that they were conducting secret negotiations to encourage it to sign a separate peace.[69] Incidentally, it has become a commonplace event in standard American reference works on Wilson and the First World War to assert that these declarations of Western Allied war aims were prompted by the publication of the secret treaties by the Soviet government.[70] Victor Mamatey, an American expert on Wilsonian diplomacy, has stated that the Fourteen Points were "to a large extent" addressed to the Bolsheviks.[71]

There is no doubt that the subject nationalities of the Austro-Hungarian Empire, regardless of ideology, sided with the Soviet stance as enunciated at Brest-Litovsk. It is also true that once it was clear that the Austro-Hungarian government would not sign a separate peace, Washington began, in mid-May 1918, to abandon the idea of preserving the Habsburg Empire. With Wilson's approval, Secretary of State Robert F. Lansing issued a statement on May 29 expressing sympathy for the Yugoslav and Czechoslovak causes. It was realized that Allied support for such national programs would create disorder in the Dual Monarchy and help speed Allied victory.[72]

However, disorder was already rampant in the Austro-Hungarian Empire, and particularly in its South Slavic provinces. Much has been written about the workers' strikes, political demonstrations, and mutinies by South Slavic soldiers and sailors in the Austro-Hungarian army which broke out from Istria and Ljubljana to Kotor. Of special interest are the so-called Green Cadres of several thousand men, deserters and returned prisoners of war from Russia, who populated the woods and fields of Croatia, Slavonia, Istria, Dalmatia, Bosnia-

Hercegovina, and Vojvodina in especially 1918, and who defied the Austro-Hungarian local authorities while they attacked big landowners and rich merchants. By the war's end some 50,000 armed soldiers were roaming the Croatian forests.[73]

It is not always easy to tell how much all these disruptive actions were inspired by political nationalism and how much by Russian social revolutionary ideology. Both factors were present. However, there are many facts that support the Russian revolutionary influence. In his monograph on the echoes of the October Revolution in the Yugoslav lands, Ferdo Čulinović has found that though many of these disorders existed even before the Russian Revolution, both their intensity and frequency increased sharply after the October Revolution. Moreover, these manifestations of anti-militarism and class conflict took on an increasingly ideological character, especially as the stream of returning prisoners of war from Russia turned into a flood.[74] Many of these men had become imbued with Russian social revolutionary ideas, and some of them were the veterans of some twenty Yugoslav Red Guard units in the Red Army.[75]

EVALUATION OF RUSSIA'S ROLE

In conclusion, if one looks at the diplomatic events between the outbreak of the First World War and the creation of the Yugoslav state on December 1, 1918, Russia's role does not appear to be significant. Tsarist Russia generally supported the Serbian cause, and it directly acted against the Yugoslav cause, especially by its participation in the secret Treaty of London with Italy. As for the Provisional Government, it lasted too short a time to be of either much help or harm to the Yugoslav cause. The Soviet government had no direct participation in the creation of the Yugoslav state and could not have, in view of its stance toward the governments of all the Great Powers, both the Western Allies and the Central Powers, and their stance toward Soviet Russia. Thus it is altogether possible for even a Soviet author such as Iu. A. Pisarev to write a whole book on the creation of the Yugoslav state and yet give comparatively little space to Russia's role.[76]

On the other hand, the same Pisarev has written a long and detailed article on just Soviet-Serbian relations during the negotiations at Brest-Litovsk and the Yugoslav problem. This and many other studies of the whole question suggest to us that if one sees the creation of the Yugoslav state as something more than the result of diplomacy and Great Power relations, the Russian factor, and particularly the Soviet Russian factor, looms much larger. It is easy, on the one hand, to agree with Mamatey, for example, when he observes that the Soviet Decree on Peace "was a demagogic gesture designed to win the support of the war-weary Russian masses," and that "even the Bolsheviks, inexperienced as they were in the ways of diplomacy, knew that peace could not be *decreed* but had to be negotiated and concluded by at least two parties."[77] Yet the Bolsheviks were experienced indeed in the ways of propaganda, and in the larger arena outside foreign offices, chanceries and departments of state, the Soviet Decree on Peace had its effect.

In the final analysis, the Yugoslav state was not created by Russia or any other Great Power. We agree with Ivo Lederer that "the Kingdom of Serbs, Croats, and Slovenes emerged with the acquiescence of the Allies, but not at their instigation."[78] Yet to the degree that external events helped to bring about the political unification of the Yugoslavs, Russia's role cannot be ignored and should not be either minimized or exaggerated. One does not necessarily have to agree totally with Tito that it was the Great October Revolution and the resulting social unrest in the Austro-Hungarian Empire that "greatly frightened the bourgeoisie in these regions and they sent their representatives to Belgrade with the petition that these regions be united with Serbia and that they create a state of the SCS—Serbs, Croats and Slovenes." It is possible to see in the Yugoslav unification of 1918 something considerably more than what Tito called "a unification of the bourgeoisie, regardless of nationality, with the aim of preventing the spread of the revolutionary movement and to ensure a division of the spoils at the expense of the working people of town and countryside."[79] And yet we should be particularly grateful to those historians, mostly Yugoslav and Soviet, who, thanks in large part to their Marxist outlook, have looked at the question of Yugoslav unification from a perspective far broader than that of diplomatic history and Great Power politics. From this standpoint Russia's influence on the events which shaped the creation of the Yugoslav state in 1918 calls for serious consideration.

Notes

1. Edward Thaden, "Public Opinion and Russian Foreign Policy toward Serbia, 1908–1914," in *Velike sile i Srbija pred Prvi svetski rat*, edited by Vasa Čubrilović, (Belgrade: Srpska Akademija Nauka i Umetnosti, Naučni skupovi Knjiga IV, Odeljenje istorijskih nauka Knjiga 1, 1976), pp. 217–230.

2. Dmitrii I. Abrikossow, *Revelations of a Russian Diplomat*, edited by George Alexander Lensen (Seattle: University of Washington Press, 1964), p. 225.

3. V.P. Potëmkin, ed., *Istoriia diplomatii*, II. *Diplomatiia v novoe vremia (1872–1919 gg.)* (Moscow: OGIZ, 1945), p. 260.

4. Bogdan Krizman, "Stvaranje Jugoslavije," in *Iz istorije Jugoslavije 1918–1948; zbornik predavanja* (Belgrade: Nolit, 1958), p. 148.

5. Michael Boro Petrovich, "The Italo-Yugoslav Boundary Question, 1914–1915," in *Russian Diplomacy and Eastern Europe 1914–1917* by Alexander Dallin et al. (New York: King's Crown Press, 1963), p. 172, f. 33. Memorandum of the Serbian Mission in Petrograd, to Sazonov, October 3, 1914, in *Mezhdunarodnye otnosheniia v epokhu imperializma:* Dokumenty iz arkhivov tsarskogo i vremennogo pravitel'stv, 1878–1917 gg., Series III (Moscow, 1931–38), Vol. V, Doc. No. 411. The abbreviation used hereafter is MOEI.

6. Ferdo Čulinović, *Dokumenti o Jugoslaviji* (Zagreb: Školska Knjiga, 1968), p. 25, "Narodna Skupština Srbije o ciljevima rata," December 7, 1914.

7. Dragovan Šepić," O misiji Lj. Stojanovića i A. Belića u Petrogradu 1915. godine," *Zbornik Historijskog Instituta Jugoslavenske Akademije,* III (Zagreb, 1960), 450.

8. Petrovich, *op. cit.*, p. 171, f. 30, Izvol'skii to Sazonov, October 30, 1914, MOEI, Doc. No. 386.

9. Petrovich, *op. cit.*, p. 163.

10. *Ibid.*, p. 172, Memorandum of the Serbian Mission in Petrograd to Sazonov, October 3, 1914, MOEI, Doc. No. 352.

11. Ante Mandić, *Fragmenti za historiju ujedinjenja; povodom četrdesetgodišnjice osnivanja Jugoslavenskog odbora* (Zagreb: Jugoslavenska Akademija Znanosti i Umjetnosti, Prilozi novijoj jugoslavenskoj historiji Knjiga 1., 1956), p. 139, Doc. No. 47, Sazonov-Supilo, Petrograd, 25 March, 1915.

12. *Ibid.*, Doc. No. 48, Supilo to Pašić, Petrograd [26 March, 1915].

13. *Ibid.*, p. 140, Schilling-Supilo, Petrograd, 27 March, 1915.

14. Dragovan Šepić, *Pisma i memorandumi Frana Supila 1914–1917* (Belgrade: Srpska Akademija Nauka i Umetnosti, Posebna Izdanja Knjiga CDI, Odeljenje Društvenih Nauka Knjiga 57, 1967), pp. 70–71, Doc. No. 40, Supilo to Pašić, draft of telegram, Petrograd, April 15, 1915.

15. Šepić, "O misiji Lj. Stojanovića i A. Belića u Petrogradu 1915. godine," *Zbornik Historijskog Instituta Jugoslavenske Akademije*, III, p. 451, f. 11, Spalajković to Pašić, March 20, 1915, telegram (Arhiv J.M. Jovanovića).

16. *Ibid.*, f. 7, Spalajković to Pašić, telegram of April 10, 1915 (Arhiv J. M. Jovanovića).

17. *Ibid.*, p. 453, f. 19, Pašić to Spalajković, Vesnić, Bošković and Ristić, telegram of April 5, 1915 (Arhiv Srpskog Ministarstva Inostranih Dela).

18. *Ibid.*, pp. 462–463, f. 44, Stojanović and Belić to Pašić, letter of May 7, 1915 (Arhiv J. M. Jovanovića). For the newspaper report, see Mandić, *Fragmenti,* Doc. No. 96, p. 176.

19. Šepić, "O misiji . . . ," p. 463.

20. *Ibid.*, pp. 463–464.

21. See the chapters by James M. Potts, "The Loss of Bulgaria," pp. 194–234, and Alfred J. Rieber, "Russian Diplomacy and Rumania," pp. 235–275, in *Russian Diplomacy and Eastern Europe (1914–1917)* by Alexander Dallin *et al.* (New York: King's Crown Press, 1963).

22. Šepić, "O misiji . . . ," p. 469, f. 59, Sazonov to Strandtmann, telegram of May 26, 1915 (Die Internationalen Beziehungen, February 8, Doc. No. 11, pp. 7–8).

23. *Ibid.*, f. 60 (Die Internationalen Beziehungen, Feb. 8, Doc. No. 32, pp. 32–33).

24. Mandić, *Fragmenti*, p. 43.

25. *Ibid.*, p. 46.

26. *Ibid.*, p. 53. Also Merritt Abrash, "War Aims toward Austria-Hungary: the Czechoslovak Pivot," in *Russian Diplomacy and Eastern Europe 1914–1917*, p. 100.

27. Mandić, *Fragmenti*, p. 50.

28. *Ibid.*, pp. 52, 53, 54.

29. *Ibid.*, p. 54.

30. *Ibid.*

31. *Ibid.*, p. 52.

32. Cited by Dragoslav Janković, *Jugoslovensko pitanje i Krfska deklaracija 1917 godine* (Belgrade: Savremena Administracija, 1967), p. 44, f. 94, Spalajković telegram of March 6, 1917, to J. Jovanović in London (Arhiv Jugoslavije u Beogradu, 80–11–316).

33. *Ibid.*, p. 46, f. 98, Pašić telegram of March 10, 1917, from Corfu to M. Spalajković in Petrograd (Diplomatski arhiv Državnog sekretarijata inostranih poslova, Ministarstvo inostranih dela Srbije, Političko odeljenje, 1917, f. VIII, Rs. Pov. No. 5716).

34. *Ibid.*, p. 47, f. 103, telegram by M. Spalajković in Petrograd, March 27, 1917 (DASIP, MID, RO, 1917, f. VIII, Rs/V. Pov. No. 1480, and *Srpske Novine,* April 6, 1917).

35. Mandić, *Fragmenti,* p. 136, Doc. No. 44, Supilo to Trumbić, Petrograd, 17 March, 1915).

36. Paul Miliukov, *Political Memoirs 1905–1917,* translated by Carl Goldberg (Ann Arbor: University of Michigan Press, 1967), p. 257.

37. *Ibid.*, p. 352.

38. Janković, *op. cit.*, citing *Srpske Novine* of March 14, 1917 (Old Style).

39. Milada Paulová, *Jugoslavenski Odbor* (Zagreb: Prosvjetna Nakladna Zadruga, 1925), pp. 314–315.

40. Janković, *op. cit.*, p. 49, f. 113, telegram of M. Spalajković from Petrograd to N. Pašić on Corfu March 25, 1917 (O.S.), (DASIP, MID, PO. 1717, f. VIII, Rs/V. Pov. No. 1427). Published, with editorial changes, in *Srpske Novine* on March 28, 1917 (O.S.).

41. *Ibid.*, p. 50, f. 114, telegram of M. Spalajković in Petrograd to J. Jovanović in London, March 28, 1917 (O.S.) (Arhiv Jugoslavije u Beogradu, 80–11–318).

42. Paulová, *op. cit.*, p. 340.

43. Mandić, *Fragmenti,* p. 56.

44. Janković, *op. cit.*, p. 54.

45. Paulová, *op. cit.*, pp. 365–366.

46. Janković, *op. cit.*, p. 54.

47. The best study of the Corfu Conference and Corfu Declaration is that by Janković, *op. cit.* See Appendix I, pp. 481–485 for the text of the Corfu Declaration.

48. *Ibid.*, p. 381.

49. *Ibid.*, p. 382.

50. Royal Institute of International Affairs, *Soviet Documents on Foreign Policy, I, 1917–1924* (Oxford University Press, 1951), p. 1, Decree on Peace, Passed by the Second All-Russian Congress of Soviets of Workers', Soldiers', and Peasants' Deputies, November 8, 1917.

51. *Ibid.*, pp. 11–12, Wireless Appeal by the Council of People's Commissars to the Peoples of the Belligerent Countries to Join in the Negotiations for an Armistice, November 28, 1917.

52. Čulinović, *Dokumenti o Jugoslaviji*, p. 61, Starčevića Stranka Prava i sovjetski dekret o miru (1917).

53. *Ibid.*, pp. 61–62, Memorandum Jugoslovenskog Kluba u Beču.

54. *Ibid.*, p. 44, Majska Deklaracija 1917. godine.

55. *Ibid.*, p. 62.

56. Janković, *op. cit.*, p. 353.

57. Royal Institute of International Affairs, *Soviet Documents on Foreign Policy, I. 1917– 1924*, p. 2.

58. *Ibid.*, pp. 8–9.

59. Janković, *op. cit.*, p. 353, f. 108, citing D. Šepić, "Pitanje tajnosti Londonskog ugovora od 1915 g.," *Zbornik Historijskog Instituta Slavonije*, II (1964), 101.

60. Janković, *op. cit.*, pp. 353–354.

61. *Ibid.*, p. 354.

62. *Ibid.*

63. *Ibid.*, p. 356.

64. Iu. A. Pisarev, "Sovetsko-serbskie otnosheniia v period Bresta i Iugoslavianskaia problema," *Voprosy Istorii*, No. 7 (July, 1973), 34–35.

65. *Ibid.*, p. 35.

66. *Ibid.*, pp. 37–38.

67. Ferdo Čulinović, *Otkliki oktiabria v iugoslavianskikh zemliakh* (Moscow: Progress, 1967), p. 42.

68. Ivo J. Lederer, *Yugoslavia at the Paris Peace Conference; A Study in Frontiermaking* (New Haven and London: Yale University Press, 1963), p. 27.

69. *Ibid.*, pp. 27–28.

70. See, for example, statements to this effect in two standard reference works, the *Harper Encyclopedia of the Modern World*, edited by Richard B. Morris and Graham W. Irwin (New York, Evanston and London: Harper & Row, 1970), pp. 375–376, and the *Concise Dictionary of American History*, edited by Wayne Andrews (New York: Charles Scribner's Sons, 1962), p. 376.

71. Victor S. Mamatey, *The United States and East Central Europe 1914–1918; A Study in*

Wilsonian Diplomacy and Propaganda (Princeton, New Jersey: Princeton University Press, 1957), p. 189.

72. Lederer, *op. cit.*, p. 31.

73. Vladimir Dedijer, Ivan Božić, Sima Ćirković and Milorad Ekmečić, *History of Yugoslavia.* Translated by Kordija Kveder (New York: McGraw-Hill, 1974), p. 499.

74. Čulinović, *Otkliki*, pp. 51 ff.

75. L. B. Valuev, G. M. Slavin, and II. Udal'tsov, *Istoriia Iugoslavii,* II (Moscow: Izdatel'stvo Akademii Nauk, 1963), p. 20.

76. Iu. A. Pisarev, *Obrazovanie iugoslavskogo gosudarstva* (Moscow: Izdatel'stvo Nauka, 1975).

77. Iu. A. Pisarev, "Sovetsko-serbskie . . ." *Voprosy Istorii,* No. 7 (July, 1973), 29–38.

78. Lederer, *op. cit.*, p. 45.

79. Josip Broz Tito, "Politički izvještaj," *V Kongres Komunističke Partije Jugoslavije; Izvještaji i referati* (Belgrade: Kultura, 1948), p. 25.

Addendum: The author regrets that at the time he wrote this paper he did not yet have access to the work by Nikola Popović, *Srbija i Rusija 1914–1918: Odnosi Srbije i Rusije u Prvom Svetskom Ratu* (Brograd ISI-Narodna Knjiga 1977).

Troubled Friendship:
Greco-Serbian Relations, 1914–1918

Domna Visvizi Dontas

GENERALLY FRIENDLY RELATIONS characterized the associations between Greece and Serbia during the nineteenth century. The first serious efforts to bring the states closer together came with the secret alliance signed at Voeslau, on 28 August 1867. Because this pact resulted from Prince Michael's personal initiative, his assassination the following year brought into question its validity, and the treaty was never enacted. Successive attempts to revive the spirit of the stillborn 1867 treaty failed, even though ties remained non-hostile.[1]

It was only in the next century that these Balkan states, both with ambitious expansionist programs, would come together. The outbreak of the Italo-Turkish War in 1911 raised once more the prospect of the collapse of the Ottoman Empire. Fears and hopes in Balkan capitals stimulated these states to join forces in an unprecedented fashion. The Balkan League of Bulgaria, Greece, Montenegro and Serbia launched war on the Sublime Porte in October 1912. But following the battlefield victories of the allies came disputes over the division of the territorial spoils from the Ottoman Empire. Greece and Serbia considered Bulgaria's ambitions unacceptable, and they embarked on negotiations for a bilateral alliance. It was this alliance, signed on June 1, 1913, which not only bound Greece and Serbia together, but also regulated their relations during World War I.

The draft-treaty which Eleftherios Venizelos, the Greek prime minister, submitted to Nihkola Pašić, his Serbian colleague, did not mention Bulgaria, but it was obvious that the two parties should unite to safeguard their mutual interests in the Macedonian region. Pašić was then also preoccupied with Serbia's defense against Austria-Hungary, whose prestige was threatened by the victory of Balkan nationalism in 1912. In an Austro-Serbian war, a Habsburg victory would signify the dismemberment, or even the vanishing of the Serbian state. Nevertheless, he did not exclude the fact that a Serbian victory might allow the unification of the South Slavs at the expense of the Dual Monarchy.[2] He therefore considered that the Greco-Serbian treaty could also be utilized as an instrument against Austria-Hungary. Venizelos was not prepared to extend the scope of the treaty, unless it included the Turkish danger against Greece. Thereupon, negotiations reached a stalemate. But, when Bulgaria's attitude hardened, during the spring of 1913, Venizelos hastened to give in to Pašić's views, and concluded a treaty against the attack of a "third party."

Venizelos' decision much disturbed the King of Greece, Constantine, who, in no case, was prepared to form an alliance which might eventually be directed against a Germanic power. The new King of Greece, who was the brother-in-law of Kaiser William II, desired to orient his country's future policy towards Germany. He told Venizelos that he was leading the country to its ruin, for in an Austro-Serbian war, Athens' aid to Belgrade would be ineffective, while Greece would be presented with considerable dangers. Venizelos, who could already look back upon a great career, and who was committed to the idea that the country's foreign policy should be on the side of Britain and France, tried to convince the King that in an Austro-Serbian war the Entente powers would intervene, and would support both Greece and Serbia. And he pressed hard for the conclusion of the alliance with Serbia. Finally, and with great reluctance, Constantine agreed and the treaty was signed on June 1, 1913. Moreover, it should be noted here that the positions taken during the meeting of the King and the Liberal party Prime Minister were of a great historical value. They revealed the spirit under which the Greco-Serbian treaty of alliance was signed. At the same time, they constituted the basis for the divergence of policy not only towards Serbia but also towards the Great powers, which was to reach dramatic dimensions during the First World War.[3]

EFFECTS OF GRECO-SERBIAN JUNE 1913 TREATY

In the treaty of June 1913 there was stipulated the mutual guarantee of protection against any unprovoked attack by a third party without specifically referring to Bulgaria. This could cover, for example, an attack on one of the allies by Austria or Turkey. Finally, each state bound itself to supply military assistance of 150,000 men and not to conclude peace subsequently, except "jointly and together."[4] No sooner was this act completed than it found an application in the Second Balkan War. Bulgaria blundered into this conflict on June 29/30, 1913, which found her fighting all the Balkan states, including Turkey. The outcome of these two wars had Greece and Serbia almost doubling their territories, Rumania receiving Dobrudja, and Bulgaria being reduced to the status of an embittered loser. The Treaty of Bucarest, signed on August 10, 1913, confirmed this new order in the Balkans.[5] This new settlement remained however incomplete on two issues: the first dealt with the demarcation of Albania's boundaries, in which Greece and Serbia both had interests; and the other involved the fate of the Aegean islands, which Greece had wrested from Turkish control during the First Balkan War.

In April 1914, Turkey, consolidated after the Balkan Wars, became very intransigent in the Aegean islands' question. Greece was not prepared to give in. When in June matters reached their peak, and Greece was about to present Turkey with an ultimatum, Venizelos appealed to Pašić for Serbia's support in the event of a Greco-Turkish conflict, in accordance to their treaty of alliance. Pašić, referring to his country's precarious economic and military situation after two years of war, emphasized Serbia's inability to become involved in a new Balkan war. But he suggested that a war could be avoided by the interference of the Great powers who had stated, in the Treaty of London of May 30, 1913,[6] that they would ultimately decide on the fate of the Aegean islands.[7]

The Greco-Turkish crisis of the spring 1914 had, on the other hand, challenged, for the first time, the real value of the Greco-Serbian treaty of alliance. Serbia declared in June 1914 that she would defend the status decided at Bucarest, but she would not assist Greece in a Greco-Turkish war for purely bilateral reasons. Serbia would however cooperate with Greece in order to defend her Macedonian interests against Bulgaria. The same proved true for Greece. Hardly a month later, upon the Sarajevo murder, Serbia and Austria-Hungary were on the brink of war—a war which developed into the great European conflagration of 1914–1918. It was Serbia's turn now to request from Greece her compliance with the treaty obligations. On 24 July 1914, the day after Austria-Hungary presented Serbia with an ultimatum, Pašić enquired of Venizelos as to how much assistance Greece would offer Serbia in an Austro-Serbian war. Venizelos' reply was that Serbia should proceed with moderation for, according to her declarations during the last Greco-Turkish crisis, she was not ready for war. He added moreover that, in the event of a Bulgarian attack against Serbia, Greece would fulfill her duties towards Serbia, and would not let the validity of the Treaty of Bucarest be questioned by the aggrandisement of Bulgaria.[8]

For the moment, Pašić was apparently satisfied with the Greek answer. A promise from, or the benevolent neutrality of, a neighbour-ing country was a commitment which he could not afford to disregard. He and Prince Alexander, the Regent of Serbia, saw in the forthcoming war the growth of Serbia and the unification of the South Slavs. They saw also, however, that if the war did not take place, Austria-Hungary would remain an immediate and constantly formidable danger.[9] The Serbian reply to the ultimatum was not satisfactory to Austria-Hungary, who, on 28 July, declared war on Serbia. Upon this, Russia sent reinforcements along her German and Austrian frontiers; on 1 August Germany declared war on Russia and on the 3rd on France;

Britain declared war on 4 August. The generalization of the war meant that each of the neutral Balkan states could no longer base its policy on the terms of the Bucarest settlement. It had to consider the general political and military situation created by a European War.

On the very day Austria-Hungary declared war on Serbia, Pašić informed Venizelos that the case was a *casus foederis* requiring Greek action.[10] On 2 August Streit, the Greek Foreign Minister, replied, without making reference to the obligations deriving from the Greco-Serbian treaty of alliance, that

> Le gouvernement royal a la conviction qu'il remplit tout son devoir d'ami et d'allié par la décision qu'il a prise d'observer vis-à-vis de la Serbie une neutralité très bienveillante et de se tenir prêt à repousser toute agression dont la Serbie pourrait être l'objet de la part de la Bulgarie.[11]

Venizelos stated, on the same day, to the French Minister at Athens furthermore that Greece would in no case associate herself with the enemies of the Triple Entente; and her active eventual participation would be decided upon receiving advice from these three powers.[12]

Venizelos' declaration was made after Germany had begun putting pressure on Greece to observe neutrality not only during the Austro-Serbian war but also in the event of a Bulgarian attack on Serbia. Germany made clear to Greece that she should not attempt an adventure against Turkey. The Berlin message was that it was in Greece's interest if Germany would join Austria against Slavism, the most formidable foe of Hellenism. On the other side, King Constantine assured the Kaiser that Greece never contemplated supporting Serbia and that she would maintain absolute neutrality.[13] At this Venizelos became very irritated, being often overbearing and sometimes reckless in his methods. On 3 August he made clear to Germany that Greece would intervene against Bulgaria in case the latter attacked Serbia, but that Greece would not move against Turkey, if she adopted a benevolent policy towards Greece.[14] No sooner had he made this statement than he concluded that the realization of the "Great Idea" (Greece's irredentist expansionist policy) could go along with Serbia's fulfilment of her dreams for a "Great Serbia." He was convinced that the immediate rôle of Greece should be an interventionist pro-Entente policy. And this because he envisaged that, in spite of the outcome of the war in Central Europe, the western maritime powers would remain unchallenged in the Near East. Consequently, Greece's fortunes were linked up with Britain and France, and thus the greater the part Greece played in the war the better able she would be to claim territorial gains when it ended. These might include, if not Constantinople itself, the Aegean islands or some parts of western Asia Minor, control of which would establish her in a strong position in the Aegean.[15]

VENIZELOS' PROPOSALS TO THE ENTENTE

With this in mind, and despite the King's opposition, Venizelos decided on an attempt to abandon neutrality. On 7 August he approached the Entente. To Russia he proposed the formation of a Balkan bloc against Austria-Hungary under the Czar's auspices. He explained that, if the Entente offered Transylvania to Rumania, Bosnia-Herzegovina and Northern Albania to Serbia, Macedonia up and including Monastir to Bulgaria, Greece would only claim Southern Albania, and the coast with Valona could be ceded to Italy. Thus the greater part of Bulgaria's aspirations would have been satisfied at the expense of Serbia, assuming this was satisfied with Bosnia-Herzegovina; Greece would have realized a portion of her territorial aspirations, and Italy would not raise obstacles. He then sounded Britain and France about their considering Greece as an ally in the event she attacked Bulgaria, if Bulgaria attacked Serbia, or if Greece were involved in the war following an attack by Turkey.[16] In support of his statement, and in accordance with Greece's treaty obligations to Serbia, he offered to Pašić the use of the port of Thessaloniki and the railway of Greek Macedonia. Also, he immediately lent guns and ammunitions to Serbia.[17]

Venizelos' proposals to Russia were most unwelcome. An extended Greece towards the East meant that at the peace conference Greece would be a rival to Russia. Russia was therefore opposed to the whole idea of Greece's active participation in the struggle (a policy which Russia pursued so long as it was possible).[18] Sazonoff, the Russian Foreign Minister, initiated to his British and French colleagues that it would be advisable, in order to gain Bulgaria to their side and modify her bellicose attitude, that the Entente should request Serbia and Greece to proceed to certain territorial concessions to Bulgaria, on the promise that, at the end of the war, they both would be compensated elsewhere.[19] As the two other partners of the Entente were undecided on their policy in the Balkans, they agreed to send to Athens a non-committal answer in which Bulgaria should not be mentioned.[20]

In the meantime in Athens, Venizelos' initiative to approach the Entente powers added to the already existing misunderstanding between the King and his Prime Minister. But as the King was under the impression that Venizelos had merely sounded out the Entente about future support, in the event that Greece backed Serbia against a Bulgarian attack, an acute crisis did not ensue. Anyhow, in the King's opinion (and that of the General Staff) the Greco-Serbian alliance was merely a necessary evil imposed on Greece by the Bulgarian and Turkish danger. It was a purely Balkan alliance and inoperative in a generalized Balkan war in which non-Balkan powers became involved. Matters, however, came to a head with the intervention of the German

Minister in Athens, who pressed on Venizelos to renounce Greece's alliance with Serbia—a demand which was immediately rejected.[21]

In this climate, on 19 August, Venizelos received the allied answer, that the three powers wished Greece to maintain neutrality so long as Turkey remained neutral, and nothing was said about Greece's integrity in relation to Bulgaria. This much disturbed him, for he was convinced that the maintenance of the Treaty of Bucarest intact was of primary importance, and that his obligations resulting from the treaty of alliance with Serbia were a secondary matter. He thought that Greece's duty at this juncture was to enter the war. He conceived then to follow another way towards this goal. On 30 August, he communicated to Pašić that from information received from Saint Petersburg, and that apprehensions created by the attitude of Turkey, this power would attack Greece with the consent of Bulgaria, so that Bulgaria would be free to attack Serbia. In such an eventuality Greece would be unable to aid Serbia. Venizelos therefore requested that Serbia concentrate, immediately, 150,000 men at the Serbo-Bulgarian frontier.[22]

The Greek approach added to Pašić's embarrassment. It was the moment when Russia declared to Serbia that she was convinced that Bulgaria's bellicose attitude would be completely modified, if Serbia, from one side, and Greece, from the other, would make territorial concessions to Bulgaria; and that both countries would be compensated elsewhere after the war. Furthermore, the Russian General Staff advocated that the Serbian army should launch a general offensive against the Austrians.[23] With these issues in mind, Pašić replied to Venizelos that Serbia was tied up with obligations towards the Entente, and that she was about to assume an offensive against the Austrians, consequently she could not detach any troops for positioning on her Bulgarian frontier. If the Bulgarian danger became imminent he intended to concentrate first on the measures to be adopted with the Entente powers.[24] With this reply Pašić underlined the fact that the Greco-Serbian alliance had now moved to a secondary place. It was that same place which Venizelos had already given to this alliance in his interventionist policy. It was maintained, however, by both leaders, as a useful instrument in undermining the allied policy of territorial concessions to Bulgaria.

Without losing time, Pašić informed Venizelos that Russia demanded from Serbia and Greece concessions to Bulgaria. Much annoyed, Venizelos threatened to resign, if the Allies demanded concessions to Bulgaria, and he was supported by public opinion in Greece. The Western allies could not face a pro-German government in Greece and hastened to state to him that no allied *démarche* would be made with that aim.[25] Venizelos, for the moment, gave in to the allied counsel for neutrality. This was to King Constantine's satisfaction, who, disagreeing with his Prime Minister's pro-Entente policy, could not afford to precipitate a crisis, having public opinion against him.[26] To crystallize the apparent understanding, the German government repeatedly assured Venizelos that neither Bulgaria nor Turkey had any aggressive intentions against Greece, asking his promise of neutrality. Giving that promise, Venizelos reserved the right to intervene in case Bulgaria attacked Serbia.[27]

Russia in the meantime convinced Britain and France that an agreement between Greece, Serbia and Bulgaria would neutralize the Bulgarian danger and it would remain only the possibility of a Turkish attack on Greece, in which case the Allies would come to Greece's aid. Persuaded that such an agreement could never materialize, unless satisfaction was given to Greece and Serbia elsewhere, the Allies, with the consent of Italy, allowed Greece to occupy provisionally Southern Albania at the end of September 1914.[28] Yet, it seemed that neither the occupation of Southern Albania by the Greek troops would make Venizelos more amenable, nor would the promise of Northern Albania lead Pašić to concessions. Both supported that if the Treaty of Bucarest were to be violated, it should be done by the three signatory powers together. But Rumania was playing her own game with both sides, the Entente and the Central powers, in order to secure the maximum rewards for a promise of benevolent neutrality;[29] and the difficulties of her 1913 partners hardly interested her. Rumania's policy and ambitions were not any more exclusively Balkan. And she had insinuated to Greece that it was to her interests to abandon her engagements vis-à-vis Serbia.[30]

REVIVAL OF DIPLOMATIC ACTIVITIES IN SOUTH-EASTERN EUROPE

Matters remained at a standstill until Turkey entered the war by attacking Russia's Black Sea fortifications, on 28 October. The Austrians, on the other hand, were about to start an offensive, which it appeared would lead to the conquest of Serbia. These new developments in South-Eastern Europe revived diplomatic activities in the area. And now it was not only Russia, who, in the early months of the war, was the only member of the Entente that devoted much attention to the Balkans. She was joined by France and Britain, who began to consider the Balkan front of great importance. Their primary objective became maintaining Bulgaria's neutrality or even having her join the Entente.[31] In the early days of November the Allies pressed on Serbia the need for territorial concessions to Bulgaria. Pašić was very perplexed: the Austrian armies were advancing into Serbian territories; he was short of necessary war materials, which he expected from France; and the Serbs were determined not to cede an inch of their territories.[32]

Before Pašić had sent his reply to the Allies, he turned to Venizelos for his military aid and war materials. The Greek reaction was prompt.

Venizelos, fearing that an entente existed between Bulgaria and Turkey, explained to Pašić that, by the time the Greek forces could reach
the Serbo-Austrian front, there would have elapsed almost two months
(the Greek troops being stationed at the moment in the Athens area).
In that interval the Bulgarian army, invading Serbia, would prevent
the union of the Greek and the Serbian forces and would expose
Greece not only to the Bulgarian but also to the Turkish danger. It was
imperative therefore that any Greek intervention should coincide with
a similar move from Rumania. As to the request for war materials,
Venizelos was unable to comply, fearing that such a despatch could be
considered as an infringement of Greece's neutrality—neutrality
which he could not abandon unless the Allies gave Greece their support.[33] It is no wonder then that Pašić, although most disappointed by
Venizelos, had been encouraged, on the other hand, to resist the
violation by Serbia alone of the Bucarest settlement of 1913. Pašić
instructed the Serbian Minister in London to state to the British government and to the Russian and French ambassadors there that he was
never unyielding to allied suggestions. But, as Serbia had carried, until
this moment, all the weight of the war in the Balkans, Serbian public
opinion would never permit its government to cede even an inch of
their territories, if Rumania and Greece would not have a share in the
sacrifice.[34]

But in the case of Greece making concessions to Bulgaria, the
Allies were divided. France and Britain saw the necessity to defer such a
demand at this juncture, to which Russia agreed very reluctantly.[35] On
4 November, the three powers asked Venizelos to come to Serbia's
aid and they would not only consider Greece as an ally, but also they
would afford her all necessary assistance. Venizelos however needed
Rumania's active cooperation.[36] Neither the allied assurance that Bulgaria would not move, nor the promise that Rumania could eventually
guarantee Bulgaria's neutrality, were satisfactory for Venizelos to come
to the aid of Serbia immediately.[37]

He had another, more serious reason, to decline this consent to the
allied overture. The Russian Minister at Athens, Prince Demidov, did
not keep it a secret that Greece should cede Serres and Kavala to
Bulgaria, acting on the suggestion of Pašić.[38] Pašić in fact wanted to
gain time, hoping to avoid finally such a sacrifice.

The allied governments were discouraged and complained that
Venizelos was encouraging Pašić to resist allied demands for Serbian
concessions to Bulgaria. The French Prime Minister Théophile Delcassé went further to state that Greece, having occupied Southern
Albania and having secured the Aegean islands, refused to make
concessions to the "general good."[39] The Greek press thereupon published articles protesting against Bulgaria for demanding territorial

acquisitions in Macedonia from Greece and Serbia in order to maintain neutrality and against the Entente for supporting Bulgaria.[40]

PROBLEMS OF GREECE AND RUMANIA

This turn of events was not in favour of Venizelos' interventionist policy, which he was determined to carry out. On 17 November he intimated to the Rumanian Minister at Athens that Greece was prepared for an understanding with Rumania on common action. On the 19th Pašić requested that Greece and Rumania join Serbia in presenting Bulgaria with an identical note, making known their intention to maintain the Bucarest settlement of 1913. They ought moreover to concert together as to their common policy in face of the Entente's insistence for territorial cessions to Bulgaria. By their overtures to Rumania, both Venizelos and Pašić aimed at forcing Bulgaria to clarify her position in the Balkans.[41] Rumania was not prepared to cooperate. At the moment, she was in pourparlers to form an alliance with Italy based on their mutual dislike of Russian predominance in the Balkans. Rumania was interested in preventing the creation of a large South-Slav state. Italy wished to expel the Greeks from Albania, and to direct their aspirations towards the Aegean. Thus the Greek and Serbian proposals to Rumania, which were eventually supported by the Entente powers, were completely fruitless.[42]

These prolonged and tedious negotiations left the Serbians unaided, now facing an Austrian offensive, and their situation rapidly becoming desperate. On 30 November, Pašić called urgently for troops to be sent by the Entente powers and he demanded formally from Greece to fulfill her treaty obligations. In a telegram to Venizelos he stated that, if the Austrians succeeded in invading Old Serbia, their way to Thessaloniki would be unhindered. Greece should therefore postpone her efforts for guarantees and send immediately eighty thousand men to Serbia's assistance.[43] Venizelos' reply was prompt: Greece would come to Serbia's aid provided the Allies directly requested her participation and guaranteed Bulgaria's neutrality and provided Rumania promised to intervene against a Bulgarian attack on either Serbia or Greece.[44]

In the meantime, this diplomatic imbroglio did not leave idle either Germany or Austria-Hungary. Fearing that new developments in the Balkans might turn the scales against them, they tried to preserve the *status quo*. To Greece they made clear that though they made overtures to Bulgaria for her entrance into the war on their side, they never promised her aggrandizement at the expense of Greece, with whose King the Kaiser was a close relative.[45] The Central Powers also requested Greece and Rumania to use their influence with Serbia and convince her that her interest was, as the Austrian troops were advanc-

ing, to conclude peace with the Dual-Monarchy. Thus Serbia would be
spared the war sacrifices, except for certain strategic points at their
frontier line. Rumania hastened to sound out Serbia; but Pašić declared that if Austria really needed to make peace with Serbia, she
should discuss it directly with her. Greece did not follow the example of
Rumania. Venizelos replied that if Serbia consented to conclude with
Austria a separate peace, she would betray the allied cause. Greece,
being a friend of the Allies, would also betray their friendship. And he
declared that he would not go any further. Venizelos' reply cut short
the intention of King Constantine to convince Serbia that the Austrian
offer could be acceptable.[46]

Following the futile attempt of Austria for peace with Serbia, on 5
December, the three allied Ministers at Athens declared to Venizelos
that if the Greek forces marched immediately in aid of Serbia, they
would guarantee Greece against a Bulgarian attack and they would
allow her, after the war, the annexation of Southern Albania, except
the area of Valona. The Allies would, furthermore, request Rumania to
associate herself in that guarantee.[47] Venizelos was now faced with
internal difficulties. His interventionist policy was openly counteracted
by King Constantine who made clear to him that Greece had first to
defeat Bulgaria and then turn to the assistance of Serbia, who, by that
time, would have been conquered by the Austrians. The King and the
General Staff moreover stated to the Serbian Minister at Athens that
the Russians could send to Serbia soldiers and guns, but Greece cannot
be deprived of them and send them to Serbia.[48] When Venizelos
learned of the interference of the General Staff, he was filled with
much consternation. He explained to the Serbian Minister that Pašić
should not consider the words of the King as a *démarche*.[49] The truth
however was that Venizelos was not prepared to intervene without
Rumania's active cooperation. Anyhow, matters in the Balkans took a
more optimistic aspect. The military successes of the Serbians, who by
15 December reoccupied Belgrade, eased his difficult situation.
Thereupon Bulgaria affirmed her neutrality.

SERBIA'S CRITICAL PROBLEMS

Despite the recent Serbian military successes, Pašić remained in a
critical situation. The Central Powers were preparing a new offensive
to annihilate Serbia. But it was not the only menace. In the last days of
December (on the 26) the Italians occupied Valona, still another threat
to Serbian national interests. As Serbia had not received the assurance
of the Allies that, at the end of the war, she would have free access to the
Adriatic, it was imperative now to secure the Vardar line which guaranteed to her another outlet to the sea by Thessaloniki.[50] The Greek
government, too, became very concerned seeing the Italians secure a
point d'appui on the Albanian coast. Athens considered that Greece and

Serbia ought also to participate in the occupation of Albania. Serbia agreed. Venizelos and Pašić decided to make accordingly a *démarche* to the allied governments.[51] This *démarche* was very unwelcome to the Allies who, by no means, could raise the Albanian question with Italy. At this moment Italy was negotiating with the Entente powers for entering the war on their side. Furthermore, events on the western front were at a stalemate and the opening of a Balkan theater seemed necessary for Britain and France. Several plans were discussed and it did not seem that agreement could be reached.

In the meantime Venizelos had alluded to the possibility of Greece's intervention against Turkey in return for certain compensations on the Asia Minor coast. This overture was not to Russia's liking. She made clear to Britian that if the Allies would find necessary to promise to Greece, in order to obtain her cooperation, the acquisition of territories, these could be in the Smyrna area. Russia stated furthermore that, if for strategic reasons the Greek army should make a landing at the Gallipoli peninsula (one of the allied plans under discussion),[52] Greece should be well-informed that the Czar would never agree to a permanent Greek base at the Dardanelles.[53] Britain thereupon deferred the subject and returned to the old plan that Greece should come to the aid of Serbia. And on 21 January 1915, Lloyd George, the Chancellor of the Exchequer in the British cabinet, declared personally to Venizelos, with whom he had developed a friendship, that the Greek forces should immediately intervene in aid of Serbia. He promised financial assistance and the cooperation of a British division of some 40,000 men, and a prompt answer. Venizelos, in face of a differentiated allied policy, had become very cautious, and he requested the official notification from the British cabinet. On the 24th the British Minister at Athens declared to Venizelos that if Greece entered the war immediately to assist her ally Serbia, the Allies would compensate her on the littoral of Asia Minor and with Cyprus as well. But these acquisitions had to be balanced by satisfactory territorial concessions in Macedonia to Bulgaria by Greece and Serbia. On her part, Bulgaria would promise her participation in the war against Turkey, or at least her benevolent neutrality. The British Minister also demanded of Venizelos not to oppose those concessions which Serbia might be disposed to make to Bulgaria, on condition that Serbia would realize her aspirations towards the Adriatic.[54]

GREECE'S DREAM: THE "GREAT IDEA"

Greek acquisitions in Asia Minor meant for Venizelos the realization of the Greek dream: the "Great Idea." Moreover, Serbia could be saved from destruction and Bulgaria, satisfied, would not risk an invasion of Serbia and eventually of Greece. What was more important for Venizelos was that Constantine, at the thought of becoming the King of a Magna Graecia, supported the plan. And they agreed to accept it on the condition that this project was combined with the assurance of Rumanian support. But Venizelos' joy was short-lived. Rumania still refused to give any promise of action.[55] Venizelos had to turn down the allied proposals. The more so as by now the King, "weak and inconsistent, hesitant and at the mercy of circumstances,"[56] under the influence of the Kaiser, preferred to adopt a line leading against the realization of Greece's *Great Idea* than to see fulfilled the pan-Serbian and South-Slav aspirations. He was convinced that the progress of Panslavism would be effected at the expense of Greek interests in South-East Europe. In point of fact, he had already made clear this conviction, and he was very concerned with Bulgaria's ambiguous and contradictory policy. And this is the reason why he distrusted Russia, who was the originator of territorial concessions to Bulgaria, and who showed now reluctance to support whole-heartedly the British project.[57] Constantine's conception, however, was erroneous. It was impressed on him by the pro-German and short-sighted General Staff. In relation to the Balkans after their wars of 1912-13, Panslavism had lost its meaning altogether. The Balkan Slavs did not think any more in terms of Panslavism of the 19th century. It was now simply a question of conflicting national aspirations. And these conflicting interests existed between Bulgaria and Greece, as well as between Bulgaria and Serbia. Greece and Serbia were not divided by such a cause.

In the meantime, it became evident to all sides that the war would not end quickly. Everywhere the combatants were mobilizing their resources and revising their plans in preparation for an offensive in the coming spring. On the diplomatic scene matters took another turn. After their futile efforts in the Balkans, the Allies precipitated their negotiations for an attack on the Dardanelles. Until such an operation could materialize, they were pressed to furnish, without fail, assistance to Serbia under an immiment danger. On 15 February they promised Venizelos the cooperation of one British and one French division to disembark at Thessaloniki, to enable him to dispatch troops to Serbia. To Venizelos this new allied *démarche* was totally unacceptable. Without guarantees against Bulgaria no Greek soldier could leave his country. And he requested Rumania's active cooperation.[58] The Allies, exasperated at this new stalemate, in the second half of February decided to proceed with operations at the Dardanelles, perhaps with Greek assistance. The news of its bombardment made a deep impression in the Balkans. In Greece, Venizelos now decided to join the Allies against Turkey. It was a far safer plan to realize his interventionist policy than to dispatch Greek forces across Serbia against the German powers—a plan which by no means whatsoever could materialize. Furthermore, Lloyd George had already insinuated to him that Great Britain did not want to see Russia predominant in the East at the end of the war, and that she would promote Greece's expansion in Anatolia.[59] France, however, believed that the operations at Gallipoli would encourage Bulgaria to side with the Allies. In such an eventuality the Greek forces would be freed to assist Serbia against Austria. Austria was in preparation now to attack Serbia in order to create a diversion to the attack against Gallipoli.[60] On 1 March Venizelos, on his own initiative, offered to send a Greek force to cooperate in the occupation of the Dardanelles, and he then informed the King and the General Staff. Constantine immediately called a Crown Council, followed by a second one (3 and 4 March 1915), which vetoed Venizelos' initiative. As a result Venizelos resigned on the following day.[61]

VENIZELOS FALLS AND RISES

The fall of Venizelos filled the Serbian and the allied capitals with echos of consternation—echoes which the new Greek government could not ignore. Demetrios Gounaris, the new Prime Minister, assured the Entente that the change was due not to a difference of views on basic policy, but to a disagreement as to the moment Greece could enter the war. And he came forward enumerating conditions, among which was Greek expansion in Albania. The Allies, involved in bringing Italy in the war, paid little attention to Greece. Parallel to these activities, Gounaris assured Pašić that the Greco-Serbian alliance would be observed in case of a Bulgarian attack—an assurance which created doubtful thoughts as to what was the real policy behind it.[62] Gounaris had in mind that, as Germany won the battle against Venizelos, she should now help Constantine to win the elections scheduled for the following June. The Greek government therefore requested Germany to defer any Austrian offensive against the Serbs until after the elections. Thus Greece would not be found in a dilemma to make known her policy of neutrality, which would influence public opinion in favour of Venizelos.[63]

Venizelos, however, did not remain out of office for long. The elections held on 13 June 1915 gave him an ample majority, but his formation of a new ministry seemed remote. By the time he won the day at the polls, Balkan problems were even more insoluble: On 10 April 1915 France and Britain had formally agreed to a Russian annexation of Constantinople and the Straits, conditional on the ultimate victory of the Entente powers; by the secret treaty of London of 26 April 1915, Italy had intervened in the war after having secured from the Allies promises of territories, included among which were lands Serbia[64] and Greece expected at the peace table; at the end of May the Entente, on Russia's initiative, had urged Serbia to cede territories in Macedonia (Egri-Palanka-Sopot-Ochrida) to Bulgaria, which was refused by the Serbian government.[65] The Allies, however, were not prepared to give in. They informed Bulgaria of their *démarche* in Nish. To Pašić's great amazement the Bulgarian press announced it before the Serbian people were aware of these diplomatic activities.[66] Sazonoff, the Russian Foreign Minister, furthermore firmly told the Greek and Serbian Ministers at Saint Petersburg that their countries should make the sacrifices to Bulgaria demanded by the Entente. This new Russian initiative produced a dangerous reaction in Nish and Athens. The Serbians talked of not participating any more in the allied cause; and the pro-German government in Athens had a good reason to defer the return of Venizelos to power.[67]

On 4 August the Allies made a simultaneous *démarche* in Nish and in Athens. To Serbia they repeated the concessions they expected from her to Bulgaria. To Greece they demanded the cession of Kavala to Bulgaria. Both countries would be compensated elsewhere after the war.[68] The Greek government endeavoured to secure the cooperation of the Serbian ministry, in order to refuse together compliance with such a demand. Pašić made clear to Gounaris that his precarious military and economic situation prevented him from resisting allied pressure indefinitely.[69] And he raised the question of Greece's treaty obligations to Serbia in the event of a Bulgarian attack. But Gounaris was satisfied to repeat the old argument that after the German forces had invaded the Serbian territories, the *casus foederis* could not be invoked.[70] What is more important was that Gounaris based his argument against the *casus foederis* on Serbia's consent that she might decide to agree to a policy of concessions to Bulgaria, undermining thus the balance of power as established by the Treaty of Bucarest. Such a policy could be interpreted as a violation of the Greco-Serbian treaty of alliance. To the Allies he made known that Greece's territorial integrity could by no means be violated.[71]

When on 23 August 1915 Venizelos again assumed the reins of power, he had to clarify the force of the Greco-Serbian alliance as it then appeared. It should be stated here that public opinion in Greece was much perturbed with allied Balkan policy and with Serbia's concessionary attitude. It seemed that Constantine's neutralist policy had to a certain extent seriously rivalled Venizelos' interventionist policy. Venizelos therefore proceeded very cautiously and in a way to carry the country with him and strengthen his position against the King. When on 30 August Pašić informed him of his decision to promise certain territorial concessions to Bulgaria in Macedonia up to Monastir, but to preserve a common frontier with Greece, he visualized concessions to Greece as well. On the following day, he declared to his Serbian colleague that he was willing to agree with the Serbian cessions to Bulgaria, if Greece was promised the Doiran-Gevgeli area and be excluded from Serbia's offer to Bulgaria. But, even if these concessions materialized, it remained to agree on what basis the Greco-Serbian alliance would remain in force—an alliance which he really desired to maintain. The Greek request for Serbian territorial concessions greatly embarrassed Pašić. This able Serbian statesman decided to play his last card to spare his country painful sacrifices. He first accepted the allied demands in favour of Bulgaria; but on so many conditions that he anticipated their rejection. He then protracted the discussions with Venizelos until Bulgaria made known her reaction.[72]

Bulgaria Complicates the Problem

Indeed, Bulgaria was not satisfied with what Serbia had offered, and, on 6 September 1915, she signed a military convention with the German powers. It was the total failure of unrealistic policy of the Allies in the Balkans—a policy which in vain was notified by the allied Ministers in Athens and Nish. Pašić remained even more exposed to his formidable foe from the north, and Venizelos with his hands tied. The King would never consent that Greece, if Bulgaria attacked Serbia jointly with the German powers, would march against Bulgaria, for such action would be interpreted as an attack on Germany. A last-minute attempt to form a Greco-Rumanian alliance to hold Bulgaria in check failed, because of Bratianu's refusal, unless the Allies sent an army of 400,000 men to the Balkans. If they could have done this, neither Rumanian nor Greek support would have been needed.[73]

The situation became more aggravated when, on 21 September, Bulgaria declared partial mobilization and Turkey ceded to Bulgaria the right bank of the Maritza River.[74] Venizelos, after much argument, convinced the King to declare immediately a partial mobilization, for the defense of Greece and independent of Greece's alliance obligations to Serbia. On 23 September, Constantine signed the decree for a general mobilization. But a state of armed neutrality was not what Venizelos wanted. He was determined to carry out his interventionist policy, if Bulgaria attacked Serbia, as he was determined to resign in the event that the Crown would not give its consent.[75] Thus decided, Venizelos proceeded to face Constantine with a *fait accompli*. On his own initiative (as he had over a year before) the previous day (22 September) declared to the representatives of the Triple Entente that in order to fulfill Greece's alliance obligations towards Serbia, they should send 150,000 men to Thessaloniki. France and Britain reluctantly agreed, but they began a new series of futile negotiations with Russia and Italy. For a moment they thought to put pressure on Bulgaria to demobilize. And this was Russia's opinion, who still found it hard to believe in Bulgarian hostility.[76] In the meantime, general mobilization in Greece was advancing rapidly and troops and war materials were forwarded to the Bulgarian frontier.[77] The King became much perturbed and made clear that he did not agree with his Prime Minister's policy; while the Bulgarian government began to fear a Rumanian attack. Germany stepped in and assured Bulgaria that both the Kings of Greece and of Rumania had promised neutrality.[78]

In the face of these developments Pašić started to despair. To put an end to inconsistent and slow policy of the Allies in the Balkans, he urged Venizelos to enter the war on the allied side, independently of Greece's treaty obligations to Serbia, but on the condition that no concessions would be made to Bulgaria. At that moment (30 September) French naval officers arrived at Thessaloniki for a reconnaissance, before allied troops landed there.[79] Venizelos was taken by surprise, as he had not yet clarified the question of concessions to Bulgaria. On the following day, he declared to the allied Ministers at Athens that no troops could land at Thessaloniki until he received formal assurance that they would not be used to compel Greece and Serbia to make concessions to Bulgaria. Only by this formal assurance would the Greek government be justified in the minds of public opinion, which would accept to facilitate the debarkation at Thessaloniki and the transfer of international troops through Greek territory to Serbia.[80] The Allies hastened to assure Venizelos that the question of concessons to Bulgaria did not exist any more, and that they were ready to join Serbia and Greece in maintaining the Treaty of Bucarest.[81] On 5 October an Anglo-French force began to disembark at Thessaloniki.

Venizelos' optimism that matters would follow the course he had chosen was unfounded. The King was adamant that Greece should remain neutral. Despite his Germanophile feelings, at this juncture he saw more clearly what the interest of his country was. With the German and Bulgarian armies ready to overrun Serbia, the Allies defeated at the Dardanelles and the Russians losing ground in Poland, there was no other way for Greece than to pursue the policy of neutrality. On 5 October Venizelos resigned, without the prospect of returning to power. With the brusque fall of Venizelos disappeared all hope of doing anything effective to save Serbia. The new Greek government, to which Pašić made an appeal for aid against Bulgaria, at once made it clear that they could do nothing for the Serbs. What is more, considering that their force at Thessaloniki was too small to bring about an amelioration to the Serbian military situation, Britain and France wished to withdraw.[82] Serbia and Russia, much annoyed, pressed them to maintain their force in that Aegean port.[83] But their long hesitation, their lack of precise military plans and the discord among the commanders of the expeditionary forces only proved that these diplomats and generals had no reason to boast of consistency and swiftness. The situation dictated otherwise.[84] It is no wonder then that Serbia was allowed to be crushed by the combined German and Bulgarian forces. Their offensive began upon the fall of Venizelos and by the end of November they had overrun the whole country.[85] The causes of this catastrophe are multilateral and it is outside the scope of this paper to enter into their details. Certainly, there is no question that the attitude of Greece facilitated Bulgaria's attack on Serbia and contributed to the destruction of her ally. The detailed study of the diplomatic documents of the period, and especially the despatches of the allied Ambassadors in Athens and Nish, prove that Serbia's downfall was due to the unrealistic Balkan policy of their governments by letting Bulgaria become the pivot of their decisions and actions. Greece's vacillation and internal division occupied a second place in the Serbian débâcle.

GRECO-SERBIAN RELATIONS

Greco-Serbian relations during this Great War did not end at this juncture towards the close of 1915. The remnants of the Serbian army, in their retreat, wished to find refuge in Greece. The pro-German Greek government vetoed this proposal, maintaining that it would give the Germano-Bulgarian forces an excuse to enter neutral Greek soil and creating further complications. The Serbs then, after an epic march through Albania reached Scutari, on their way to the port of Valona. In Scutari they were faced with another disappointment. Italy, now the fourth member of the Entente, showed her clear hostility to the quartering of Serbian troops in Valona. Prince Alexander and Pašić were in despair, and with them their destitute soldiers. They complained bitterly to the French that the Allies had abandoned them and that they had lost all hope of regaining their national soil and their independence.[86]

In face of these developments, the French took the initiative to give way to the Serbian despair.[87] They suggested that the island of Corfu would be a speedy and realizable solution to this acute problem. The negotiations which ensued showed that the Allies remained as unrealistic as before in their attitude towards the Balkans. Now the pivot was not Bulgaria but Italy, on which the Triple Alliance oscillated. They acted in the Balkans as their main concern was Italy's satisfaction. Finally, by February 1916, the Allies, after having presented Greece with a *fait accompli*, had completed the establishment of the Serbian troops at Corfu.[88] Their reorganization was the task of British and French detachments which made their quarters on the island too. But Italy could not miss an opportunity to participate in a project which might eventually, perhaps, give her rights to Corfu. She convinced France and Britain that a small Italian force should participate in the work of rehabilitating the Serbians. With the experience of Italian inhumanity at Scutari, Pašić declared to the French that it would be desirable that the Italians abstain from having an active role in Serbian reorganization. The echo of his words was lost in the air. The Italians had their share in the Serbian reorganization. Prince Alexander felt a great consternation, and he intimated that the Italians had Machiavellian designs to the detriment of the Yugoslav union and that they wished to bring about the destruction of the Serbian race. To the French Minister to his kingdom he made clear that the Serbians did not feel all that bitter against the Greeks but they loathed the Italians. And he stated that "we must remain friends with the Greeks."[89]

Matters at Corfu did not develop without reaction from Greece. Her government and King had protested strongly against the establishment of the Serbs at Corfu. But they accepted finally the *fait accompli*, as a gesture to the Serbians. What created great dismay in Greece was the appearance of Italian soldiers on the island. Government and opposition—and Venizelos personally—made France and Britain responsible for any demonstrations of the people, in the case of annexationist Italian propaganda in Corfu. But the Protecting Powers remained unmoved.[90] Thus Greece anticipated events which took place much after the regrouped Serbian troops left the island and were transported to Thessaloniki, in May 1916. Needless to say, this transport was not effected without another tumultuous discussion between the Allies and the Greek government.[91]

The arrival of the Serbian forces, some 115,000 men, at the Aegean port perturbed the Germano-Bulgarian armies in Serbian Macedonia. Their generals decided on a prompt action in order to obstruct any moves northwards of the allied forces. They therefore took over, on 28 May, from the Greek King's garrison the important Fort Rupel, at the head of the Struma valley—an event with unpredicted results in the north of Greece. Venizelos could not remain idle. He instigated pro-Venizelist officers at Thessaloniki, who at the close of 1915 had formed a National Defense Committee, to demonstrate against the authorities of the King, under the protection of the Serbian and French troops. Thereupon, the French Commander declared the city in a state of seige. It was this movement that prompted Venizelos to take up with the Allies the possibility of his setting up a provisional, pro-Entente government in Thessaloniki. The allied governments considered that the change should take place in Athens by the appointment of a pro-Entente ministry. Upon pressure, in the summer 1916, the pro-German Prime Minister Skouloudis was replaced by the pro-Entente Zaimis. The result was that the two factions (pro-German and pro-Entente) were confronting each other, ready for a civil war. The situation deteriorated when on 18 August the Bulgarians began operations in eastern Macedonia, just at the time when the French Commander at Thessaloniki, General Sarrail, had at long last completed preparations for a Serbo-Allied offensive in western Macedonia. This offensive he hoped to co-ordinate with Rumania who, finally, agreed on 17 August to join the Allies.[92] The entry of Rumania into the allied bloc gave hopes to France and Britain that Greece would join too. No such decision was forthcoming. The French were exasperated. The Serbo-Allied offensive was delayed, and the Bulgarians were about to occupy Kavala. Thus, after a trivial incident, French marines landed at Piraeus on the pretext to protect French property. On 11 September, Kavala was surrendered to the Bulgarians by the royalist forces. There was no other solution for Venizelos than to set up a provisional government in Thessaloniki, where he arrived on a French man-of-war.[93]

Venizelos inaugurated this new period of his troublesome career with a declaration on the political orientation of the movement. He wanted to build up an army in order to recover the territories occupied by the Bulgarians, and to fulfill Greece's obligations to Serbia, thus removing the stigma for the Greek nation.[94] This declaration followed a *Te Deum*, during which there were pronounced blessings for the Greek Royal Family, the Prince-Regent of Serbia Alexander, the Provisional Government of Greece and the governments of the Allied Powers.[95]

VENIZELOS OPPOSES BULGARIA AND GERMANY

Matters thereupon developed rapidly. The Serbo-Allied forces entered Serbian Macedonia and began a successful advance. On 19 November they conquered Monastir. Venizelos hastened to congratulate Pašić, reasserting his unaltered friendship for him and his people and to extend his wishes for the formation of a Greater Serbia. Equally warm was Pašić's reply to Venizelos.[96] Thus encouraged, Venizelos declared, on 24 November, that he considered his provisional government in a state of war with Bulgaria for having attacked Serbia, the ally of Greece, and for having devastated national territories, contrary to her promises. He also declared his government at war with Germany for having incited Bulgaria to attack Serbia and for having acted against Greece, by violating the guarantees given to the Greek government in respect to the towns of Kavala, Seres and Drama.[97] And Venizelos concentrated on organizing his administration and army, with allied aid. Greece became two separate states, each one with its own government and its own army. Civil war was threatened. The French were anxious to install Venizelos at Athens and to induce the King to abdicate. Neither Britain nor Russia, however, was willing to let the situation deteriorate even further. The Serbs, in turn, became most perturbed in face of the French attitude in Greece. The French Commander Sarrail contemplated withdrawing his troops from Monastir for a march against Athens, and he was urging his government. The

British could not see this urgency and they advocated that the change
in Greece should take place by peaceful means, because they were not
certain if the majority of population were Venizelos' adherents. The
Russians, though involved in the consolidation of their new régime,
were against overturning the Greek throne. What is more, the Russian
Foreign Minister, Teretchenko explained to the British Ambassador in
Petrograd, in rather strong terms, that it was impossible to think of
withdrawing troops from Monastir in order to be used in Greece. At
this moment, Russia was organizing a new offensive against the Germans and it was essential that the Serbian front should be kept in full
strength. Encouraged by the Russian attitude, the Prince-Regent declared to Petrograd that, in case the Western Allies withdrew their
troops from Monastir to direct them to Athens, he would have to
conclude a separate peace with Austria-Hungary—an eventuality
which would have led Rumania to follow suit. The Russian government
thereupon warned the French and the British cabinets that it was
adverse to their Greek policy. On the one side, the weakening of the
Monastir front would overturn the balance of the eastern front with
dangerous consequences. On the other side, a violent change of régime
in Greece might result in a civil war. And what is more, the Russians
made clear that France and Britain could not interfere in Greece
without the consent of Russia who was one of the three Protecting
Powers—a principle which should be observed.[98] Serbia was thus
spared another serious setback. Greece also was spared a civil war.

GREECE'S INTERNAL POLITICAL STRUGGLES

In the meantime in Athens events had taken a dramatic turn.
Constantine was not prepared to yield so easily. And Greece became
the arena in which the German Powers and the Western Allies strug-
gled to dominate, competing to bend Constantine's government to
their will by threat and pressure. The Germans had intensified their
efforts to retain him on the throne. The French and the British had
tried to reconcile the "old" Greece with the "new." Failing in these
endeavours, they began to press for stringent measures against the
Athens government, leading to the control of the armed forces. The
Greek government refused to comply with these demands. The Western Allies insisted by threatening a landing of their troops, but
Constantine seemed unbent. On 1 December 1917, they landed detachments which were confronted by the royal troops and induced
them to retire to their ships. On the 7th the Allies declared the blockade
of royalist Greece; but Constantine still did not depart from his position
of neutrality. And the first six months of 1917 were characterized not
only by the political struggle for dominance but also by the sufferings of
the Greek people. Famine and unemployment plagued Greek society.[99] Finally, Constantine succumbed to pressures exercised by the

French Senator Jonnart,[100] acting as high commissioner of the Protecting Powers. He abdicated in favor of his second son, Alexander. And, on 27 June 1917, Venizelos returned to Athens as prime minister of a forcefully unified Greece.

Greece was now officially on the side of the Allies. The closing scene of the internal drama was Venizelos' appearance in the Chamber of Deputies on 26 August. In front of satisfied, but also of dissatisfied, deputies, he delivered a memorable speech, in which he defended his policy since the Balkan Wars. He proclaimed the sacred character of the international agreements and Greece's alliance obligations vis-à-vis Serbia; and he addressed a fraternal greeting to the heroic Serbian nation. He expressed his conviction that the Greek people were ready for any sacrifice in order to participate in the universal struggle for liberty by the side of the Allies, with the aim of reestablishing national honour, of reconquering lost national territories and of defending national interests.[101]

By then there was still little progress recorded on the Balkan front. The army which Venizelos had formed with British and French aid in Thessaloniki had not succeeded in uprooting the Bulgarians in the Struma region. The Serbian forces, too, were disheartened and politically divided and their activities almost at deadlock. French troops were dissatisfied with their Commander-in-Chief. So serious was the situation along the whole length of the Macedonian front that the question of maintaining the army of the Orient in being had become a highly controversial issue both within and between the allied Governments. Such a situation made Venizelos very anxious and he intimated to Pašić his wish to put into force the Greco-Serbian alliance treaty, in order to safeguard their national interests at the peace settlement. But Pašić stated in a very cordial letter to Venizelos that, still in exile, he was unable to commit himself.[102] However, Venizelos felt that he ought to tighten his relations with the Serbians. On his return from Paris and London, where he secured allied financial aid for Greece's actual participation, he paid a visit to Pašić at Corfu and informed him personally of his contacts in the western capitals.[103]

At the close of the year 1917 there seemed to be an enterprise of peace, a peace of conciliation, a peace without victors and losers. It appeared such a peace would be unfavourable either to Greece or to Serbia. Bulgaria had launched a campaign of pleas and protests in Paris and London, aiming at impressing on the Allies that she should be given the hegemony in the Balkans. France and Britain were tempted to consider Bulgaria's ambitions. They thought that if they detached Bulgaria from the Central Powers, peace would be certain in their favour. They were led into this line of thinking by the failure of the spring 1917 offensive on the Macedonian front. Matters became more serious, when on 25 December 1917, Lloyd George, making a declara-

tion in the House of Commons on the general situation and on the aims
of the Allies, did not refer to the national aspirations of Serbia and
Greece. It was the prospect of negotiations between the Allies and
Bulgaria which prevented him from doing so. The result was that in
Athens the royalists declared with triumph why should the Greeks fight
on the allied side. Venizelos' situation became very embarrassing. Pašić
also was faced with a political crisis. He was attacked by opponents as
being too weak to defend Serbian interests. On 28 February he was
compelled to resign. The Allies were hesitating to commit themselves;
but they did not wish Greece without Venizelos and Serbia without
Pašić. On 23 March Pašić formed a new government. On 7 April France
and Britain declared to Greece that they would remain devoted to their
duties as Protecting Powers and first they would afford all assistance for
the liberation of her territories.[104]

To Venizelos this declaration was vague and unsatisfactory. The
Allies were still wavering and undecided. He turned to Pašić in order to
combine their efforts and press Britain and France for action. On 22
April the Prince-Regent of Serbia paid a visit to Athens. His discussions
with Venizelos could not lead to concrete results. Prince Alexander
made clear that, being in exile and depending on the French troops to
proceed with the liberation of his country, he was not on the same
footing with the King of Greece.[105] However, they agreed that Greece
and Serbia could play "a fruitful double-game between the Allies and
the German Powers," at least, as a means of pressure.[106] They therefore
let leak in Paris and London that, according to the Greco-Serbian treaty
of alliance, they might consider a separate peace with the German
Powers "jointly and together."

WESTERN POWERS SUPPORT GREECE AND SERBIA

On 17 June the new French Commander-in-Chief, Franchet d'Es-
pérey, arrived at Thessaloniki, and on the 18th the Western Powers
assured Greece and Serbia that they would remain their faithful
friends.[107] Thereupon military preparations proceeded at a quick
pace, and on 14 September the offensive was finally launched. The
Serbs stormed the western and the eastern slopes of the Vetrenik while
French colonial troops carried the strongpoint of Dobropolje. At the
same time, Greek and British troops began to move forward on
the front of Doiran and entered the town. By the 25th of September the
Bulgarian troops had been forced off Greek soil; and by the 29th the
Serbs had captured Skopje. By that date enemy resistance had ceased
almost everywhere. On the previous day Bulgaria, in a state of revolution, had sent delegates to Thessaloniki to sue for peace. War seemed at
an end. Pašić, who was indeed a great statesman and much experienced
in the inconsistent diplomacy of the Allies in the Balkans, proclaimed,
on 1 December 1918, a Yugoslav state to include Serbia, Montenegro,

Slovenia, Croatia and Bosnia, thus facing the Allies with a *fait accompli*.[108] It was to the great delight of Venizelos, who envisaged that it would soon be Greece's turn to realize her national aspirations fulfilled in the Aegean. Venizelos' and Pašić's wartime collaboration was sealed on 14 July 1919, when Greek and Yugoslav detachments marched together with the allied troops under the "Arc de Triomphe" in Paris.

EVALUATION OF GRECO-SERBIAN ALLIANCE

True it is that the application of the Greco-Serbian treaty of alliance created many controversial problems. Yet it contributed to the collaboration of its two chief actors, Venizelos and Pašić, despite the Powers. In insisting, in 1914 and 1915, on the maintenance of the Greco-Serbian alliance, Venizelos and Pašić never thought in terms of only being faithful to an act which, at the moment, had more or less a narrow scope. They considered it as an instrument for the pursuit of their pro-allied and eventually expansionist policy, and as an instrument to undermine the unrealistic pro-Bulgarian allied policy. The creation of a Great Serbia, at the end of a victorious war, would balance the formation of a *Magna Graecia* in the Aegean. Serbia and Greece were not divided over conflicting territorial claims. The Serbs looked for expansion westwards and the Greeks eastwards. In Albania, where both countries had interests, there would have been few difficulties had the Great Powers allowed these two states to negotiate a settlement.

By pursuing the maintenance of the Greco-Serbian alliance and by insisting on the faithfulness to the 1913 Bucarest settlement, both Pašić and Venizelos respected the value of the acts which closed the Balkan Wars, for regional stability and security of their nations. And what is more, their peoples could never consent to a change of the *status quo*, which was gained by long wars, satisfying thus their national aspirations. There were the considerations which underlay the pursuance of the Greco-Serbian treaty of alliance, in spite of the heavy storms, and allowed this treaty to survive in the interwar period.

Notes

1. Domna Dontas, *Greece and the Great Powers, 1863–1875*, Thessaloniki, 1966, pp. 89–90, 115–6, 130.

2. Pierre Renouvin, *Les Crises du XXe siècle*, Series: *Histoire des Relations Internationales*, Paris, 1953–1969, Vol. VII, p. 25.

3. George B. Leon, *Greece and the Great Powers, 1914–1917*, Thessaloniki, 1974, pp. 14–5; A.-F. Frangulis, *La Grèce. Son Statut international, son histoire diplomatique*, Paris, n.d., 2nd edition, Vol. I, pp. 100–102.

4. Edouard Driault-Michel Lhéritier, *Histoire diplomatique de la Grèce, de 1821 à nos jours*, Paris, 1925–6, Vol. V, pp. 115–7; See text of the Treaty in *British Documents on the Origins of the War 1898–1914*, G. P. Gooch and Harold Temperley, eds., London, 1927–38, Vol. IX, Part II.

5. See text of the Treaty in *British Foreign and State Papers*, Vol. CVII, pp. 663–670 and in *Documents Diplomatiques Français*, third series, Vol. VII, No 601.

6. Driault-Lhéritier, *op. cit.*, Vol. V, pp. 103–114.

7. *Ibidem*, pp. 156–8; Frangulis, *op. cit.*, Vol. I, pp. 110–4; Leon, *op. cit.*, pp. 13–4.

8. Frangulis, *op. cit.*, Vol. I, pp. 136–7.

9. M. S. Anderson, *The Eastern Question, 1774–1923: A Study in International Relations*, London, 1966, p. 310.

10. Leon, *op. cit.*, p. 20.

11. Frangulis, *op. cit.*, Vol. I, pp. 140–1.

12. A.M.A.E. (Archives du Ministère des Affaires Etrangères de France), Série: Guerre 1914–18, *Correspondence Politique, Grèce*, 244, f. 2, tel. No. 111, very confidential, Halgoenël to Delcassé, Athens, 2 August, 1914. *Note:* Austria-Hungary in fact was using all her influence at Sofia, so that Bulgaria remained idle for the moment (Karl Kautsky, *Documents allemands relatifs à l'origine de la Guerre*. Collection complète des Documents officiels, trad. Max Montgelas-Walter Schucking, Paris, 1922, Vol. III, pp. 27–28.

13. See documents published in Frangulis, *op. cit.*, Vol. I, pp. 142–147. *Note:* Referring to Frangulis, one should remember that the purpose of this publication was to defend King Constantine's policy during World War I.

14. Kautsky, *op. cit.*, Vol. IV, p. 53.

15. Georges Ventiris, *Greece, 1910–1920* (in Greek), Athens, 1970, Vol. II, p. 221; Anderson, *op. cit.*, pp. 320–1.

16. Leon, *op. cit.*, pp. 33, 36–7. *Note:* So anxious was Venizelos to act at this juncture that he told the French Minister in Athens that, even in the case of a negative allied answer, he had decided to resign rather than not comply with Greece's obligations to Serbia (A.M.A.E., *Grèce*, 244, f. 4, tel. No. 117, Deville to Delcassé, Athens, 12 August, 1914).

17. A.M.A.E., *Grèce*, 292, ff. 7–22, note annexed to the report "Sur la politique germanophile du Roi Constantin" of 1 May, 1917; Emanuel Roucounas, *Foreign Policy, 1914–1923* (in Greek), Athens, 1978, pp. 178–9.

18. Anderson, *op. cit.*, p. 321.

19. A.M.A.E., *Serbie*, 370, ff. 4–5, tel. Delcassé to the French Minister at Nish, Paris, 25 August, 1914; *ibidem*, f. 3, copy, Delcassé to Deville (Athens), Paris, 29 August, 1914; *Documents Diplomatiques Secrets Russes, 1914–1917* (d'après les Archives du Ministère des Affaires Etrangères à Petrograd) trad. du Russe par J. Polonsky, Paris, 1928, p. 117, Sazonoff to the Russian Ambassador in Paris and London, secret tel. No. 2149, Saint Petersburg, 12 August, 1914; and Sazonoff to the Russian Minister in Nish, Athens, Bucarest, Paris and London, Saint Petersburg, 17 August, 1914, secret tel. No. 2273.

20. A.M.A.E., *Grèce*, 244, f. 5 tels. 603 and 609, Delcassé to the French Ambassadors in London and Saint Petersburg, Paris, 13 August, 1914; *ibidem*, f. 6, No. 430, Paléologue to Delcassé, Saint Petersburg, 14 August, 1914; Constantin Sakellaropoulos, *The Shadow of the West. The History of a Catastrophe* (in Greek), 2nd edition, Athens, 1960, pp. 19–20.

21. Leon, *op. cit.*, pp. 38–39.

22. No. 28017, Streit to Alexandropoulos (in Nish), Athens, 18 August, 1914, cited in Frangulis, Vol. I, pp. 155–6.

23. A.M.A.E., *Serbie*, f. 3, tel. No. 381, Delcassé to Deville, (in Athens), Paris, 29 August, 1914; *ibidem*, f. 8, Boppe to Delcassé, Nish, 3 September, 1914.

24. Leon, *op. cit.*, p. 56; Frangulis, *op. cit.*, Vol. I, p. 157.

25. A.M.A.E., *Grèce*, 244, f. 27, tel. No. 150, Deville to Delcassé, Athens, 12 September, 1914.

26. See for details in Leon, *op. cit.*, pp. 60–78.

27. A.M.A.E., *Grèce*, 244, copy, Boppe to Delcassé, Nish, 20 September, 1914; Leon, *op. cit.*, p. 80.

28. Leon, "Greece and the Albanian Question at the Outbreak of the First World War," *Balkan Studies*, 11:1 (1970), pp. 61–80.

29. Anderson, *op. cit.*, pp. 316–7.

30. A.M.A.E., *Grèce*, 244, f. 26, tel. No. 109, copy, Blondel to Delcassé, Bucarest, 8 September, 1914.

31. *Mezdunarodnye otnosheniya v epokhu imperializma. Dokumenty iz arkhivov Tsarkogo i Vremennogo Pravitelstv, 1878–1917 gg*, Series III, 1914–1917 gg, Vol. VI, p. 8, aide-mémoire of the British Ambassador in St. Petersburg to the Foreign Ministry, 21 November, 1914.

32. Frangulis, *op. cit.*, Vol. I, p. 165.

33. *Ibidem*, Vol. I, pp. 165–6; A.M.A.E., *Grèce*, 244, f. 59, copy, Delcassé to Deville, Bordeaux, 16 November, 1914.

34. A.M.A.E., *Serbie*, 370, f. 52, No. 1043, copy, Cambon to Delcassé, London, 16 November, 1914.

35. *Mezdunarodnye ... op. cit.*, Vol. VI, pp. 89–90, tel. No. 672, Benckendorff to Sazonoff, London, 3 November, 1914.

36. The Allies were more than convinced that the key for the solution of the Balkan problem at this moment was Rumania's entering the war on the allied side (copy of tel. Grey to British Ambassadors in Bordeaux, Bucarest, Nish and Sofia, London, 17 November, 1914, in *Mezdunarodyne ... op. cit.*, Vol. VI, pp. 91–2).

37. Venizelos to the Greek Ministers in London, Bordeaux and Saint Petersburg, Athens, 24 November, 1914, cited in Frangulis, Vol. I, pp. 165–6; A.M.A.E., *Grèce*, 244, f. 60, No. 197, Deville to Delcassé, Athens, 18 November, 1914.

38. Leon, *op. cit.*, p. 83.

39. *Ibidem*, p. 83.

40. A.M.A.E., *Grèce*, 244, f. 74, Deville to Delcassé, Athens, 30 November, 1914.

41. Leon, *op. cit.*, pp. 83–84; Frangulis, *op. cit.*, Vol. I, pp. 166–7.

42. Anderson, *op. cit.*, p. 317; No. 1828, Psychas to Venizelos, Bucarest, 8 November, 1914, cited in Frangulis, *op. cit.*, pp. 167–8.

43. A.M.A.E., *Serbie*, 370, f. 78, tel. No. 358, Boppe to Delcassé, Nish, 30 November, 1914.

44. Leon, *op. cit.*, p. 90.

45. No. 2830, confidential, Theotokis to Venizelos, Berlin, 24 November, 1914, cited in Frangulis, *op. cit.*, Vol. I, pp. 164–5.

46. A.M.A.E., *Serbie*, 370, f. 82, tel. Delcassé to Boppe, Paris, 3 December, 1914; *ibidem*, f. 92, tel., Boppe to Delcassé, Nish, 7 December, 1914; *ibidem*, f. 94, tel., copy, very conf., Deville to Delcassé, Athens, 7 December, 1914.

47. A.M.A.E., *Grèce*, 244, f. 78, allied communication to Venizelos, 5 December, 1914; *Mezdunarodnye ... op. cit.*, Vol. VI, p. 148, Sazonoff to the Russian Ambassadors in

Nish, Sofia, Bucarest and Athens, Saint Petersburg, 19 December, 1914, tel. No. 4076.

48. Leon, *op. cit.*, p. 91; A.M.A.E., *Grèce*, 244, f. 82, tel. No. 221, Deville to Delcassé, Athens, 9 December, 1914.

49. A.M.A.E., *Serbie*, 370, f. 100, tel. No. 223, copy, Deville to Delcassé, Athens, 11 December, 1914.

50. *Ibidem, Serbie*, 370, f. 121, tel. No. 434, Boppe to Delcassé, Nish, 29 December, 1914.

51. *Ibidem, Grèce*, 244, f. 105, No. 7, Deville to Delcassé, Athens, 6 January, 1915.

52. See for details in Leon, *op. cit.*, pp. 98–105.

53. A.M.A.E., *Grèce*, 244, f. 111, tel. No. 60, Paul Cambon to Delcassé, London, 12 January, 1915; *ibidem*, f. 113, tel. No. 61, very conf., Paléologue to Delcassé, Saint Petersburg, 13 January, 1915.

54. Grey to Elliot, Foreign Office, 23 January, 1915, cited in Frangulis, *op. cit.*, Vol. I, pp. 172–3 and in Leon, *op. cit.*, p. 107.

55. Psychas to Venizelos, very conf., Bucarest, 4 February, 1915, cited in Frangulis, *op. cit.*, Vol. I, pp. 177–8; *Mezdunarodnye . . . op. cit.*, Vol. VII, pp. 223–5, Demidoff to Sazonoff, Athens, 28 February, 1915, very conf.

56. As the French Admiral Dartige described him. See A. Pingaud, *Histoire diplomatique de la France pendant la grande Guerre*, Paris, 1938–40, Vol. I, p. 157.

57. A.M.A.E., *Grèce*, 244, ff. 72–3, Olivier Taigny, the French member of the International Commission for control of Greek finances, to the Quai d'Orsay, Athens, 28 November, 1914.

58. Raymond Poincaré, *The Memoirs of Raymond Poincaré 1915*, transl. by Sir George Arthur, London, 1930, pp. 32–6; *Mezdunarodnye . . . op. cit.*, Vol. VII, pp. 255–6, Demidov to Sazonoff, Athens, 1 February, 1915, conf. tel. No. 53.

59. Benckendorff to Sazonoff, London, 19 March, 1915, tel. No. 153, in *Mezdunarodnye . . . op. cit.*, Vol. VII, p. 395; *The Diary of Lord Bertie of Thame, 1914–1918*, ed. by Lady Algernon Gordon Lennox, London, 1925, Vol. I, pp. 126–7. *Note:* Sazonoff had communicated to Grey Russia's claims to be presented during the peace conference. (Sazonoff to Benckendorff, Saint Petersburg, 19 March, 1915, tel. No. 937, in *Mezdunarodnye . . . op. cit.*, Vol. VII, pp. 392–3).

60. A.M.A.E., *Grèce*, 244, f. 163, Delcassé to the French Ambassadors in London, Saint Petersburg and Athens, Paris, 4 March, 1915.

61. See for details on the Crown Councils, though biased, in Frangulis, *op. cit.*, pp. 179–203; also for the more complete story in Leon, *op. cit.*, pp. 125–139.

62. Frangulis, *op. cit.*, (Vol. I, pp. 207–55) devotes a chapter to Gounaris' foreign policy, but the result was that neither the Allies nor Serbia could trust a pro-German government. In fact they considered the fall of Venizelos as a German victory.

63. Leon, *op. cit.*, p. 186.

64. Pašić complained bitterly to the Ministers of the Triple Entente (A.M.A.E., *Serbie*, 371, f. 105, tel. No. 320, Boppe to Delcassé, Nish, 6 May, 1915).

65. *Ibidem, Serbie*, 371, f. 181, tel. No. 392, Boppe to Delcassé, Nish, 30 May, 1915; *ibidem, Serbie*, 372, ff. 33–4, No. 421, Boppe to Delcassé, 9 June, 1915.

66. *Ibidem, Serbie*, 372, f. 4, tel. 399, Boppe to Delcassé, Nish, 2 June, 1915.

67. *Ibidem, Serbie*, 372, f. 100, No. 487, Boppe to Delcassé, Nish, 29 June, 1915; *ibidem, Grèce*, 245, f. 19, No. 275, Deville to Delcassé, Athens, 11 July, 1915.

68. *Ibidem, Serbie*, 372, ff. 171–2, Allied Note to the Serbian Government; Leon, *op. cit.*, p. 195.

69. No. 7953, Alexandropoulos to Zographos, Nish, 7 August, 1915, cited in Frangulis, *op. cit.*, Vol. I, pp. 252–3. *Note:* It is worth noting here that the Austrians, too, were in difficulties with the Germans. Conrad had been irritated that Germany took such preponderance in the area; he resented depending on Bulgaria and considered making a separate peace with the Serbians, in order to contain these ambitions. Austria-Hungary and Germany also quarrelled over matters of peace. The Germans hoped to win the war outright. This meant an offensive in the West. The Austrians were not nearly so pledged to this end—on the contrary, an outright German victory would worry them almost as much as an outright allied victory (Norman Stone, *The Eastern Front, 1914–1917* , London, 1975, p. 243). With this in mind, the Austrian Government sounded the Serbian Government, through the Greek Foreign Minister, as to the possibility of signing a separate Austro-Serbian peace—a proposal which remained without answer. (A.M.A.E., *Serbie*, 372, f. 181, No. 346, confidential, Jaunez to Delcassé, Athens, 18 August, 1915).

70. *Ibidem, Grèce*, 245, f. 108, No. 372, Guillemin to Delcassé, Athens, 31 August, 1915.

71. See for a detailed account, Leon, *op. cit.*, pp. 197–206.

72. *Ibidem*, pp. 211–4, there is an excellent detailed account on the matter.

73. Anderson, *op. cit.*, p. 329.

74. Leon, *op. cit.*, p. 218.

75. Statement made in Yannina by Venizelos' Finance Minister. (A.M.A.E., *Grèce*, 245, f. 132, No. 45, Dussap to Delcassé, Yannina, 23 September, 1915).

76. Frangulis, *op. cit.*, Vol. I, pp. 266–270; Anderson, *op. cit.*, pp. 329–330.

77. A.M.A.E., *Grèce*, 245, f. 140, tel. No. 115, Leon to Guillemin, Thessaloniki, 25 September, 1915.

78. Leon, *op. cit.*, p. 232.

79. *Ibidem*, p. 237; Frangulis, *op. cit.*, Vol. I, p. 270.

80. Poincaré, *op. cit.*, p. 249; No. 10148, Venizelos to the Allied Ministers at Athens, 1 October, 1915, cited in Frangulis, *op. cit.*, Vol. I, pp. 274–5.

81. Leon, *op. cit.*, pp. 240–1.

82. A.M.A.E., *Grèce*, 246, f. 127, tel. No. 590, Guillemin to Delcassé, Athens, 21 October, 1915.

83. *Ibidem, Grèce*, 246, ff. 39–44, extract from a letter by Taigny to the Quai d'Orsay, Athens, 6 October, 1915. See for a detailed account in Leon, *op. cit.*, p. 245–269. Anderson (*op. cit.*, p. 331) wrote that: "The history of the allied occupation of Salonica is one of the best examples of the military idiocies which can be committed in a search for political advantages."

84. Joseph J. Joffre, *Les Mémoires du Maréchal Joffre, 1910–1917*, Paris, 1922, Vol. II, pp. 117–140 and 179–186; David Lloyd George, *War Memoirs*, London, 1936, Vol. VI, p. 3200; Poincaré, *op. cit.*, pp. 252, 257; Stone, *op. cit.*, p. 221.

85. See for details of the allied retreat from Serbia in Capitaine Canudo, *Combats d'Orient-Dardanelles-Salonique (1915–1916)*, Paris, 1917, pp. 169–272.

86. A.M.A.E., *Serbie*, 395, f. 11, Boppe to Briand, Scutari, 27 December, 1915.

87. *Ibidem, Serbie*, 395, f. 5, telephone message by Joffre to the Quai d'Orsay, Scutari, 22 December, 1915.

88. *Mémoires du Maréchal Joffre, op. cit.*, Vol. II, pp. 186–9.

89. A.M.A.E., *Serbie*, 395, f. 205, No. 3, Boissonnas to Briand, Corfu, 12 February, 1916.

90. *Ibidem, Serbie*, 395, ff. 28–9, tel. No. 52, copy, Guillemin to Briand, Athens, 8 January, 1916.

91. *Mémoires du Maréchal Joffre, op. cit.*, Vol. II, pp. 295–7. The Serbian troops were under the leadership of the Prince-Regent, while Pašić and his ministers remained at Corfu until the end of the war.

92. Joffre, *op. cit.*, Vol. II, pp. 311–315.

93. See for details in Douglas Dakin, *The Unification of Greece, 1770–1923*, London, 1972, pp. 212–4.

94. A.M.A.E., *Grèce*, 286, ff. 157–8, No. 133, Graillet to Briand, Thessaloniki, 12 October, 1916; *Ibidem, Grèce*, 286, ff. 177–8, tel. No. 197, Graillet to Briand, Thessaloniki, 14 October, 1916.

95. *Ibidem, Grèce*, 287, f. 169, tel. No. 214, Graillet to Briand, Thessaloniki, 9 November, 1916.

96. *Ibidem, Grèce*, 288, f. 53, copy, Venizelos to Pašić, 19 November, 1916 and f. 54, copy, Pašić to Venizelos, 22 November, 1916.

97. *Ibidem, Grèce,* 288, ff. 56–7, No. 223, Graillet to Guillemin, Thessaloniki, 24 November, 1916.

98. Driault-Lhéritier, *op. cit.,* Vol. V, pp. 298–9.

99. Dakin, *op. cit.,* pp. 214–5.

100. Yannis Mourelos, *La Mission Jonnart et la déposition de Constantin 1er de Grèce (Juin 1917),* a thesis, University of Paris-Sorbonne, 1978, *passim.*

101. The complete text of Venizelos' speech is to be found in Leon Maccas, *Cinq ans d'histoire grecque, 1912–1917,* Paris, 1917.

102. A.M.A.E., *Grèce,* 277, f. 132, Graillet to Ribot, Thessaloniki, 8 October, 1917; *ibidem, Grèce,* 277, f. 179, de Billy to Ribot, Athens, 15 October, 1917, where there are to be found copies of the letters exchanged between the two Prime Ministers.

103. *Ibidem, Grèce,* 278, f. 17, No. 202, Lorgeon to Briand, Corfu, 2 November, 1917; Driault-Lhéritier, *op. cit.,* Vol. V, pp. 323–4.

104. A.M.A.E., *Serbie,* 388, ff. 220–1, Nos. 116, 117, Fontenay to Briand, Corfu, 21 and 23 March, 1918; Driault-Lhéritier, *op. cit.,* Vol. V, p. 326.

105. A.M.A.E., *Serbie,* 389, f. 65, No. 164, Fontenay to Pichon, Corfu, 21 April, 1918; *ibidem, Grèce,* 282, ff. 181–2, No. 113, de Billy to Pichon, Athens, 28 April, 1918.

106. Driault-Lhéritier, *op. cit.,* Vol. V, p. 328.

107. *Ibidem,* Vol. V, p. 332.

108. Dimitrije Djordjevic, *The History of Serbia, 1800–1918* (in Greek), (Thessaloniki, 1970), pp. 404–16.

George D. Herron and the Italian-Yugoslav Rivalries during the Final Stages of World War I, 1917-1919: Some Observations Based on Documents from the Herron Papers

Fritz Fellner

> The most of my time these days seems consumed in trying to meet with some degree of adequacy the wide disappointment amounting almost to bitter resentment that has arisen among various Slav nationalities in response to the recent pronouncements of Mr. Lloyd George and President [Woodrow] Wilson. It is our President who has occasioned the deepest disappointment because his word is looked upon as being more specific and comprehensive as well as more authoritative and final than the word of any other statesman.... Many representatives of these nationalities are in Geneva and delegates from each have called upon me to express and discuss their national anxieties and despairs. I think it is my duty to present to you their several states of mind.[1]

THESE WORRIED DELIBERATIONS are the introduction to a lengthy report sent by George D. Herron to the American chargé d'affaires in Bern on January 25, 1918. Herron continues his letter with a passionate description of the disappointment created among the émigrés from the Habsburg Monarchy by the War Aims speech delivered by Lloyd George on January 5, 1918, and Wilson's proclamation of the Fourteen Points a few days later—declarations which were considered by politicians and historians in the years after the war as having been the signal for the dissolution of the Habsburg Monarchy.

Herron's report proves that the representatives of Central European nationalities living in exile interpreted this proclamation, not without justification, as a threat to their political aims which at the moment of the proclamation of the Fourteen Points transcended the claim of autonomy and were directed towards full independence from Habsburg rule. Recent research has shown that the War Aims declaration of Lloyd George and the Proclamation of the Fourteen Points by Wilson were not only provoked by the Russian Peace Aims proposals of December 1917, but were at the same time intended to find a way to preserve the Habsburg Monarchy by re-organizing her along reformed constitutional lines and by granting autonomy to the various national groups. After Russia's withdrawal from the united front against German imperialism, the Allies were in greater need for a counterweight against German power in Eastern Europe than before 1914. Lloyd George's statements in regard to the conservation of a reformed Habsburg Monarchy and President Wilson's reform program of Point X should be seen and interpreted in the context of this political situation. The public declarations made by the Allied statesmen were part of a complicated net of confidential and private contacts established during the years 1917 and 1918 and were used to probe the intentions of Allies, Associates and enemies. These informal contacts and secret talks were held mostly in Switzerland which had become the center of secret conspirative and espionage activities,

> not only because of her central geographic position nor only because of her historic toleration and hospitality toward the political missionaries of all nations. Indeed it may be said that Switzerland was the war's real psychic center. . . .[2]

HERRON'S EARLY ACTIVITIES

George D. Herron, from whose pen this description of the Swiss atmosphere exuded, spoke from personal experience: sometime in the course of the year 1915 Herron had moved from Fiesole near Florence, Italy, where he had led the life of a free-lance intellectual, to Geneva. Within a short time Herron had established the reputation of being close to President Wilson, even of being a sort of personal, confidential representative of the American President in Europe. This reputation was never questioned and was accented by many scholars dealing with the secret peace feelers extended in Switzerland in 1917–18.[3] No one has ever bothered to check this reputation or to investigate the role which the American George D. Herron claimed to have played as mediator or intermediary between the rivaling nationalities. In the 1920's George D. Herron donated a selection of his private political papers to the Hoover Library, now Hoover Institution on War, Peace and Revolution. Based on these papers supplemented by information from Herron's friends and some other documents, a young American historian, Mitchell Pirie Briggs, published a study of Herron's role in the European settlement in the aftermath of World War I.[4] Briggs accepted the documents which were put at his disposal at their face value without probing into the many contradictions apparent in Herron's account of his life and his activities. Herron, who would eventually end up on the political stage of international intrigue, was born in 1862 in Montezuma, Indiana, the son of poor but pious Scottish parents. Briggs has managed to sketch Herron's life story along the visible dates, but failed to thoroughly examine the nebulous periods in which many of the changes in his life took place.

After travelling in Europe for a few years Herron decided to enter the ministry. Although he never received a formal education, Herron was awarded the degree of Doctor of Divinity from Tabor College, whereupon he became a minister in Burlington, Iowa. At Burlington he managed to impress the wealthy widow of a railroad tycoon, Mrs. E. D. Rand, and her daughter, Miss Carrie Rand. Mrs. Rand endowed a professorship in Applied Christianity for him at Grinnell College, where Miss Rand became Dean of Women while Herron pioneered a social interpretation of Christianity—he had become a Socialist some-time earlier and later campaigned for E. V. Debs, the Socialist candidate for the presidency. Herron's relationship with Miss Rand led to a scandal which ended in a divorce from his first wife. He married Miss Rand and the newlyweds moved to Italy where Herron lived as a free-lance writer propagating Christian socialist ideas in various jour-nals and magazines and apparently living from his wife's wealth. Why Herron moved to Geneva after Italy's entrance into the war cannot be established. His second wife died in 1914 and although this can be seen as a possible reason, it might well be that his activities made it necessary for him to move to a neutral country. Documents in the Herron Papers at the Hoover Institution show that Herron acted as an informant for Allied governments and as a propaganda agent for the U.S. State Department. He regularly supplied the British Foreign Office and British Secret Service with information dealing with the various clan-destine activities in Switzerland for which he received a monthly stipend of 1,000 francs "for secretarial help."[5] He also kept in close contact with the Italian embassy at Bern. It was not without reason that Herron, in donating his papers to the Hoover library, stipulated that the volumes dealing with Italy, Serbia, Albania and Bulgaria should not be made accessible before 25 years after the donation. This stipulation explains why Herron's role in regard to the Adriatic problem had not been dealt with by his biographer Briggs and has not yet been inte-grated into our knowledge of political activities in this area in 1917/19. From these documents Herron emerges as an intermediary in inner-Italian intrigues, and as a propagator of the political interests and objectives of the Italian Prime Minister Orlando and the socialist Minis-ter Bissolati in their conflict with the Italian Foreign Minister Sonnino. The antagonism between Orlando and Bissolati on one hand and Sonnino on the other hand had its basis in the imperialistic tendencies of Sonnino. The personal and political quarrels among the three politi-cians centered around the question of an Italian expansionist policy in the Balkans and Herron apparently played a provocative role in the interplay of party politics, personal rivalries and imperialistic tenden-cies:

> Because of friendship I had with different men in Italy and afterward with Serbian representatives in Geneva, I often found myself, during the early part of the war, in a mediatory position between spokesmen of these

nations. These representatives would sometimes meet in my house in Geneva and I would try to get them to some kind of agreement.[6]

Herron had especially close relations with Ambassador Paulucci and other members of the Italian embassy, most of whom belonged to a younger generation of diplomats. Herron also kept close contact with Professor G. A. Borghese, who was in charge of Italian propaganda. According to Herron's reports these men

> ... were all greatly troubled by the apparent ignorance of the govern-
> ment in Rome regarding the importance of the conflict between Italy and
> the Yugoslavs over Adriatic territories.

Herron indicates in the preface to the collection of his documents (he has required that all those using his papers first study it) that he was substantially and in a constructive way involved in achieving a revision of the Italian attitude towards South Slav national aims. He specifically claims to have been instrumental in organizing the Congress of Op-pressed Nationalities in Rome in the spring of 1918 where the so-called Pact of Rome was concluded. The documents in the Herron papers furnish no proof for that claim,[7] but there can be no doubt that the Herron Papers deposited in the Hoover Institution are only part of a far larger collection of papers which Herron drafted and distributed or received during his four years of political activities in Switzerland. Checking through his papers one can point to lacunae. Using Herron's papers as a beginning point, one should try to search for material concerning his activities in the national archives in Washington, London, and Rome.

TRANSITION FROM WAR TO PEACE

The climax of Herron's activities occurred during the years of transition from war to peace, especially from spring 1918 to spring 1919. Herron established links with pacifists in Austria, Hungary, Germany and the Netherlands and arranged for informal peace talks with Heinrich Lammasch and Julius Meinl from Austria, Wilhelm Mühlon, Friedrich Foerster and Ludwig Quidde from Germany and Jong von Beek and Donk from the Netherlands. In 1915 and 1916 Herron published some pamphlets explaining the political ideas and objectives of Woodrow Wilson. As a result of these activities he estab-lished a reputation as being Wilson's personal representative in Europe and became the target of wooing by the opponents of German im-perialism and the propagators of liberation for the suppressed nationalities in Central Europe. This was particularly true of the exile politicians of the Slav nationalities who hoped to gain influence on Wilson's decision-making through George D. Herron—or at least gain access to his advisors. Herron did nothing to discourage them, though his papers clearly show how unjustified the widely held impression regarding his relationship to Wilson actually was.[8] Although the men seeking his support thought of him as an honest broker who could be trusted to present their ideas to the President, Herron in fact behaved in a rather insincere and deceitful way. A characteristic example of his double-dealing can be found in a letter dated December 27, 1917, to the Italian embassy in Bern, in which he tried to refute accusations of having made anti-Italian statements. He emphatically denied supporting the preservation of the existing Habsburg monarchy:

> There is not in Europe a more anti-Austrian person than myself. I have . . . absolutely defended Italy's claims and stood against Austria. . . . The only excuse for such reports goes back to the visit of Professor Foerster. . . . Austria had let it be announced (privately) that she was ready to reconstitute herself on the basis of the American States, to concede the Irredenta to Italy and to unite the Serbs in a larger Serbia. It may have been a deception, but Americans were willing to listen—if there was any chance of cutting off Austria from Germany and ending the war on Italy's frontier. But to be ready to receive . . . Austria's practical surrender to the Allies and their cause, is very far from being pro-Austrian. . . . But so far am I from being pro-Austrian, I have become absolutely convinced after all these considerations of Austrian possibilities that the only way to European peace or to European freedom or democracy is through absolute dismemberment of the Austrian Empire. That is my present unqualified position; and it is the thing I shall advocate in America; and I believe that anything short of Austrian dismemberment will be a failure of the war aims of the Allies.[9]

A few weeks later Herron had long talks with Professor Lammasch, who returned to Austria convinced that Herron was an ardent supporter and friend of Austria, which had every chance of having its existence guaranteed if it would carry out some constitutional reforms.[10] Herron continued to present himself to visitors from the German parts of the Habsburg Monarchy as a true friend of a democratic reformed Habsburg Empire, while at the same time reporting to the State Department that all his informers from the non-German nationalities were united in their conviction that the dissolution of the Austro-Hungarian Empire was inevitable. This dissolution, he wrote in a letter dated April 19, 1918, could result either

> . . . by a complete collapse of the whole political and social system as in Russia or the break-up may proceed through the revolution of each of the several states or at least through revolution on the part of the Czechs or Yugoslavs.

In this letter Herron appears to be particularly impressed by the unification aspirations of the Southern Slavs, "who are entering into a racial unity that has no precedent in their past." These aspirations for national unification had been invigorated by the recently signed agreements between Yugoslav and Italian representatives.[11]

SLAVIC REACTION TO THE FOURTEEN POINTS

An equally pro-Yugoslav sentiment is shown in the report from January 25, 1918, quoted at the beginning of this article, in which Herron communicated to the State Department the disappointment with the Fourteen Points which representatives of the Slav nationalities felt. Alexander Z. Yovitchitch and Nikola Stoianovitch had come to him as delegates of the Southern Slavs and had raised complaints concerning the fact that according to their impression

> . . . all smaller nations had been abandoned by the Allies for the sake of detaching Austria from Germany and obtaining a premature and inconclusive peace. They considered that the whole principle of the right of each nationality to choose its own political condition and affiliation had been forsaken, if not betrayed. The problem of an early military victory over Germany had swallowed up, so they thought, President Wilson's primary object of winning the world for democracy. The Serb peoples or the Yugo-Slavs as they had agreed to call themselves, feel that their complete integration and independence as a sovereign nation should have been specifically declared as an indispensable part of Allied programme. They believe that this is due to them from Europe and that it is an act of justice. . . . If any people since civilization began deserved to have its demands satisfied, it is the Serbian people. The Serbs are indeed a people whose history is a perpetual martyrdom . . . for seven long and terrible centuries they have had to live with one hand at the sword and the other on the plough. Time after time they have saved Europe from the Turks only to be betrayed and torn into fragments by the Habsburgs or the Magyars. . . . And repeatedly have the Serbs been prevented from achieving their freedom and unity by the conflicting interests of European diplomacy. . . .[12]

Herron reported that in a second meeting he succeeded in explaining to the Yugoslav delegates the positive aspects of the Fourteen Points, demonstrating to them the advantages implied in the possibilities contained in them, possibilities which

> . . . leave the way open for their future union and development and which can be stipulated in the following five points:
>
> First, the addition, upon the Dalmatian coast, of the port and territory which would insure their economic future.
>
> Second, the implied privilege of Serbia and Montenegro instantly to unite themselves.
>
> Third, the hope of ultimate union with Bosnia and Herzegovina and Croatia—a hope which would become open to them through the democratization of the Austrian-Empire. . . .
>
> Fourth, the wide scope of decisions presented to the Peace Conference by the demand that the relations of the Balkan States to one another be determined by friendly counsel along historically established lines of allegiance and nationality.
>
> Fifth, and most important of all, that the indispensable basis of the peace which President Wilson proposes is the Society of Nations. . . .[13]

In addition to his talks with Yugoslav representatives Herron had meetings with Czech and Polish emissaries and he recapitulated the impressions he had gained from the discussions in the conclusion

> that all Slavic people hold two or three principles in common: a) the dismemberment of the Austro-Hungarian Empire . . . is a sine qua non of a European, b) Prussia has to be reduced to a smaller size, and c) strategic and natural borders are obsolete in view of the establishment of the Society of Nations.

YUGOSLAV-ITALIAN NEGOTIATIONS

The Herron Papers do not disclose to what degree Herron actually collaborated in the implementation of the Italian-Yugoslav rapprochement which climaxed in the signing of the Pact of Rome, but they make it apparent that the Yugoslav-Italian negotiations were part of a personal rivalry and political antagonism between Orlando and Sonnino on the Italian side similar to the rivalry between Pasitch and Trumbitch on the side of the Southern Slavs and that these personal conflicts determined, to quite an extent, the relationship of Italy and of the Southern Slavs to the Allied Great Powers.

The visit which Trumbitch paid to Herron in Geneva on September 25, 1918, certainly has to be considered in light of these rivalries. Herron sent an extensive report on Trumbitch's visit to the State Department and this document sheds some discerning light on the bizarre political situation at the moment of the collapse of the Central Powers:

> Dr. A. Trumbitch came from Rome into Switzerland, about two weeks ago, but remained secluded in the Ticino, baffling every effort of his own and the Italian Legations in Bern, to come into contact with him for a time: when he came to Bern, however, he saw Mr. Wilson, and Mr. Dulles, before his subsequent visit to me.

> Day before yesterday, he sent me word, that he wished a strictly confidential interview, and that he wished neither the members of the Serbian Central Committee nor the Italians to know of his presence in Geneva. He came yesterday, on his way to Paris, and remained with me for three hours; during which time all the questions at issue between Italy and Yugo-Slavia were exposed by Dr. Trumbitch, and discussed at length. The point of the confidential discussion was this: can or will America take any steps toward enforcing a complete and just settlement on the part of Italy with the Yugoslavs, especially as regards the whole Adriatic and Dalmatian problem? I can only, at this writing, state briefly the chief presentations of Dr. Trumbitch.

> I. The entire Serbian Italian question, which it was thought the Congress of Rome had disposed of happily and finally is back in the melting-pot. Negotiations are practically back where they were before the Congress was held. This is not generally known; but it is the truth about the present situation. . . . As a consequence, new bitterness, new strife, and potential new disasters loom ahead of the Allied cause in South-Eastern Europe.

II. The crux of the matter is the presence of Signor Sonnino in the Italian Foreign office . . . [Sonnino] still stands for an Italian imperialist policy. He not only has no sympathy with, he has fundamental antipathy to, the aspirations of the Yugoslavs for National unity and racial integration. He secretly believes in, and works for, the preservation of Austria—except that part of Austria which he believes should go to Italy. . . . Signor Sonnino believes in the Triple Alliance today just as much as he did before the war. He does not believe in American disinterestedness; nor does he desire American influence in Europe. He is a constant obstacle in the path of America and the Entente, and his presence is a constant peril to the pursuit of their ultimate war-aims.

III. Italy has never really renounced the Pact of London. There are, of course, many noble and generous Italians, who individually renounce this Pact, but neither Sonnino as Foreign Minister, nor the Italian Government as a whole, have taken this step. And Dr. Trumbitch has no doubt that Italy intends to secure the fulfillment of as much of this Pact as the conditions involved in the conclusion of the war make possible. Rather than accept the fulfillment of the Pact of London, every remaining Serbian or Yugoslav would fight to the death.

IV. Now, overtopping all this, is the military question. Dr. Trumbitch conceives it highly possible, if not altogether probable, that Germany is preparing for a powerful and conclusive offensive on the Italian front. . . . The German hope and purpose are to deal Italy such a decisive blow as to take her out of the war. The food reserves of Lombardy, the wealth of Milan and Turin and the port of Genoa would be in German hands. There would be an Italian debacle closely resembling the debacle of Russia, according to Germany's plan. Thus again the Fates would favour Germany at the critical moment, as they did in the Russian failure at the previous critical moment. Germany would hope to gain at least two years time by this conclusive blow at Italy. Now the only guarantee against such a result is the presence of an American army in Italy before the first of March. Dr. Trumbitch agrees with me that Italy cannot sustain this large German offensive alone, and that an American or English army is necessary on the Italian front, in order to save the Allied cause from prolonged disaster. . . .

V. Now the fateful and conclusive question is: can America, can England, avail herself of this critical situation to enforce: (1) the renunciation on the part of the Italian government, of the Pact of London; (2) a just and final settlement of the issues between Italy and Yugoslavia—even, say, of committing the whole matter to an American Commission; (3) indirectly compelling the removal of the chief obstacle to a true co-operation between Italy and America, between Italy and Serbia—namely, Baron Sonnino at the Italian Foreign Office?

VI. Dr. Trumbitch explained to me, with maps he brought with him, the military and naval situation, and presented a plan by which a small but well-equipped American or English naval expedition could take possession of the Adriatic and utterly destroy the remnants of the Austrian fleet. It was also possible to land an expeditionary force at Sebenico; which expedition could rally all the Yugoslav forces, and accomplish an overthrow of Austria. . . . There are today, he says, 150,000 well armed Yugoslav deserters from the Austrian army hiding in the forests of Serbia and the hinterland behind the mountains of Dalmatia. These have no way of making connection as yet with the troops at Salonica. But an army, say of 100,000 Americans, landing at Sebenico, would find an amazing number of troops rallying to its standards and would find the whole of Bosnia, Herzegovina and Croatia rising instantly in revolution, and coming to this army's support. He would like to present this plan to General Pershing and the American General Staff and I have written to Ambassador Sharp, suggesting that he secure for Dr. Trumbitch this opportunity.

VII. In conclusion, let me say that the opinions of Dr. Trumbitch are worthy of the most serious consideration by our government, and especially by the President. Dr. Trumbitch is the most able, the most intelligent, the most envisioned and the most trusted of all Yugoslav leaders. If the union of the Yugoslavs in a great nation becomes an accomplished fact, Dr. Trumbitch is the probable first prime minister.[14]

SOUTHERN SLAV AMBITIONS

No doubt, the competition for the strategic entrenchment of territorial aspiration had begun and apparently Herron stood in the center of the Southern Slav ambitions. At least that is where he claims to have been: in the "Preparatory Remarks" to his Papers he records that during the attempts to bring about the unification of the three groups of Southern Slav exiles his home in Geneva was the stage of mutual Yugoslav intrigues:

> I recall the time when all Yugoslav chieftains met in Geneva to form a government and how, upon a single afternoon, three different sets of these Yugoslav government creators were seated in different rooms of my house in Geneva, neither set knowing that the other two were present, each set coming to intrigue against the other and to try to reach President Wilson through me. . . .[15]

Herron wrote this account some time after the signing of the peace treaties at a time when, according to his own testimony, he had abandoned the Yugoslav cause in deep disappointment:

> . . . I began my work with all my sympathies intensely with the Serbs and my predilections against the Bulgarians. By the end of the war and the Peace Conference this state of mind had completely reversed itself. My contact and experience with these two peoples convinced me that the Bulgarians were deeply wronged throughout the war and by the peace and that the Serbs were utterly untrustworthy. They were also responsible to a much larger degree than America is aware for the precipitation of the war. I became acquainted with the infidelity of the Serb peoples toward each other as well as their treachery and violence toward other peoples. At one time, for instance, Trumbic, their first Foreign Minister and most reputable of all Yugoslav statesmen, came to an explicit agreement with me as to the terms of peace with Italy which the Yugoslavs were ready to accept, and then went to Paris and flatly perjured himself relying on French support and corruption as well as the support and innocence of President Wilson. . . .[16]

In the moment of the capitulation of the Central Powers Herron had once more been spokesman for Yugoslav claims. On November 2, 1918, he sent an urgent appeal to the State Department communicating Yugoslav and Czech demands for armistice conditions.[17] In his accompanying letter Herron mentions that "members of the seven nationalities meeting together here in Geneva in the persons of some fifty delegates" had made him "President of their conference" and that he had "promised to do whatever I found possible to indorse their proceedings to those in authority in our government." Herron pushed the demands of the Czechs and Yugoslavs by using an argument which weighed heavily with the U.S. government: he pointed to the

> imminence of the Bolsheviki peril to all Europe east of the Rhine. The peril is becoming more portentous and monstrously near every moment Germany is systematically instructing her remaining two million Russian prisoners in the Bolsheviki philosophy. Regular courses of instruction are given by officially appointed teachers. Then, by one mode and another the more intelligent of these supplied with immense sums of German money are slipped into different countries of Europe. The members of the provisional governing committee of the Yugoslavs state that, if they are put into immediate possession of all their territories, with complete control over the troops and civil authorities in those territories and if their ports are opened immediately to food supplies from the Allies, they can hold South-Eastern Europe from the threatened Bolsheviki revolution and prevent the dissolution of civil order in all the former Austro-Hungarian nationalities and the Balkans. . . . The Czechoslovaks also declare that, if they are placed in immediate possession of their own territories, they can hold back the Bolsheviki invasion of Europe by Russia and prevent the dissolution of Hungary. . . .

Whether this letter and the Yugoslav-Czech armistice proposals ever reached the State Department could not be established and is of little significance since it could not have influenced the decisions at that late date. The very next day the Italians concluded the armistice with the military representative of the Habsburg Monarchy according to their own territorial aspirations and political interests. A few days later in a memorandum entitled "The New Nations and the Bolsheviki" in which Herron discussed the future of the Balkans he surprisingly enough presented himself as an outspoken opponent, even enemy of Yugoslav aspirations.[18]

HERRON'S EFFORTS TO INFLUENCE AMERICAN DELEGATION

Throughout the following months, in which the Allied delegations discussed the problems of the peace settlement in Paris, Herron tried desperately to gain influence in the American delegation and especially on Wilson, pushing a definitely anti-Yugoslav and pro-Italian policy. On March 17, 1919, Herron turned directly to President Wilson:

May I add to this, without seeming intrusive or impertinent, a word about the Yugo-Slavs and the Italians. I have been, as perhaps you may remember from some of my reports of nearly two years ago, pro-Serbian. I have done everything possible for these people, even to the extent of expending upon their needs no small portion of what small fortune I still possess, but they are now manifesting themselves as the most greedy and chauvinistic and intriguing of all the nationalities, and they are being stimulated to this by certain French intrigues and financial interests. Your whole program for the Society of Nations has no worse enemy than these same Yugo-Slavs at the present time. . . . On the other hand, the younger Italians . . . are the best supporters of the League of Nations and of your whole program. . . . I wish you could see your way to inviting to a personal interview the Marquis Durazzo, Secretary to the Signor Sonnino and the Italian Foreign Office, who is at the Hotel Edward VII. He is the grandson of the great Marquis Durazzo who fought with Mazzini, and is one of the coming men of the Italian future.

It is because of what I see in Italy, because of the true support which I believe our American idea will have in this new Italy, that I beg you not to be deceived by the Yugo-Slav pretensions at this time, and to give to Italy the utmost consideration in this Adriatic dispute. Against all my former predilections, I have come to believe that Italy is much nearer the right than the Yugo-Slavs.

Also I believe that the future peace of Europe and the hope of a democratic Europe is a good deal more assured by our relying upon Italy than it is by our relying upon France. . . . [19]

Herron's efforts were to no avail. The anti-Italian mood in the American delegation was too strong—the letters which Charles Seymour, one of the delegation, wrote to his family during his stay at Paris show that this anti-Italian attitude was to no small extent determined by irrational emotions.[20]

Herron apparently was not discouraged; he not only continued to propagate the Italian cause by sending reports and memoranda to Paris, but in the moment of crisis in the conflict between Wilson and the Italians, in the Fiume-crisis from March to May 1919, he tried in newspaper interviews to expose the Yugoslav claims to Fiume as economically as well as ethnically incorrect. An interview given in early April to the correspondent of the Agence centrale at Lucerne, a Yugoslav propaganda agency in Switzerland, led to an excited newspaper controversy with the Yugoslav Minister Kramer[21] and caused the Yugoslav Foreign Minister Ante Trumbitch to write a personal letter to Herron to justify in an extended way the Yugoslav claims to all of Dalmatia and Istria including Rijeka and Trieste.[22] In his rejoinder Herron identified himself with the Italian position and accused Serbia of acting in bad will. It is characteristic of Herron's activities that he sent copies of his letter to Trumbitch not only to President Wilson, but also to the Italian embassy at Bern with a request to have it forwarded to

Prime Minister Orlando, and to the British consul at Geneva asking him to transmit this document to the British Foreign Office.[23]

SIGNS OF RESIGNATION AND DISAPPOINTMENT

Herron's letter to Trumbitch shows the first sign of resignation and disappointment over the realization that all his efforts to gain influence on the decision-making process in world affairs had remained without success. Hidden in his explanation of the interview we find in this document the best description of Herron's wartime activities written in his own words:

> . . . I want to disabuse your mind of any thought that anything I have said may have had any effect whatever upon the mind of the President or the minds of the American Peace Commissioners. I am not a delegate to the Peace Commission, nor have I been in any way officially attached to it, nor have I been his counsellor. It is true that I have, for nearly three years upheld him in every possible way, especially in the public press of Europe, because I believed that upon him as upon no other man in the secular history of the world, the destiny of mankind immediately depended. For this reason has grown up the legend, which I have done my utmost to destroy, but seemed unable to do so, that in advocating his idea and his opportunity I am in some way speaking his mind and acting in some official or semi-official capacity. Such is not the case and even though I have betimes expressed my opinions to him about this or that phase of the European situation, I have no reason whatever for supposing that any opinion of mine has ever had the slightest influence upon him or upon the American Commission for the negotiations of peace. In fact, there is scarcely anything I know of in which the decision of the American Peace Commission has not been different from what I hoped such decisions would be. . . . Peace has not been made on the basis of the Fourteen Principles, but on a basis of compromise. . . . [24]

Some time before Herron had written to President Wilson to express to him his personal disappointment with the course the Paris Conference had taken and only a few days before Herron wrote to Trumbitch that he had received a letter from Woodrow Wilson saying:

> I am sorry that you are so deeply discouraged about the work of the conference. It is undoubtedly true that on the whole we have been able to keep tolerably close to the lines laid down at the outset and I am confirmed in this opinion by the judgment of many conscientious men about me, by whose conscience as well as by my own I tried to be guided. The treaty which ends so terrible a war must unavoidably seem harsh towards the outlaws who started the war, but when details are read and understood I believe that the indignation will be largely removed.[25]

Herron's activities in Geneva and his attempts to take the lead in the reshaping of the national order in the Adriatic sphere were no more than ephemeral meddling behind the stage of world history. But his papers throw new light on the difficulties which made the settlement of all the conflicting claims so complex and dissatisfying to all parties concerned.

Notes

1. Herron Papers (H.P.), vol. III, Austria I, p. 1. This article is based on research done in the archives of the Hoover Institution on War, Revolution and Peace, Stanford, Calif. I am indebted to the staff of the archives and library and in particular to Mrs. Agnes Peterson for their assistance and their hospitality which made it possible for me to carry on intensive research work while being the first Austrian guest professor holding the Austrian chair at Stanford University.
2. H.P., vol. I, Germany I, Preparatory remarks, p. 2.
3. Cf. Benedikt, Heinrich: Die Friedensaktion der Meinl-Gruppe 1917/18. Die Bemühungen um einen Verständigungsfrieden nach Dokumenten, Aktenstücken und Briefen.–Grau: 1961; in regard to the history of Yugoslavia cf. Zivojinovic, Dragan.: America, Italy and the birth of Yugoslavia (1917–1919).–New York 1972, p. 55.
4. Briggs, Mitchell Pirie: George D. Herron and the European Settlement.–Stanford: 1932.
5. H.P., vol XI, Doc. XXIII. Cf. also Briggs, European Settlement, pp. 31–32.
6. This and the following quotations are taken from H.P. vol. I, Germany I, Preparatory Remarks, pp. 14–15.
7. H.P., vol. I, Preparatory Remarks, p. 15. Cf. Briggs, p. 28 who did not have permission to see vol VI, though vol. VI does not contain any documents which give any conclusive evidence on Herron's activities in this connection.
8. Cf. especially H.P. vol. XII as well as other volumes passim. Herron apparently did not meet Wilson personally before 1919, cf. H.P. vol. VI, Italy and Serbia.
9. H.P. vol. VI, Italy, Doc. V, Letter Herrons to Marquese Durazzo, Dec. 27, 1917.
10. H.P., vol. III, Austria, Cf. Benedikt, Die Friedensaktion der Meinl-Gruppe. Benedikt had copies of the Herron Papers at his disposal.
11. H.P. vol. III, Austria, Doc. XXV.
12. H.P. vol. III, Austria I, Doc. I.
13. Ibid.
14. H.P. vol. VI, Italy and Serbia, Doc. IV, Herron to State Department, September 27, 1918.
15. H.P. vol. I, Preparatory Remarks, p. 5.
16. Ibid., p. 29.
17. H.P. vol. II, Czecho-Slovakia, Doc. IV, IVa, and V.
18. H.P. vol. VI, Italy and Serbia, Doc. VI.
19. H.P. vol. VI, Italy and Serbia, Doc. XII.
20. Cf. Seymour, Charles: Letters from the Paris Peace Conference. Edited by Harold B. Whiteman Jr.—New Haven: Yale Univ. Press 1965.
21. H.P. vol XXVII, Supplementary, Italy and Serbia, Doc. VII.
22. H.P. vol. VI, Italy and Serbia, Doc. XIV, April 14, 1919.
23. Ibid., Doc. XIX,XXII, XXIII, XXVI.
24. Ibid., Doc. XX.
25. H.P. vol. I, Doc. XV, April 28, 1919.

Unifying the Yugoslav Economy, 1918–1921: Misery and Early Misunderstandings

John R. Lampe

THE AMERICAN VISITORS to present-day Yugoslavia may find its socialist institutions foreign to their own experience but often feel kinship with its federal form of government. Perhaps the most enduring Yugoslav response to visitors who mistake their own empathy for easy understanding is to remind them that the Socialist Federal Republic of Yugoslavia is not only a country of six republics, but also of five nationalities, four languages, three religions, two alphabets, and one party trying to reconcile them.

This well-known litany, with the number of the first and last items neatly reversed, can also serve as an introduction to the initial problems of unifying the first Yugoslavia after World War I. Complicating the economic unification of the new Kingdom of Serbs, Croats and Slovenes (KSCS) in late 1918 was a further progression of diversities: six custom areas, five currencies, four railway networks, three types of banking systems, two governments, and one comparative advantage (livestock) in foreign trade.[1] Even the last, lone element was not, as we shall see, one that bound the Yugoslav lands comfortably together.

The miseries of the First World War far surpassed the burden of the Revolutionary War on the young American state. They made the reconciliation of diversity more difficult. The loss of Yugoslav life and property was enormous, if not precisely known. Serbia alone suffered over one million dead, a third of its prewar population, and saw up to one-half of its prewar wealth destroyed. From 1912 forward it fought two Balkan wars in Macedonia, several campaigns on its own territory, endured enemy occupation and preserved its army for the Salonika front and victorious reentry in 1918. The former Habsburg lands in the first Yugoslavia had lost several hundred thousand dead, mainly on the Italian front, and a like number taken prisoner, mainly on the Russian front. One fifth of their prewar wealth had been destroyed.

In these disparate war damages lay the source of several economic misunderstandings between the component parts of the new KSCS that created political hostility. Serbia had suffered more than the former Habsburg lands, even if its claims to the Paris Peace Conference are reduced substantially.[2] In the absence of prompt or satisfactory reparations, Serbian representatives were tempted to feel that the "northern territorities" owed the new state compensations for what their previous Austro-Hungarian rulers had done. From the viewpoint of Croatian and Slovenian representatives, however, their own devotion to the Yugoslav idea and their eventual overthrow of Habsburg authority deserved recognition. Their economies had undoubtedly lost more than they gained during the war, especially when we add the onerous terms under which private firms and especially agricultural landholders were forced to do business with Habsburg military authorities.[3]

PREWAR ADVANTAGES AND WARTIME DISADVANTAGES

The northern commercial interests also lost the prewar advantage of doing business in a large customs union of 51 million people with a stable currency. The new Yugoslav state was one quarter that size and could not stabilize the value of its dinar until 1924. Setting aside market size and postwar monetary problems, moreover, the component parts of the new state had developed no prewar momentum toward a unified Yugoslav economy on which they would draw. Certainly their respective business communities had failed to do so. Slovenian industry and agriculture were tied to Trieste or Gratz by the Südbahn rail line, in the fashion that the Macedonian hinterland was linked to Thessaloniki. Now all these cities were permanently placed outside of Yugoslav territory. Italian occupation separated Rijeka, its port facilities and shipbuilding industry, from Croatia and Dalmatia for most of the interwar period. The late Rudolf Bićanić regarded separation from this ring of important commercial centers just across its new boundaries as one of the major economic trials facing the first Yugoslavia.[4]

Although not connected before 1914 to any city in this ring, independent Serbia had seen its comparative advantage in foreign trade develop along lines that ran dangerously parallel to those of the former Habsburg lands. The surge of grain exports, passing 40 percent of total value for 1906–10, that carried Serbia through its Tariff War with Austria-Hungary was surprisingly not the problem. According to regrettably indirect indications, the Hungarian Agricultural Revolution of the nineteenth century had effectively barred grain from Croatia/ Slavonia on the Vojvodina from Austrian or Hungarian markets.[5] Livestock and processed meat constituted the source of prewar comparative advantage shared by virtually all the Yugoslav lands. By the end of its Tariff War in 1911, Serbia had been able to process half of its 23 million dinars (equivalent to French francs) in meat exports. Virtually all of them had gone either to Austria-Hungary or to Germany. But so in 1910 had thrice that value in just livestock from both Croatia/ Slavonia and the Vojvodina, twice as much from Slovenia and almost that from Bosnia-Hercegovina: all together over eight times the value of Serbian meat exports, nearly ten if we include Croatian meat fats and other by-products.[6] Serbian and Bosnian plums, another 10-20 percent of the respective prewar export values, also went primarily to Central European destinations. So did the Croatian, Slovenian and Bosnian timber that accounted for a similar share of prewar exports from the three Habsburg territories, each of whose total export value surpassed the Serbian figure.[7]

Clearly these Central European markets would have to remain open and active if the new Yugoslav economy were to maintain the prewar exports of its component parts. That they did not once normal trade resumed in the 1920's is a matter of record.[8]

More important for our purposes is the discouraging effect that the Central European direction of these pre-1914 exports had on creating any impetus within the respective commercial communities, even when in largely native hands, for trade or investment in the other Yugoslav lands. Croatian exports to Serbia, for instance, fell short of half a million crowns in a total that exceeded 150 millions. My research has revealed only one instance of Croatian investment in Serbia, and then only a million crowns from the Serbian Bank in Zagreb.[9] In addition, the well-known rivalry between Austrian and Hungarian interests made sure that there would be precious little interaction between the Slovenian and Croatian economies and repeated friction over what to do about the joint Austro-Hungarian venture in Bosnia-Hercegovina.[10] In the absence of a badly needed monograph on the wartime experience of these several economies, the general record of the Habsburg war effort can be taken as preliminary evidence that the coordination of Croatian, Slovenian and Bosnian development did not improve much between 1914 and 1918.

More certainly, the Austrian occupation of Serbia between 1915 and 1918 made no significant effort to coordinate its economy with those of the other Yugoslav lands. Habsburg authorities persuaded a delegation from the Zagreb Chamber of Commerce to visit Belgrade in February 1916 to examine possible connections, but the unrepaired rail and road networks made even transportation to and from Serbia so unpromising that the delegation declined to pursue any projects.[11] Professor Djordjević's survey of the occupation makes it clear that Habsburg authorities never had any sort of plan, even an exploitative one, for developing the productive resources of the Serbian economy. Only the army had ever expected a prolonged occupation. After some discussion, the military left the Bor copper mines and the Smederevo-Niš rail line to German exploitation as a price for the latter army's evacuation. The Hungarian civil governor who at least allowed the Belgrade municipal government to reconvene was forced to quit his post unreplaced in 1916, under pressure from the Austrian army's

high command. Their officers left most of the undamaged industrial
plant to lie idle. A few token "agricultural stations" were set up and
manned with prisoners of war while the remaining peasants tried to
grow as little as possible for fear of requisitions. Coal and nonferrous
mines were heavily worked but then flooded or set afire when the
retreat began in the fall of 1918. The several Austrian banks that
opened branches in Belgrade during the war took no interest in promoting local enterprises. The one institution established by the occupying army's authorities that touched the entire economy was a system of
requisition and rationing. A central warehouse was set up in Belgrade
for collecting requisitioned food, textiles and metals. It sent them on to
Austria-Hungary for the war effort. Another branch of this "centrala"
provided Belgrade with rations of meat and other foods that shrank as
the city's population climbed back to 50,000, over half its prewar level,
by mid-1917.[12]

In sum, their experience before and during the First World War
cannot be said by any stretch of the imagination to have prepared the
Yugoslav lands in general and its business interests in particular for
economic integration immediately afterwards. Yet that is precisely the
task that they were forced to undertake, along with the recovery from
the war and the adjustment to a more divided and protectionist European economy that burdened the rest of the continent as well.[13]

The rest of this brief analysis carries the pursuit of economic
integration only as far as the official formation of the Kingdom of
Serbs, Croats and Slovenes in 1921. The paucity of past Yugoslav
scholarship on the sweep of the new state's formative experience is
partly explained by the compartmentalization of research within the
present republics. Lack of statistical data is another major obstacle.
Reliable, countrywide aggregates of production and trade were simply
not collected until after 1921. What we have before then comes from
scattered, often biased or inadequate sources.[14] The period is, all the
same, too important to ignore.

The present paper relies on largely secondary sources to examine
the major sectors in the Yugoslav economy between 1918 and 1921. It
seems appropriate to group the interrelated experiences of agriculture
and foreign trade, of transportation and mining, and of industry and
banking. Within all three pairings we find inadvertent frictions developing between Serbia and the former Habsburg territories of Croatia,
Slavonia and Slovenia. These misunderstandings, especially over industry and banking, would feed not only on the aforementioned disparity in war damages but also on the difficult conditions peculiar to the
immediate postwar period throughout Central Europe.

PEASANT UNREST AND CROATIAN AGRICULTURAL TRADE

One condition that characterized much of Habsburg territory as
the war drew to a close was a growing body of peasant deserters from

local garrisons. They chose to keep their weapons and roam the countryside in bands rather than return to their villages. Once the war ended and Austro-Hungarian troops withdrew from their former Yugoslav lands, these so-called "green cadres" could take the law into their own hands from the Vojvodina across Croatia and Bosnia-Hercegovina to Slovenia. In his recent study of the Srem, Nikola Gaćeša joins another careful Yugoslav scholar of the period, Dragoslav Janković, in doubting that such peasants' initial seizures of Jewish property and Austrian or Italian estates can be given a coherent revolutionary or socialist character.[15] The threat of the green cadres was in any event sufficient to prompt the Narodno Vijeće in Zagreb, the only effective government in the western Yugoslav lands by November 1918, to attempt unsuccessfully to mobilize these peasants and thus bring them under its control. Failing this, the National Council asked the Serbian government to send troops. They arrived in mid-November, 1918. The troops restored order that would last only until prisoners of war began returning from Russia in February 1919.

The Narodno Vijeće had anticipated further unrest. In November it already abolished *kmetsva*, or indentured sharecropping, and proclaimed that large holdings would be redistributed. This is not the place to examine the subsequent agrarian reform and resettlement in all its aspects and regional variations. The reform is the one economic aspect of this immediate postwar period to have received extensive treatment in Yugoslav historiography. It seems relevant to the present inquiry only where the redistribution went into effect quickly. Legal redistribution began first in Croatia/Slavonia, including the Srem, and the Vojvodina under the basic legislation of February 1919 and further regulations in April. One result of the progressive breakup of all holdings over 57 hectares (100 Hungarian jutars) was to reduce the size of harvests and the raising of livestock. According to Bićanić, the agricultural faculty of the University of Zagreb calculated that total agricultural output in Croatia/Slavonia declined 20 percent from its already reduced wartime level during the period 1918–1921.[16]

Another result of this rapidly spreading redistribution was most probably to prompt non-Yugoslav owners not yet affected to sell their existing livestock and grain as quickly as possible, not only for the highest price but with no thought for replenishing the herds or crops. The flow of such goods to food-starved postwar Austria and Hungary, long their principal markets anyway, was thus accelerated by the agrarian reform.

That flow had not ended with the Habsburg collapse in October of 1918. The Yugoslav lands found themselves at the war's end with six separate customs areas, for Croatia/Slavonia, Slovenia, Dalmatia, Bosnia/Hercegovina, the Vojvodina, and Serbia and Montenegro combined. Acting mainly through the food rationing *centrale* set up under Habsburg control or occupation, these areas enforced complex regulations that restricted trade between their territories more effectively than any level of tariffs might have. Grain shipments from Vojvodina to neighboring Serbia were for instance "nearly impossible." Supposedly the same regulations applied to trade with Austria and Hungary, but the higher prices initially available in their badly drained economies made the effort worthwhile. Some governing bodies simply charged fees for exemptions to the regulations. The first combined Yugoslav government was able to agree on the creation of a single customs union, with free internal trade and external trade on the basis of the prewar Serbian tariff, only in March 1919. By then the pattern was set. A renewed ban on all exports to Austria or Hungary was quickly amended to exempt border areas until the Paris Peace Conference fixed final frontiers. This, plus an unclear division of responsibility between civilian and military authorities in Belgrade for granting exemptions to the ban, allowed grain and livestock to continue moving northward from Croatia and the Vojvodina while food shortages persisted in other Yugoslav lands. Blame for the shortages was assigned variously to the government in Belgrade, to the exporting areas or to their Jewish merchants who were presumed to have special ties to Austria and Hungary.[17]

In Zagreb, however, the population as a whole bore a heavy burden for the city's having become the largest single focal point for such trade. Prices for all foodstuffs shot up eighteenfold over their prewar level by mid-1919, even before the conversion from crowns to dinars, thus surpassing the increase in Belgrade through 1922. By that time, Zagreb's prices were 40 to 60 times their prewar level.[18] More apparent to the other Yugoslav lands was the fact that in the process Zagreb had become the center for exports from and imports to the emerging new state. How could it have been otherwise, though, with the major ports of Trieste and Rijeka in Italian hands and Belgrade cut off by rail from the western territories and Central Europe until the bridge across the Sava River could be rebuilt? That arduous task was not completed until October 1920, partly with the assistance of an American army engineer.[19] Even the Zagreb's greater proximity than Belgrade's to Vienna and Prague meant that the 30–40 percent of Yugoslav export value and 40–50 percent of imports derived from Austria and Czechoslavakia throughout the 1920's would favor the commercial development of the Croatian capital. During 1920, the proportion of total export value shipped to those two countries was exactly 50 percent, largely consisting of grain, livestock and other foodstuffs.[20]

RAILWAY REPAIR, THE COAL CRISIS AND BELGRADE'S INDUSTRY

Rebuilding the bridge across the Sava River was only one part of the widespread repair needed to restore the Serbian and Macedonian railway network to prewar length. Its mileage had been the shortest of

all the independent Balkan states save Montenegro. Its combined
mileage per capita, moreover, had amounted to just one third of
the ratios for the networks in Croatia/Slavonia and even Bosnia/
Hercegovina. The new construction needed to end this latter imbalance and properly connect the four Yugoslav networks exceeded the
total prewar length.[21] Some lines would still remain to be built after the
Second World War.

By the fall of 1918, the one major standard-gauge line in Serbia,
the Belgrade-Niš section of the Orient Express's route, had been damaged beyond hope of use. Retreating Bulgarian troops had requisitioned or destroyed the system's central repair yards in Niš. Neither
the line nor the yards could operate again until August 1919.[22] In the
meantime, Belgrade was cut off from Skopje and also the source of its
wartime supplies, the Aegean port of Thessaloniki. Other Serbian and
Macedonian lines, typically narrow-gauge, were also damaged. Paris,
someone said, was closer to Belgrade than Mladenovac. All this, plus
losses of rolling stock, had wiped out over half the prewar assets of the
combined Serbian and Macedonian network.

When the new state's first provisional government was forced to
resign in August 1919, critics cited delays in the restoration of rail
service as one of its most serious failings. Yet those delays extended to
the Hungarian network in Croatia and the Vojvodina as well as to
Serbia and Macedonia. Complaints from all these areas would persist in
the National Assembly until 1922. Rapid resumption had proved possible only on the Austrian network in Slovenia and on the separate,
largely narrow-gauge network in Bosnia-Hercegovina. The latter's
service was repeatedly disrupted during 1919 by strikes.

Elsewhere the prevailing shortage of rolling stock that the war
effort had created in all the southern Habsburg lands was compounded by the aptly named coal crisis. Both Slovenia and Bosnia-
Hercegovina had their own supplies of the soft coal that locomotives
burned. Croatia had mainly lignite mines, the Vojvodina nothing and
Serbia several severely damaged lignite and hard coal mines. Austria
and Hungary were just as badly fixed. Traffic from Zagreb to Vienna
and Trieste was continually interrupted during 1919 for lack of coal.
The new government's efforts to import the necessary amounts from
Czechoslovakia as part of reparations foundered on Yugoslav exclusion from the Allied Control Commission for dividing up such supplies
from the former Habsburg lands.[23]

The coal crisis confronted Serbian industry, already concentrated
in Belgrade, with a double disadvantage. In addition to soft coal for rail
transport, the shortage extended to lignite. The private mines around
Belgrade were too badly damaged to resume production until 1920 or
later. Croatian output of lignite, from mines concentrated near Zagreb,
continued to increase annually during 1919–21 from a wartime level

that already exceeded that of 1913.[24] Fuel for heating buildings or running streetcars and some types of industrial machinery was thus available in Zagreb. Belgrade's factories stayed without heat, electricity or steam power through most of 1919.

Compounding special problems of Belgrade's industry was the surprising lack of state support during this obviously difficult period. Was not the new Yugoslav government, even before the Vidovdan Constitution of 1921, based in Belgrade and heavily reliant on an army and ministries who were still essentially Serbian? Without question. But no European government, as Sir John Hicks has pointed out, had useful experience in directing production in the private sector to meet a given public target until the mobilization of entire economies during the First World War.[25] The forced evacuation of the Serbian army and government in 1915 denied the small state even the possibility of that new experience. Little wonder that the Serbian army command, in complete charge of rail traffic and repairs until January 1919, and the new Ministry of Transportation found themselves squabbling over the authority to control the railroad's coal supplies through the rest of the year, or that private mine owners could persuade the Ministry of Trade and Industry to allocate no more than a modest three million dinars to help reopen the lignite mines whose production would have gone so far toward solving Belgrade's coal crisis.[26]

The city's industrial owners, far from manipulating the government's policies behind the scenes, had hardly been able to influence it at all during or after the war. At least this is the lesson that emerges from the experience of the Serbian *Industrijska Komora*, or Industrial Chamber, that had been founded in Belgrade before the war and that Djordje Vajfert, Injat Bajloni and Belgrade's other industrialists dominated.[27]

The Chamber set up headquarters in Paris in 1916, after the evacuation. Its counterparts for trade and artisan crafts were in Nice. Moreover, the Serbian army and state apparatus were on Corfu and then in Thessaloniki. The army's *Vojno-privredna direkcija*, or Military-Economic Directorate, successfully resisted civilian influence even from the Ministry of Trade and Industry. The government's list of priorities for postwar recovery (plan is too strong a word) put agriculture at the top and industry near the bottom. The Paris Chamber's efforts to limit note issue by the Narodna Banka failed. Inquiries on the extent of war damage in Serbia went unanswered even after the government had returned in the Fall of 1918.

The Industrial Chamber returned to Belgrade itself in December but still exercised no perceptible influence. Although invited to an official Yugoslav conference about the signing of compensating agreements with Austria and Hungary, its representatives were unable to change provisions that largely ignored Belgrade's badly damaged industrial facilities. The only effect of their objections was to prompt the Serbian-controlled Ministry of Trade and Industry to call a second conference that included only 5 Serbian representatives among a total of 55. The Chamber's demands for nationalization of all former Austrian- or Hungarian-owned firms throughout the country and its warnings against the threat to Serbian recovery from Croatian or Slovenian industry fell on deaf ears. So did its protests over Serbian army purchases from foreign rather than Serbian suppliers and over the favoritism accorded the railways and the tobacco monopoly in allocations of coal or lignite. The Chamber's conversion to a Yugoslav-wide organization later in 1919 changed neither its basically Serbian character nor its lack of influence. Its only accomplishment appears to have been the resumption of prewar *povlastice*, Serbian tax and tariff exemptions for individual enterprises. They had not made much impact then and did not include the massive credits and technical assistance that rapid postwar recovery would have required.[28]

Interestingly, the *Industrijska Komora* suffered not only from poor political connections but also from insufficient funds to carry out any progra·ıs of its own. The ability of its most powerful members to reestablish their own individual enterprises in Belgrade (the Vajfert brewery and the Bajloni flour mills in particular) testified to their unwillingness or their unpreparedness to offer industrial recovery collective support even through their own organization.

BANKING AND THE INDUSTRIAL ASCENDANCY OF ZAGREB

Industrial firms in Zagreb did not need to rely on state support. Instead they drew on capital from private banks to establish a position of primacy in Croatian and even Yugoslav industry that had only begun to emerge before the First World War. A variety of metal- and woodworking, meat and chemical processing, and cotton textile enterprises had led the way in a surge after 1900 that had seen the number of Zagreb's industrial firms double by 1910. Their total varies with the definition of what were the city limits but at most amounted to 79, versus at least 63 in Belgrade at the same time. Rising mainly at the expense of the declining Slavonian timber industry, this maximum number of enterprises still amounted to just one-third of the total for Croatia/Slavonia. By 1926 that fraction had risen to one-half, and the number of Zagreb's industrial firms to ten times their prewar level, versus a two- or three-fold increase for Belgrade. Only Slovenia could approach the rough notion we have of capital invested in Croatian industry for the mid-1920's. This capacity was scattered among smaller towns rather than concentrated in its central city of Ljubljana. Serbian industrial capital was concentrated in Belgrade but fell short of half the

Croatian and Slovenian totals of over two billion dinars apiece.[29]

One reason for this increased imbalance was obviously the location of the latter two areas between Yugoslavia's major trading partners during the 1920's, Italy for exports and, as we have seen, Austria and Czechoslovakia for imports. Exports earned investable capital and imports brought in the machinery and materials needed for manufacture. The faster demobilization of formerly Habsburg troops than of the Serbian army may have made more labor available to Croatian and Slovenian firms.

Another reason was the financial situation of the immediate postwar years. It is of special interest here because of the misunderstanding and mistrust it created between the commercial communities of Zagreb and Belgrade. The conflict between the private banks of the former and the state banks of the latter has endured in a socialist context to the present day.

This last and most portentious misunderstanding had its origins in the objective necessity for the new Yugoslav state to create a single currency and a single bank to issue it, in the fashion of any modern nation. The combined value of the German marks, Bulgarian leva and Montenegrin perper that the war had scattered across the eastern half of the country was too small compared to the supply of Serbian dinars either in circulation or safe-keeping to pose a serious postwar problem. The sum of Austro-Hungarian crowns was far larger, exceeding in Serbia alone half the face value of all dinars and amounting to more than twice that value in both Croatia/Slavonia and the Vojvodina.[30] Yet under no circumstances could any reasonable observer have expected that the bank notes of a recent enemy and now a defunct state could become the currency of the first Yugoslavia. The Serbian dinar was the only choice, unless the risky business of creating an entirely new currency were to be attempted. No one appears even to have suggested it.

Two questions remained to be settled. At what rate of exchange would the conversion of crowns to dinars take place? How could the existing Serbian bank of issue become one that represented all the Yugoslav lands? Let us consider them in that order.

While Serbian authorities were suggesting 10/1 to 20/1, Croatian and Slovenian representatives argued for rates of conversion that ranged from three crowns for one dinar down to one for one. But the initial Serbian decision in November 1918 to allow the use of crowns to continue in the western Yugoslav lands at two crowns per dinar, based on their respective official values in Swiss gold francs, revealed the problem posed by such a low rate. Crowns from Vienna and Budapest, where its market rate of exchange was rightly expected to decline rapidly, began finding their way south to Zagreb and Ljubljana. Some last new issues of crown notes and the willingness of the French army command in Budapest to accept and use them to cover expenses in the Vojvodina added to the flow.[31]

To stop this influx, Serbian authorities began, in December 1918, to require that all Austro-Hungarian crowns in circulation be rubber-stamped for Yugoslav use by the end of January 1919. The total stamped by that date amounted to 5,323 million crowns, with the 1,949 million in Croatia/Slavonia and the 1,689 million in the Vojvodina accounting for two-thirds.[32] Complaints immediately spread through the western Yugoslav lands, including a riot in Slovenia, over the confusing use of different colored stamps in different places, the lack of local control over the stamping and the resulting ease of counter-feiting. A different method of marking than this *žigosanje* was clear-ly needed if the conversion of crowns to dinars was to be accepted throughout the Yugoslav lands. From September 1919 through Janu-ary of 1920, a second marking with postage-style adhesive stamps was therefore undertaken and at a lower rate of exchange. This *markiranje* made four crowns equal to one dinar, now the rate of exchange on the Viennese market, but the Serbian-dominated government also charged a tax of 20 percent of the value of all crowns that made the real rate of exchange 5/1. Bonds given in return for the 20 percent tax would not mature for 10 years and would supposedly stem the growing use of Yugoslav crowns for speculation on Vienna's active currency ex-change.[33]

Some Serbian observers of the time dismissed the hardship in-volved in what became the final rate of conversion by calling the major Yugoslav holders of Habsburg crowns wartime speculators and profiteers. One Slovenian response seems closer to the truth: wartime speculators had typically sought to amass wealth in the form of goods, property or gold, leaving the mass of savers whose deposits made up the majority of Slovenian and Croatian bank liabilities to absorb the main losses from conversion.[34]

Before considering the actual response of these savings banks to the dilemma of conversion, we should take note of another strategy that Slovenian and Croatian financial interests might have pursued but chose not to. The actual conversion of rubber- and then adhesive-stamped crowns to dinars took place during 1920 under the auspices of the new bank of issue, the Narodna Banka Kr. Srba, Hrvata Slovenaca. True, the bank had been founded in January 1920 with the staff and reputation of the Narodna Banka Kr. Srbije, just returned from Mar-seilles in early 1919. Its prewar reputation was based not only on sound European-style financial practice but also on surprising independence from the Serbian government. The independence derived in turn from the bank's ownership by private stockholders.[35] Nine months of discussion in 1919, some in Zagreb, between officials of the Serbian bank and representatives from the other Yugoslav lands produced apparently general agreement that the new bank should be organized along the same principles. The existing 10 million dinars of capital stock in the Narodna Banka Kr. Srbije was to be augmented by another 40 million dinars worth of 500 dinar shares.

The attempted issue of just half that amount in 1920 and again in 1921 offered the larger western Yugoslav banks the chance to obtain a controlling interest in the issue of new dinars and perhaps in the final conversion of crowns. Yet, like Austrian interests at the time of the Serbian bank's founding in 1884, they declined to do so.[36] Serbian stockholders of the existing 20,000 shares from the old Narodna Banka admittedly had the right, despite protests from the "northern areas," to buy three of the new shares for every one they already owned, or three-quarters of total new issues projected. But they did not, probably could not, exercise those rights. The first issue of 40,000 new shares in October 1920 saw just 4,421 sold, with only 1,033 in Serbia.

The 800 sold in Croatia/Slovenia were fewer than the total in Slovenia and Bosnia/Hercegovina as well as in Serbia. The further 11,735 shares sold from May 1921 forward, with only half of the price now payable in gold and the rest in banknotes over a five-year period, attracted a similar distribution of buyers. Only when the Narodna Banka made the entire purchase price payable in bank notes on a delayed basis, in February 1922, was the entire issue finally sold. Serbian buyers, principally banks, took almost three-quarters of them. That the subsequent distribution of credit from the Narodna Banka through the 1920's would favor banks in general and Serbian ones in particular comes then as no surprise.[37] The natural northern resentment of the new central bank's distribution of credit deserved to be tempered for two reasons. First, the Serbian banks were not just the Narodna's largest shareholders but also continued to hold most of their liabilities in current accounts or especially bills of exchange. Their transfer to or rediscounting by the Narodna Banka Kr. Srbije had been the latter's principal prewar types of interest-earning asset.[38] Second, the northern banks had made the rational economic choice in 1920–22 to forego the uncertain market value of central bank shares, the government's first claim on central bank credit and most important the shares' maximum dividend of 10 percent to deal in more profitable assets. Already in 1920, while Serbian banks were recording profits that averaged 3.5 percent of paid-in capital, Slovenian banks were averaging 12.7 percent and Croatian ones 25.4 percent.[39]

The assets of the Croatian banks demand special attention. Their direction toward industry, especially in Zagreb, and the ensuing profits appeared to contemporary observers in Belgrade as final proof that the Croatian economy was still riding a wave of prosperity that had begun with wartime profits from serving the Austro-Hungarian war effort. In reality, these industrial profits were a phenomenon of the immediate postwar period. We have already noted one of their origins. The Zagreb-centered agricultural trade with the desperately reduced economies of Austria and Hungary generated profits that could be spent to import machinery and materials needed for manufacture. But who would effect the transfer and how exactly could it take place?

Enter the half-dozen large Zagreb savings banks whose prewar assets already exceeded those of any Serbian bank. Their prewar profits had come mainly from mortgage loans whose interest surpassed the 4–6 percent paid on mortgage bonds and the 2–5 percent paid on savings deposits, together over two-thirds of their liabilities. As long as the crown remained a stable currency, these deposits could be considered the long-term liability needed to cover the issue of 5–50 year bonds.[40] Most of these bonds presumably permitted mortgage loans to the larger agricultural estates to furnish them the capital needed to bring the raising of livestock up to high Hungarian standards and, as we have seen, to push their export value to twice the celebrated Serbian total. Now the impending agrarian reform promised to break up those estates at the same time that the crown had ceased to be anything resembling a stable currency. Its rapid inflation made even the 6 percent mortgage bonds of the prewar sort seem unattractive investments. Savings deposits nonetheless continued to grow, doubling for all Croatian banks during 1920 to twenty times the Serbian total.

Where to place these liabilities and to earn more than the high 8–10 percent interest rates needed to attract them? In joint-stock shares whose values and dividends could move with inflation, came back the answer from established European standards of financial practice. The Croatian explosion of joint-stock investment included a great deal of new stock in the major Zagreb banks. Most of the major banks attracted an unknown, perhaps significant quantity of funds from Austrian and especially Hungarian estate owners selling off their property before it could be redistributed. But only one of these banks was under clear foreign control, the *Havatska zemaljska*, now *Jugoslovenska banka* of Prague's famous *Živnostenska banka*. The biggest Zagreb bank, the *Prva hrvatska štedionica*, remained as before the war essentially in native Croatian hands. It quickly became the largest investor in industrial stocks, supporting 51 firms by 1921.[41] The largest group of these enterprises were related to woodcutting or processing, reflecting the final transfer of the timber industry from the noble estates to commercial management in Zagreb. The absence of any state regulation for these incorporations until 1922 attracted funds from the rest of the Yugoslav lands as well as from Austria and Hungary. By 1921 the Zagreb banks controlled 57 percent of Yugoslav joint stock capital, versus 20 percent for Serbia. The proportion of Serbian bank investment in industrial stocks was smaller still, given the banks' wartime debts and need for postwar credit that bound them so closely to the Narodna Banks.[42]

During the rest of the decade this first imbalance receded to 31/24 but large savings deposits and industrial investments continued to distinguish Croatian bank liabilities and assets from their Serbian counterparts. Data for 1924–27 shows that 60 percent of Croatian bank liabilities and assets were so distributed. Four-fifths of Serbian assets remained in the current account overdrafts and bills of exchange that preserved their prewar dependency on acceptances and discounting from the central bank in Belgrade.[43]

To summarize, what had happened was the following. The Zagreb banks had become the focal point for private investors, foreign and domestic, seeking to hedge against the conversion from crowns to dinars and the agrarian reform while still taking advantage of the industrial investments and trading opportunities that the breakup of the Habsburg monarchy afforded anyone doing business with the former core-economies of Austria and Hungary. The advantage derived from the dynamics of that breakup, and from the Croatian and Slovenian responses to it. In Belgrade, however, responses were understandably mistaken for initiatives to maintain presumably high wartime profits. The general Serbian reliance on reparations or public policy to effect rapid postwar recovery had proved fruitless despite military victory and essential control of the central government. Industry and mining received little state assistance. Their slow recovery made the success of the private sector in the western Yugoslav lands seem all the more galling, especially considering the circumstances of military defeat within which it was achieved.

Notes

1. The six customs areas consisted of Serbia (combined with Macedonia and from November 26 Montenegro), the Vojvodina, Croatia/Slavonia, Slovenia, Dalmatia and Bosnia-Hercegovina. The five currencies were the Serbian dinar, the Austro-Hungarian crown, the German mark, the Bulgarian lev and the Montenegrin perper. The four railway networks were the Serbian and Macedonian combined, the Austrian network in Slovenia, the Hungarian network in Croatia/Slavonia, Dalmatia and the Vojvodina, and the joint Austro-Hungarian network in Bosnia-Hercegovina. The three banking systems were the Serbian commercial banks based on short-term bills of exchange, the Croatian and Dalmatian savings banks based on long-term mortgage loans and bonds, and the Slovenian cooperative savings banks on the Raiffeisen model of mass participation. The prewar Serbian administration and the new Narodno Vijeće formed in Zagreb in October 1918 by Croatian, Slovenian and Habsburg Serb representatives were the two governments. On the six political parties, more if we count the two Moslem organizations, that added to the problems of economic integration, see the useful summary in Joseph Rothschild, *East Central Europe Between the Two World Wars* (Seattle, Wash.: Washington University Press, 1974), pp. 204–13.

2. A judicious appraisal of the 7–10 billion dinars claimed for Serbian war damages is found in Smiljana Djurović, "Industrija Srbije na početku privrednog života Kr. Srba, Hrvata i Slovenaca" (The Industry of Serbia at the Start of the Economic Life of the Kingdom of Serbs, Croats and Slovenes), *Istorija XX veka* (History of the Twentieth Century), X (Belgrade, 1969), pp. 190–93. The official estimates presented by Serbian authorities to the Paris peace conference are in Srpski Centralni Komitet, *Srbija po imovnom pogledu pre, za vreme i posle svetskog rata* [Serbian Wealth before, during and after the World War] (Geneva, 1918), pp. 79–115.

3. See V. Stipetić, *Kretanje i tendencije u razvitku poljoprivredne proizvodnje u područjr NR Hrvatske* [Movements and Tendencies in the Development of Agricultural Production in the Area of the PR Croatia] (Zagreb, 1959), p. 83; Toussaint Hočevar, *The Structure of the Slovenian Economy, 1848–1963* (N. Y.: Studia Slovenica, 1965), pp. 132, 145.

4. Rodolf Bićanić, "Ekonomske promene u Hrvatskoj izazvane stvaranjem Jugoslavije, 1918" [Economic Changes in Croatia Occasioned by the Creation of Yugoslavia, 1918] in *Prilozi za ekonomsku povijest Hrvatske* [Contributions to the Economic History of Croatia] (Zagreb, 1967), p. 84.

5. See Chapter 9, "The Economic Development of the Imperial Borderlands to 1914," in John R. Lampe and Marvin R. Jackson, *An Economic History of the Balkan States: From Imperial Borderlands to Developing Nations* (forthcoming from Indiana University

Press). On the Hungarian Agricultural Revolution, see L. Katus, "Economic Growth in Hungary during the Age of Dualism, A Quantitative Analysis," in E. Pamlényi, ed., *Social-Economic Researches on the History of East-Central Europe* (Budapest, 1970), pp. 35–87, and Scott M. Eddie, "Agricultural Production and Output per Worker in Hungary, 1867–1914," *Journal of Economic History* XXXVIII, 2(June 1968), pp. 197–222.

6. Stipetić, *Kretanje*, pp. 79–97, 143–45; Bićanić, "Ekonomske promene u Hrvatskoj," pp. 86–87.

7. Ch. 9 in Lampe and Jackson, *Economic History of the Balkan States* (forthcoming).

8. The effect of interwar Italian and Austrian tariffs on Slovenian milk and meat exports respectively are cases in point, according to Hočevar, *Structure of the Slovenian Economy*, pp. 116–17, 144. For aggregate trade and tariff data on the 1920's, see Ch. 10 in Lampe and Jackson, *Economic History of the Balkan States* (forthcoming).

9. John R. Lampe, "Serbia, 1878–1912," in Rondo Cameron, ed., *Banking and Economic Development: Some Lessons of History* (N. Y.: Oxford University Press, 1972), p. 161.

10. Virtually none is noted in Hočevar, *Structure of the Slovenian Economy*, pp. 58–113, in Igor Karaman, *Privreda i društvo Hrvatske u 19. stoleću* [The Economy and Society of Croatia in the 19th Century] (Zagreb, 1972), or in Peter Sugar, *The Industrialization of Bosnia-Hercegovina. 1878–1918* (Seattle, Wash: University of Washington Press, 1963), pp. 43–97.

11. Djurović, "Industrija Srbije," p. 18.

12. Dimitrije Djordjević, "Austro-ugarski okupacioni režim u Srbiji i njegov slom" [The Austro-Hungarian Occupation of Serbia and Its Fall] in Vasa Čubrilović *et. al.*, eds., *Naučni skup u povodu 50-godišnjice raspada Austro-ugarske monarhije i stvaranje jugoslovenske države* [Scientific Gathering on the 50th Anniversary of the Fall of the Austro-Hungarian Monarchy and the Creation of the Yugoslav State] (Zagreb, 1969), pp. 206–23. Also see Vasa Čubrilović, ed., *Istorija Beograda*, III (Belgrade, 1974), pp. 47–56, and Djurović, "Industrija Srbije," pp. 178–93.

13. For a good recent summary of the war's immediate economic consequences, see Derek H. Aldcroft, *From Versailles to Wall Street, 1919–1929* (Berkeley, Calif.: University of California Press, 1977), pp. 11–77.

14. Djurović "Industrija Srbije," 169–72.

15. Nikola Gačeša, *Agrarna reforma i kolonizacije u Sremu, 1919–1941* [Agrarian Reform and Colonization in the Srem, 1919–1941] (Novi Sad, 1975), pp. 36–45; Dragoslav Janković, "Društveni i politički odnosi u Kr. SHS uoći stvaranje SRPJ (komunista), 1 Dec., 1918–20 April, 1919" [Social and Political Relations in the Kingdom SCS on the Eve of the Creation of the SWPY (Communists), Dec. 1, 1918–April 20, 1919], *Istorija XX veka*, I (1969), pp. 37–44.

16. Bićanić, "Ekonomske promene u Hrvatskoj," pp. 95–96.

17. Janković, "Društveni i politički odnosi," pp. 28–34, 54–56; T. Timet, *Stanbena izgradja Zagreba do 1954* [The Building Construction of Zagreb to 1954] (Zagreb, 1961), pp. 153–54. On the food shortages in postwar Austria and Hungary, see Ivan Berend

and G. T. Ranki, *Economic Development in East-Central Euope in the 19th and 20th Centuries* (N. Y.: Columbia University Press, 1974), pp. 174–75.

18. Mira Kolar-Dimitrijević, *Radni slojevi Zagreba od 1918 do 1931* [The Working Classes of Zagreb from 1918 to 1931] (Zagreb, 1973), pp. 299–304; Čubrilović, ed., *Istorija Beograda*, II, p. 200.

19. A. Panitch, "The Railway Systems of the SCS Kingdom," *Belgrade Economic and Financial Review* (Belgrade, Jan., 1924), p. 1; Djurović, "Industrija Srbije," p. 196.

20. D. Knežević, "Trgovinske razmene izmedju Kr. SHS i Republike Austrije u toku 1920 g. "[Trade Relations Between the Kingdom SCS and the Republic of Austria during 1920], *Zbornik Filosofskog Fakulteta Beograda*, 1 (Belgrade, 1970), pp. 683–97; J. Petrovitch, "The Character of the Foreign Trade of the S. H. S. Kingdom," *Belgrade Economic and Financial Review* (Dec., 1923), pp. 10–12; Bićanić, "Ekonomske promene u Hrvatskoj," pp. 86–87.

21. Serbia had 31 kilometers of railway per capita and Macedonia just 18 in 1910, versus 82 for both Croatia/Slavonia and Slovenia and 74 for Bosnia-Hercegovina. See Table 9.5 in Lampe and Jackson, *Economic History of the Balkan States* (forthcoming). On the estimated need for postwar construction, see Panitch, "The Railway Systems," pp. 2–4.

22. Until then, French army vehicles provided the one means of modern transport between Belgrade and Niš. Hungarian officials had promised as part of the armistice to send 3,000 skilled workers to repair the rail and telegraph networks, but only a small fraction ever came. Demands for German rolling stock went unmet, and the small Allied deliveries consisted of food and clothing collected by volunteers. See M. Avramovitch, "The Railway Situation in the Balkans," *Manchester Guardian Commercial: The Reconstruction of Europe* (Manchester, Sept. 7, 1922), pp. 407–8; Djurović, "Industrija Srbije," pp. 15, 196–98; M. Milenković, *Železničari Srbije, 1918–1920* [The Railway Workers of Serbia, 1918–1920] (Belgrade, 1971), pp. 14–15.

23. Only a few thousand tons of coal trickled in during 1919, mainly from the Tešen area of Czechoslovakia. Large-scale deliveries of 800 tons a month from Hungary did not begin arriving, as reparations, until September, 1921. Smiljana Djurović, "Kriza uglja na teritoriji Kr. Srba, Hrvata i Slovenaca 1919 g." [The Coal Crisis on the Territory of the Kingdom of Serbs, Croats and Slovenes, 1919] *Acta historico-oeconomica iugoslaviae*, II (Zagreb, 1975), pp. 68–81; Berend and Ranki, *East-Central Europe*, p. 184. On the general European coal shortage after the war, see Aldcroft, *From Versailles*, pp. 60–61.

24. Stevan Kukoleća, *Industrija Jugoslavije, 1918–1939* (Belgrade, 1941) pp. 105, 348–52; Josef Lakatoš, *Industrija Hrvatske* [The Industry of Croatia] (Zagreb, 1924), pp. 18–19.

25. Sir John Hicks, *A Theory of Economic History* (N. Y.: Oxford University Press, 1969), pp. 99, 162–63. On the English experience with planned production during the First World War, see Arthur Marwick, *The Deluge, British Society and the First World War* (N.Y.: W. W. Norton, 1970), pp. 151–88.

26. Djurović, "Kriza uglja," pp. 77–81, and "Industrija Srbije," pp. 204–6.

27. Ibid., pp. 184–210.

28. On the prewar Serbian experience compared to that of Bulgaria and Romania, see John R. Lampe, "Varieties of Unsuccessful Industrialization: The Balkan States Before 1914," *Journal of Economic History*, XXXV, 1 (March, 1975), pp. 80–81.

29. On the pre-1914 period, see Lampe, "Serbia, 1878–1912," p. 125, and Karaman, *Privreda*, p. 319. On the 1920's, see Novak Popović and Dušan Mišić, *Naša domaća privreda* [Our Domestic Economy] (Belgrade, 1929), pp. 369–70; Kukoleća, *Industrija Jugoslavije*, pp. 75, 319; Timet, *Stanbena izgradnja Zagreba*, p. 151; Čubrilović, ed., *Istorija Beograda*, III, pp. 231–32.

30. See note 32 below.

31. Miodrag Ugričić, *Novčani sistem Jugoslavije* [The Monetary System of Yugoslavia] (Belgrade, 1967), p. 95; Janković, "Društveni odnosi." pp. 34–36; Leo Pasvolsky, *The Economic Nationalism of the Danubian States* (N. Y.: Macmillan, 1928), pp. 109–11.

32. *Narodna Banka, 1884–1934* (Belgrade, 1935), pp. 140–44.

33. F. G. Steiner, "Vienna as an Exchange Market for the Succession States," *Manchester Guardian Commercial: Reconstruction in Europe* (April 20, 1922), pp. 37–38; Ugričić, *Novčani sistem*, pp. 98–100; Kolar-Dimitrijević, *Radni slojevi Zagreba*, pp. 184–87.

34. Hočevar, *Structure of the Slovenian Economy*, p. 122.

35. See Lampe, "Serbia, 1878–1912," pp. 137–43.

36. Ibid.; *Narodna Banka, 1884–1934*, pp. 93–116; Ugričić, *Novčani sistem*, p. 97.

37. Smiljana Djurović, "Struktura aksionarskih društava u Beogradu izmedju 1918–1929 g." [The Structure of Joint-Stock Companies in Belgrade between 1918–1929], *Acta historico-oeconomica iugoslaviae*, IV (1977), p. 147.

38. Lampe, "Serbia, 1878–1912," pp. 143–50.

39. Timet, *Stanbena izgradnja Zagreba*, pp. 147–48.

40. See T. Timet, "Razvitak hipotekarnih i komunalnih zajmova . . . kod novčanih zavoda u Hrvatskoj i Slavoniji [The Development of Mortgage and Communal Loans . . . Among the Banks in Croatia and Slavonia] in *Prilozi*, pp. 143–262.

41. Ibid.; Timet, *Stanbena izgradja Zagreba*, pp. 147–51; Kolar-Dimitrijević, *Radni slojevi Zagreba*, pp. 36–38. On a similar boom in industrial stocks for Viennese banks in the immediate postwar inflation, see Pasvolsky, *Economic Nationalism*, pp. 164–70.

42. *Jugoslovenski Kompas, 1919–1920*, II (Zagreb, 1921), pp. 3–25, 140–45, 312–33; *Narodna Banka, 1884–1934*, p. 105; Djurović, "Struktura aksionarskih društava," pp. 150–58; Bićanić, "Ekonomske promene u Hrvatskoj," pp. 101–2.

43. Popović and Mišić, *Naša domaća privreda*, p. 55.

Language, Ethnicity, and Nationalism: On the Linguistic Foundations of a Unified Yugoslavia

Henrik Birnbaum

FEW, IF ANY, FACTORS have proven themselves as strong a nation-building force as language, the common mother tongue of a whole people. The native language shared by one's fellow countrymen not only, by virtue of being the most natural and sophisticated means of communication, is the strongest link holding together the fabric of a nation in its everyday life but also, as the vehicle of a people's verbal creativity—its national literature and, frequently, its time-honored oral tradition—it symbolizes and lends artistic expression to the supreme national values cherished by the people of a country, of a state.

When in 1918 the formation of the Kingdom of the Serbs, Croats, and Slovenes was proclaimed in Belgrade, the very name chosen for the new multinational state carried with it a good deal of the problems of ethnicity and nationalism which have plagued Yugoslavia throughout the first sixty years of its existence or, in other words, to this very day. The change in name to the admittedly more apt (if in some respects not quite accurate) designation Kingdom of Yugoslavia instituted in 1929—incidentally, for questionable political reasons—did little to affect the strained ethnolinguistic situation of the state as a whole. Even the far-reaching structural changes reflecting the new socialist and federal reality of the postwar period—some of them not implemented until recently—have only to a limited extent reduced the inherent ethnic tensions which continue to exist and occasionally flare up into open confrontation in today's Yugoslavia and which find their expression, in part, in the linguistic mosaic which the country presents. With all due respect for the much greater expertise commanded by some native Yugoslav scholars in the field, it is perhaps not altogether inappropriate if an outside observer with genuine sympathy for the whole of Yugoslavia may venture to contribute a few hopefully dispassionate remarks pertaining to the linguistic foundations of a unified Yugoslav state.

Specifically, the largely controversial and often emotionally charged issues that will be briefly addressed here are the following: (1) the Slavic languages of Yugoslavia and their South Slavic setting; (2) Serbo-Croatian—one language or two? (3) the language of Dubrovnik and its past; (4) Kajkavian, its present status and historical position between Croatian and Slovenian; (5) the Torlak dialects of Serbian; (6) the status of Macedonian; (7) the non-Slavic languages of Yugoslavia, notably Albanian and Hungarian; (8) language standardization and language planning in Yugoslavia. In surveying these problems we will not so much be concerned with pointing to any particular conceivable solutions to unresolved and as yet unanswered questions (though some will be mentioned at least in passing) but will rather attempt to simply state the relevant facts in as objective terms as possible. Only in closing a few suggestions or, rather, comments will be made, comments based on the present linguistic situation of Yugoslavia with a view to its integrated political structure as a federation of interdependent, unified republics.

THE SLAVIC LANGUAGES OF YUGOSLAVIA AND THEIR SOUTH SLAVIC SETTING

Though usually not translated, Yugoslav literally means 'South Slavic' of course, and the name Yugoslavia would therefore denote 'the land of the Southern Slavs.' Obviously, this term is somewhat imprecise as Yugoslavia, the homeland of several South Slavic nationalities to be sure, does not encompass all of the Southern Slavs; the vast majority of the Bulgarians do not, as we all know, live within the borders of Yugoslavia. In this connection it should be remembered that standardized literary languages crystallized only relatively late in the South Slavic area, at least when compared with some other Slavic languages, and, even more so, with some other languages of Europe. Essentially, the South Slavic languages as literary standards are a creation of the 19th century, a result of the national revival and, indirectly, the collapse of the Ottoman rule in the Balkans; and, as is generally known, standard Macedonian was not established and officially recognized until the end of World War II. The dialectal basis and, in general, the spoken form of the South Slavic languages have therefore been particularly important and to this very day dialectal divisions, notably that between the ekavian and the (i) jekavian varieties of standard, i.e., štokavian, Serbo-Croatian, also play a prominent role in the determination of accepted variants of the standard language. As a result of this significance of the dialectal foundations of the South Slavic linguistic area the borderlines between the South Slavic languages, Slovenian, Serbo-Croatian, Macedonian, and Bulgarian, are not—other than in their established literary form where they coincide with political borders— always very sharp or easy to draw. On the contrary, it can be said that from a dialectical point of view the entire South Slavic territory, stretching from the Eastern Alps to the Black Sea, forms one continuous whole marked by gradual transitions rather than by abrupt change-overs from one language to another. Thus, to take a few examples, while the borders between literary and official Slovenian and Croatian (or, to be precise, the Croatian variant of Serbo-Croatian; cf. below) or between Serbian, on the one hand, and Macedonian and Bulgarian, on the other, are of course well established and ascertainable in space, the corresponding dialectal isoglosses separating the Slovenian dialect area from that of kajkavian Croatian or the Torlak dialects of Serbian from Macedonian and Bulgarian are frequently not so easy to identify and the precise nature of the bundles of isogloss lines required to posit a genuine shift from one language to another (and not merely from one dialect to another within the same language) is not always readily clear. To some extent, this of course has to do with the difficulties inherent in any clear-cut definition of the concept of language as opposed to dialect.[1]

In any synchronic, descriptive classification of the Slavic languages, South Slavic is usually subgrouped into, on the one hand, Slovenian-Serbo-Croatian and, on the other, Macedo-Bulgarian or, in other words, into a northwestern and a southeastern branch. While such a classification, taking into account the modern standard languages only, certainly is valid in purely synchronic terms, it is far from sure that it is applicable in diachronic or historical (and prehistoric) terms as well. Rather, the expansion of the ancestors of the Southern Slavs into their presently settled areas is now usually believed to have followed two main tracks: one through present-day Romania into the heartlands of the Balkans, the other one through the passes of the Carpathians (and possibly also through those of the Sudeten Mountains or, at any rate, through the so-called Moravian Gate separating the Carpathian and Sudeten Mountains), first into what is now Czechoslovakia, and from there on to Pannonia (today's Hungary) and the adjacent areas of the Eastern Alps (present-day eastern and southern Austria and northwestern Yugoslavia) and further into the western regions of the Balkans. It was presumably here, in what is now Yugoslavia, that the Slavs coming from the north and northwest met and mingled with other, westbound Slavic tribes moving in from the littoral of the Black Sea and its hinterland. The two ethnic names, that of the *Croats* and that of the *Serbs* (or, in a phonetic variant, *Sorbs*), of which at least the former probably is of Iranian origin—at first designating, it would seem, an ethnically different social layer in charge of the forebears of those Southern Slavs—whereas the latter's etymology remains obscure and controversial (an Iranian origin being only one among several suggested explanations), still testify, to some extent, to this path-crossing. Until about 1000 A.D. the ethnonym Croats (*Hrvati,*

Chorvati, etc.) was used both for the predecessors of the contemporary South Slavic Croats and for some Slavic groups who were settled on the northern slopes of the Carpathian (and possibly Sudeten) Mountains; cf. the so-called White Croats of Slavic medieval historical sources. Similarly, Serbs (*Srbi, Sorbi, Serbi,* etc.) is not only the name of one of the Balkan Slavic peoples but also, in a slightly different form, that of the Western Slavs of Lusatia, settled between Silesia and Saxony in today's East Germany, the remnant of a once numerous Slavic ethnic group occupying in the Early and High Middle Ages an area stretching from the central Oder and the Neisse (Nysa) in the east to the Saale in the west. Possibly, as has been suggested by the Soviet etymologist O.N. Trubačev, we are dealing here with a people which was "occidentalized" at a relatively late date. An early attestation of this ethnonym as *Sérbioi,* (or *Sérvioi,* in Constantine Porphyrogenitus' famous work *De administrando imperio,* chapter 9; mid-10th century) still seems to denote an East Slavic tribe (but probably not, in a distorted form, the East Slavic tribe of the *sěverjane*).[2]

Even though Serbs and Croats today speak, essentially, one and the same standard language, albeit in two variants (for details and discussion, see below), it is therefore quite conceivable that their forebears partly entered the Balkans along different routes, the Proto-Serbs (or, at any rate, a portion of them), along with the ancestors of the Slavs of Bulgaria (not to be confused with the Altaic Bulgars or Proto-Bulgarians), from the northeast, originating from what is today the western portion of the Ukraine, the Proto-Croats, along with the Proto-Slovenes, from the north and northwest, Pannonia and the East Alpine region where they had come from an area north of the Carpathians and, possibly, the Sudeten. Some scholars have therefore even posited a 'Pannonian Slavic' and a 'Daco-Slavic' transitional phase in the prehistory of South Slavic, that is, prior to the arrival of the Southern Slavs in the territories of their more permanent settlement (rather than conceiving of 'Pannonian Slavic' and 'Daco-Slavic' as actual onetime transitional dialects between North and South Slavic, something which, on insufficient grounds, also has been suggested). True, it is not possible to retrace in detail all the migratory routes and it is certainly possible that some of the Proto-Serbs, too, entered the Balkans proper (i.e., crossed the Danube) coming from eastern Pannonia. The basically uniform Serbo-Croatian language or, rather, its underlying—locally, to be sure, differentiated—dialect basis may thus very well be the result of a secondary convergence and/or partial coterritorial symbiosis of two Late Common Slavic dialects and their speakers in the second half of the first millennium A.D. The subsequent divergent evolution of Serbian and Croatian is, as we know, largely due to well-established historical factors (among them, the influence of the Byzantine vs. the Western cultural and ecclesiastic orbit, manifesting itself, most overtly, in the use of two alphabets, the Cyrillic and the Latin; different consequences of the Turkish conquest; the varying extent of linguistic Balkanization.)[3]

SERBO-CROATIAN—ONE LANGUAGE OR TWO?

In the preceding paragraphs reference has been made, a couple of times, to the fact that Serbs and Croats today still "essentially speak one and the same standard language" and to the "basically uniform Serbo-Croatian language." At this point, however, it would seem fair to raise the question whether such assertions are indeed justified or whether they do not, at best, represent merely one of two (or more) conceivable views, another one presumably claiming that Serbian and Croatian by now in fact constitute two different, if admittedly very closely related and thus in many respects quite similar languages. As we all know, this question is really at the heart of the very complex and at times highly emotionalized language controversy in Yugoslavia, with all its implications and ramifications. Compared to it, most other linguistic problems present in today's Yugoslavia appear minor and relatively harmless though by no means always noncontroversial or lacking in certain sensitivities (cf. below). Yet it is the question just raised, namely, whether the language spoken and written by a vast majority of Yugoslavs (to wit, about 15 millions as compared to slightly under 3 millions using Slovenian or Macedonian and just over 2 millions claiming a non-Slavic language as their native tongue; for more precise figures, see below) remains fundamentally one language, with two accepted standard variants, or whether it—as even some serious scholars would rather make us believe—by now actually has split into two separate languages about to enter upon distinct evolutionary courses, that, in particular during the last two decades or so, has been one of the hottest issues debated in Yugoslavia. Publications by highly resepcted linguists such as the collective volume *Hrvatski književni jezik i pitanje varijanata* (special issue no. 1 of the journal *Kritika*, Zagreb, 1969, with contributions by the internationally renowned scholars R. Katičić, Lj. Jonke, and others), D. Brozović's *Rječnik jezika ili jezik rječnika? Varijacije na temu varijanata* (special issue no. 2 of the same Zagreb journal, 1969), the same linguist's *Standardni jezik*, Zagreb, 1970, or P. Ivić's *Srpski narod i njegov jezik*, Belgrade, 1971, whatever their specific merits in many respects, have certainly not contributed to ease existing tensions or to calm already excited—not to say, incited—minds of people concerned. Also, in this connection it has not been helpful, of course, that this linguistic question has been allowed to be blurred at times by being coupled with broader issues of decentralization vs. concentration of political power, greater or lesser liberalization throughout the country, tightening or relaxing of the controls of the Party and the central state

organs, not to speak of other tensions, historical-political and economic, continuing to exist and, occasionally, to be reinforced in the
relations between Serbs and Croats. Clearly, such factors are only
indirectly related to the question whether, on purely scientific grounds,
it is more correct to go on reckoning with one unified (though varie-
gated) Serbo-Croatian language or to now assume the existence of two
separate languages (and not only variants), Serbian and Croatian.[4]

From a strictly linguistic point of view there cannot really be any
serious doubt, it would seem to me, that it is appropriate to continue to
consider Serbo-Croatian (or Croato-Serbian, as it is referred to in
Croatia[5]) one language, granted the definitional issue of what in fact
constitutes a language, previously hinted at, remains problematic.
From this point of view, then, I would suggest, the relevant situation in
Yugoslavia bears, with some qualification, comparison with, say, British
vs. American English or, for that matter, French as spoken in France as
opposed to that heard in Canadian Quebec or the Spanish of Spain as
compared to that of Latin America, even though the overseas (and,
historically, colonial) dimension is missing when it comes to the Serbo-
Croatian situation. To be sure, some people may indeed prefer to
consider the Queen's English and the speech of New York City or Los
Angeles (let alone that of Texas or Alabama) two different languages
altogether, and I, for one, am familiar with the relatively recent fad of
German publishing houses to mark some of their translations as "aus
dem Amerikanischen—not, nota bene, Englischen—übersetzt," to
take just one example. Yet I would think that most reasonable people
still rather consider the two accepted standard varieties of English used
on both sides of the Atlantic as essentially representing but one language. Similar considerations must apply, I would imagine, to French
and Spanish. Transposed, *mutatis mutandis,* to the Yugoslav reality, while
the separating distance in space between the two variants is missing
here, what is added, by the same token, is an element of historically
conditioned emotionalism (if not, frequently, outright resentment and
hatred) which, fortunately, today is lacking in the internal dealings of,
for example, the Anglo-Saxon (also, specifically, known as the English-
speaking) world. But reduced to its purely linguistic aspect, it would
seem that there is not really that much difference: Serbian and Croatian in their respective štokavian standard varieties, too, continue, at
least for the time being, to be two facets of one and the same literary
language, the mutual-intelligibility test, sometimes resorted to in such
instances, providing merely one criterion.

Admittedly, however, this claim is in need of some further qualification. In addition to the strictly linguistic point of view concerning this
matter there is another, sociolinguistic dimension to this whole problem; and seen in this light, things may, as a matter of fact, turn out quite
a bit different.

After much public debate, an amendment, adopted in 1972, was added to the constitution of the Socialist Republic of Croatia establishing as the official language on the territory of that republic the Croatian literary language (*hrvatski književni jezik*) which was defined as "the standard form of the national language (*narodni jezik*) of the Croats and Serbs in Croatia which is called Croatian or Serbian."[6] This amendment was subsequently incorporated in the new constitution of 1974 (art. 138, sec. 1), and the wording of the new federal constitution of the same year was accordingly altered so as to reflect this change and to give each constituent republic the right to designate which language or languages will enjoy official status on its respective territory.[7] Taking into account the wishes of Croatian cultural personalities and politicians concerned with language problems, these legal acts thus brought to a close, at least on the face of it, the occasional quite sharp and bitter controversy regarding the name and status of the standard language used in Croatia. While acceding to the demands advanced by prominent Croatian linguists and writers in their pertinent declaration of 1967 to the effect that the standard language in use in their republic be called Croatian rather than Croato-Serbian (or Serbo-Croatian), the new formulation of the law has not really resolved any truly linguistic issues since the individuals and authorities concerned in Serbia, Bosnia-Hercegovina, and Montenegro (Crna Gora) continue to maintain that the language spoken in their republics is identical with that of the Republic of Croatia and that it should be called Serbo-Croatian or Croato-Serbian. This latter attitude has particular bearing, of course, on the many Serbs living in Croatia. As R. Dunatov in his dispassionate and well-argued sociolinguistic analysis of the Serbo-Croatian language controversy and its present ramifications and predictable consequences, based to a large extent on the tenets of the Prague School and its followers concerning the various functions of standard languages, has pointed out, the practical language dilemma must be particularly strongly felt in Bosnia-Hercegovina where a veritable ethnic mixture of the population prevails, especially in the larger towns and cities. Here, *c.* 40 percent of the inhabitants claim "Moslem," another *c.* 37 percent Serbian, and approximately 20 percent Croatian ethnicity. Most of the "Moslems" and the Croats of this republic use the (i)jekavian pronunciation and adhere to all or most of the other characteristics of the Croatian standard of Serbo-Croatian. The Serbs of Bosnia-Hercegovina are also predominantly (i)jekavian speakers (in which respect they therefore differ from the ekavian speakers of Serbia) but otherwise they share lexical and grammatical features with the Serbian standard variant. Dunatov then goes on to list and discuss the options open to the development of the standard language in that republic, several of which seem highly problematic to say the least.[8] And, sharing Magner's view that "making predictions about Yugoslavia is a notoriously hazardous business," Dunatov nonetheless concludes his discussion by venturing two points: (1) The Croats will continue to develop their standard, for which they have achieved its own name, independently of other republics. In fact, vigorous new efforts in the field of language normation are now underway. Nothing suggests that the Croats will ever want to return to the "one-language with two variants" option. (2) At least for the foreseeable future precisely this option (also referred to as the Novi Sad Agreement) will be adhered to by the other republics, Serbia, Montenegro, and Bosnia-Hercegovina. Only in the latter, owing to its particularly complex and difficult linguistic situation, a decision to adopt one lexical and orthographic norm may be forthcoming. Rather than applying questionable linguistic parameters, Dunatov resorts to Ivić's sociolinguistic criteria according to which there can be no doubt as to ●he autonomy of present-day Slovenian vis-á-vis contemporary Croatian (the two belonging to different ethnic groups and using different standard languages; for some further discussion, cf. also below). Accepting at the same time Brozović's view that variants may very well function as standard languages, he therefore also sees no reason why one should not argue "for the autonomy of the Croatian standard vis-á-vis the Serbian."[9] Given these premises, it must consequently seem conceivable, if not outright likely, that what today is merely the Croatian variant of one Serbo-Croatian literary language one day, as a result of careful and directed language planning, will indeed emerge as a full-fledged separate language—Croatian—different in some crucial respects from the remainder of the language from which it took its origin, this latter then having every right to claim its own unambiguous name—Serbian. There is, as a matter of fact, much that suggests precisely such a direction for future development of Serbo-Croatian. Such secondary, politically motivated, deliberate divergence in language evolution certainly does not lack contemporary parallels; cf. only, for example, the recent emergence of a Moldavian literary language (in Soviet Moldavia, established after World War II) with a clearly Romanian base or, for that matter, the creation of standard Macedonian, its historical foundation undoubtedly being essentially Bulgarian (cf. below).

THE LANGUAGE OF DUBROVNIK, PAST AND PRESENT

Turning now to some relatively minor issues involving the languages of Yugolsavia, we may, for a moment, dwell on one particular problem of Serbo-Croatian linguistics—the language of Dubrovnik. To the extent that there is indeed a problem here at all, it is a historical one. For today, the standard language used in the city of Dubrovnik and its immediate environs is of course (i)jekavian Štokavian or, in other words, the Croatian variant of Serbo-Croatian; also, as we all know, the alphabet in use there is the Latin one. While there is little doubt therefore as to how to classify the current standard language of Dubrovnik, its past presents something of a puzzle. I am not so much concerned here, obviously, with the fact that Dubrovnik and its adjacent territory officially became a part of Croatia only in the new, post-World War II Yugoslavia while in the interwar period it belonged to the region of Mantenegro (*Zetska banovina*) Rather, what I am referring to here is the controversial question as to which was the earliest dialect basis in Dubrovnik for the written Serbo-Croatian language, (i)jekavian Štokavian (as is the case today) or ikavian Čakavian, as has also been suggested in view of the fact that the earliest Ragusan vernacular poetry (by such outstanding Renaissance poets as Džore Držić or Šiško Menčetić, to mention just the best ones) betrays some čakavian dialectal traits. At the same time, prose of that period is written in (i)jekavian Štokavian. If we consider that, in a historical (and, to be sure, not entirely accurate) perspective, Štokavian has often been considered as primarily representing the Serbian variant of Serbo-Croatian whereas Čakavian and Kajkavian, again in oversimplified historical terms, have been identified with its Croatian variant (Čakavian in coastal or Dalmatian Croatia and its hinterland, Kajkavian in inland or Pannonian, later Slavonian, Croatia, the present nonstandard status of these dialects as well as their considerably shrunk area being a result of later developments), it is understandable that the question of the precise nature of the early literary language of Dubrovnik can easily be drawn into the overall nationalistic issue of Serbian vs. Croatian with many emotional overtones. This quesiton is further complicated by the fact that, in addition to using the Latin script, Cyrillic was used exclusively in Slavic writings up to the late 15th century in the Republic of St. Blasius, particularly in its official and business dealings with Bosnia and Serbia but in part also in other diplomatic correspondence (whereas the records of the central administration of the city republic were all in Latin). By contrast, Glagolitic writing—flourishing more or less unimpeded along the Central and North Dalmatian coast and, especially, on the Croatian littoral (*Hrvatsko Primorje*) and in the Kvarner archipelago (where the island of Krk was the main stronghold of medieval and later Glagolitism)—has left only few and, in general, fairly insignificant traces in and around Dubrovnik, mostly in some minor churches and monasteries on nearby islands. By the same token, there can be no doubt that Dubrovnik, while also maintaining some literary ties with Bosnia, Serbia, and Montenegro (the former Duklja/Dioclea or Zeta), in its cultural and intellectual outlook was primarily oriented toward the west, Italy in particular.

Personally, I am inclined to share the view of those—M. Rešetar and P. Ivić, foremost among them—who do not believe in the existence of an actual earlier Čakavian substratum in and around Dubrovnik but assume that Štokavian, in its (i)jekavian variety, was indeed the earliest form of Serbo-Croatian spoken in the streets of the ancient city and its vicinity. These scholars have therefore explained the čakavian component in the language of the early Ragusan poets as due to an artificial and deliberate importation or transplantation of North Dalmatian literary standards to the vernacular poetry produced in the merchant republic, a phenomenon certainly not without historical parallels. However, I do not see this issue as one where one really has to decide between labeling the language of 15th-16th century Dubrovnik as either Serbian or Croatian; yet if one had to make a choice (which I do not think one should) it would rather have to be Serbian.[10] But in fact, I would almost consider it something of a historical distortion to insist on assigning either label—and it is only in view of the recently adopted official usage of the term 'Croatian literary language,' pointing, if it is to make some sense, to the future rather than to the past, that one has to caution against any possible extension of this term to an area and a period where it does not rightfully belong. Similar considerations would, however, not necessarily apply to the literature of Dubrovnik in the late Middle Ages and through the Renaissance and Baroque epochs. Here, on the strength of literary and general cultural rather than linguistic criteria, it would seem legitimate to consider Ragusan literature part of the Croatian literary heritage—the seeming contradiction notwithstanding.

THE PERIPHERAL DIALECTS OF SERBO-CROATIAN: KAJKAVIAN AND TORLAK

Remaining for a while with the central problematics of Serbo-Croatian linguistics as it pertains to questions of ethnicity and national identity so crucial to Yugoslavia as a whole and the preservation of its federal statehood, we may now briefly review a couple of controversial issues relevant to the most peripheral dialect areas of Serbo-Croatian, those of Kajkavian in the northwest and of Torlak in the southeast. Specifically, the discussion has centered here for some time on the question whether these dialect groups can in fact be considered purely Serbo-Croatian, in a diachronic as well as synchronic terms, that is to say, historically and structurally, or whether they do not rather qualify as genuinely transitional and mixed—Kajkavian in relation to Slovenian, Torlak in relation to Macedonian and Bulgarian. These questions assume particular significance, of course, when it is remembered that the capital of Croatia, Zagreb, is located in the heart of the Kajkavian area and that such old Serbian political and cultural centers as Niš and Prizren are on Torlak territory. While in certain respects posing similar problems and calling for approach and solutions along, in part, analogous lines, the two sets of questions just raised are nonetheless too different in their specifics to allow for a combined treatment. They will therefore be dealt with separately here.

As is well known, Slovenian is among the Slavic languages which have suffered the greatest territorial losses in early historical times. If, at least for the sake of argument, we equate Proto-Slovenian with a Late Common Slavic dialect which for want of a better term we may call Early Alpine Slavic, it is readily clear that this dialect or, rather dialect cluster at one time must have been spoken over a fairly large area covering not only present-day Slovenia but also a good portion of today's eastern, southern, and central Austria (the provinces of Carinthia and Styria, as well as parts of Lower and Upper Austria, Salzburg/ Salzkammergut, and Burgenland) in addition to, presumably, extending into western Hungary (Transdanubia, at least south of Lake Balaton).[11] While the gradual retreat of the Alpine Slavs from what is today Austria (with the exception of parts of Carinthia and some minor areas in Styria) can be traced in historical sources with some degree of accuracy (certain details remaining in need of clarification, to be sure) and we at least know of the major events putting an end to the predominance of a Slavic population in Pannonia—namely, the advent of the Magyars in the last decades of the 9th centuryand their permanent settling in the area in the course of the 10th century—we are, generally speaking, less well informed, at least in terms of extra-linguistic evidence, when it comes to the crystallization of Slovenian proper in its present homeland.[12] Notably, the process of separation which occurred between what is now, on the one hand, Slovenian, the standard language as well as its several dialects, and, on the other, the kajkavian variety of Serbo-Croatian (occasionally also referred to as *kaj*-Croatian) is still not fully elucidated and merely the main lines of this process are more or less known.

While the Serbian linguist A. Belić considered Kajkavian the result of dialect mixing, with Slovenian as well as Serbo-Croatian elements present, and I. Popović in his aforementioned history of Serbo-Croatian sketched a different, complex, and by and large not very persuasive concept of the emergence of Kajkavian, Slovenian, and Čakavian (considering the latter two as belonging to the same sub-branch!), the majority of linguists who have studied the problem of the origin of Slovenian and Kajkavian adhere to a view which is at variance with the two just referred to. With minor differences this more generally held view was or is espoused by such well-known Slavists as N. van Wijk, A. Marguliés, F. Ramovš, F. Sławski, and P. Ivić. Essentially it amounts to the notion that Slovenian proper and Kajkavian go back to the same dialectal origin, and that Kajkavian can be considered a secondarily Croatized Slovenian (and hence a language now clearly different from Slovenian) or, as Ramovš once put it, a language "wrestled by Serbo-Croatian from Slovenian." Most characteristics which set off Kajkavian from Slovenian—Ivić has counted eleven such major features—are of relatively recent date and can be traced back roughly to the 10th through 15th centuries. By the same token, the shared features of the two languages and dialect areas may well go back to a period of common development prior even to their speakers' arrival in their present areas of settlement. P. Ivić put it succinctly when he wrote:

> The region near the Slovenian border in western Croatia belongs among the most intensely differentiated dialectal areas of the Serbocroatian language territory. This region is crossed by the historically most important bundle of isoglosses in the Slavic Southwest. This is a bundle marking the boundary between the Kajkavian area (which includes the Slovenian language and the Croatian Kajkavian dialectal group) and the Štokavian and Čakavian dialectal groups. It is striking to see how sharp this boundary is; one remains impressed by the almost absolute absence of really transitional dialect types.[13]

And subsequently, returning to the same topic, Ivić had this to add:

> Since there was no specific political link between Slovenia and the Kajkavian area in northern Croatia before the 16th century, and since the geographic conditions in the present habitat of Slovenians and Kajkavians would not favor their common linguistic development, distinct from that of their eastern and southern neighbors, it seems likely that their common linguistic features stem from the propinquity of their ancestors in the period preceding their settlement in what is now Yugoslavia.[14]

While Ivić thus has no doubts as to the origin and time of the features which Slovenian and Kajkavian share, he nonetheless clearly recognizes—primarily on sociolinguistic grounds, as we have seen—the autonomy of present-day Slovenian vis-à-vis Croatian, including its Kajkavian speakers whose Croatization as regards the use of the standard language therefore must be considered to be of such extent as to warrant their now being counted as part of the Croatian linguistic community rather than representing a deviant dialect group of Slovenian.[15]

Turning now to the opposite end of the Serbo-Croatian linguistic spectrum, that is, to the Torlak (or Prizren-Timok) dialect group of Serbian, the historical premises are here basically quite different from those found in the far northwest. There can be little doubt, it would seem, that the Torlak dialects are genuinely transitional between, on the one hand, Serbian and, on the other, Macedonian and Bulgarian. What remains controversial, to some extent, is whether it is their origin and historical basis or their more striking present structural-typological characteristics that should be considered decisive when labeling this dialect group essentially Serbian or Macedo-Bulgarian; also, if Serbian, its relation to other major dialect groups of Serbo-Croatian raises some questions.

It is only natural, of course, that Bulgarian linguists of an earlier generation (such as B. Conev and S. Mladenov) would count the Prizren-Timok dialects among the local variants of Bulgarian. More recently, from a structural-typologocial point of view, these dialects were considered Macedo-Bulgarian rather than Serbian also, for example, by such an acknowledged specialist in South Slavic dialectology as F. Sławski who wrote: "From a contemporary point of view, these are already dialects of the Bulgarian-Macedonian type, marked by virtually all the Balkanisms characteristic of the Bulgarian-Macedonian group."[16] As to the origin and earliest evolutionary phase of this dialect group it is now generally agreed, however, that they were Serbian. Thus discussing the transitional status of Torlak between Serbian and Bulgarian (Macedonian as an independent language and not merely a specific dialect cluster then not yet being seriously considered), the great Dutch Slavist N. van Wijk in one of his famous lectures read at the Sorbonne in the 1930s reached this conclusion:

> Cette répartition des particularités linguistiques des deux langues n'admet qu'une seule conclusion, à savoir: que le dialecte de transition était serbe à l'origine, mais que dans la suite, il a traversé avec le bulgare une période d'évolution commune.[17]

The question thus arises which criteria, the historical or the contemporary (and typologically more striking), to attribute greater significance when attempting to put a label—Serbian or Macedo-Bulgarian—on the Torlak dialect group. It may not come as a surprise, of course, that Yugoslav—Serbian and Croatian—linguists have counted the Timok-Prizren dialects among the Serbo-Croatian. This was true of A. Belić as well as M. Rešetar; but it was only P. Ivić who has attempted to provide a modern theoretical justification for this classification. Though, in principle, contending that "one must group present-day dialects according to their present-day and not according to their erstwhile status"[18] Ivić nonetheless considered the—admittedly numerically much more weighty—genetic criteria decisive for the classification of the Torlak dialects when he wrote:

> It is clear, at any rate, that the dialects of the Prizren-Timok zone entered the evolutionary sphere of the Balkan *Sprachbund* and that this shift is essentially not older than the 15th century. Consequently, the main isoglosses which connect the Prizren-Timok dialects with Bulgarian and Macedonian are chronologically secondary in relation to those which mark the closeness of these with the other štokavian dialects. Therefore, even though they are valid for a description of the typological (structural) characteristics of the dialects, these isoglosses nonetheless have no significance as regards the origin of the dialects.

And, in a methodologically important footnote, he added

> And the great linguistic importance of structural phenomena notwithstanding, they cannot provide the basic criteria for defining the closeness of language types. In this respect the central place belongs to

the statistic measurement, i.e., the sum total of the concrete agreements and differences in the data itself of which a language is made up. If one were to take into consideration exclusively structural criteria, one would arrive at the most absurd conclusions, e.g., that the Macedonian and Bulgarian dialects are closer to Aromunian and Romanian than to the Slavic languages.[19]

In the 1956 Serbo-Croatian edition of his survey of Serbo-Croatian dialectology, Ivić, although recognizing Torlak as a well-defined dialect group, still considered it part of štokavian Serbian, in this respect following his teacher A. Belić. It should be remembered here, incidentally, that, prior to the crystallization and official recognition of Macedonian as an independent literary language, Belić also claimed all of the dialects now generally considered Macedonian as being essentially Serbian. Only two years later, in the 1958 German edition of his dialectology, Ivić reclassified the Torlak dialects as a distinct, major dialectal group on a par with the other three major dialect groups of Serbo-Croatian, Štokavian, Čakavian, and Kajkavian while pointing to the old organic connections with Štokavian and, in fact, their common origin.[20] This quadripartition of the Serbo-Croatian dialects, earlier strongly advocated by M. Rešetar, is now prevalent among Yugoslav dialectologists. Perhaps, to accurately characterize the status of Torlak in a nutshell, it would be fair to say that the dialects subsumed under this name are essentially Serbo-Croatian, in which framework they hold a position equivalent with other major dialect groups, but that in terms of the progression of their Balkanization (in the linguistic sense) they are as much a full-fledged member of the Balkan *Sprachbund* as are Macedonian and Bulgarian (among the South Slavic languages; or Romanian, with Macedo-Romanian or Aromanian and Megleno-Romanian, and Albanian among the non-Slavic languages of the Balkans). In this context it should be noted, however, that the Balkanization of Serbo-Croatian as a whole has already made considerable inroads, and that parts of both the Kosovo-Reseva and the Šumadija-Vojvodina dialect groups are increasingly drawn into the orbit of Balkan Slavic in the narrow sense.[21]

THE STATUS OF MACEDONIAN

Whereas the question of the status, mutual relationship, and rights of the Serbian and Croatian standard variants of Serbo-Croatian and their speakers is primarily an internal Yugoslav or even intra-Serbo-Croatian affair, and the same is true also of a proper assessment of the nature of the language spoken, now and in the past, in Dubrovnik and its environs, the problems of the peripheral dialects of Serbo-Croatian, Kajkavian and Torlak, briefly touched upon here, have dimensions which in part at least go beyond the narrow purview of Serbo-Croatian linguistics and language policy and, to some extent, even beyond the sociolinguistic and political issues of Yugoslavia as a whole. Thus, the problem of defining the proper place of Kajkavian pertains, as we have seen, both to Serbo-Croatian and Slovenian while the analogous problem as far as Torlak is concerned not only bears upon the relationship between Serbo-Crotian and the most recent Slavic literary language, Macedonian, but also has been a matter of controversy between Yugoslav (primarily Serbian) and Bulgarian linguists and politicians. The linguistic aspect of the so-called Macedonian question, too, carries broader international—in the first instance, Yugoslav-Bulgarian—implications.

As is generally known, it is a fairly widespread opinion, voiced in particular in Bulgarian circles, that Macedonian, as a standard literary language, is an artificial creation without any base in linguistic and, consequently, ethnic reality. By the same token, it is a view over and over repeated especially in Yugoslavia, by politicians as well as scholars, that Macedonian not only very much exists today but that it is in fact as old as Slavic literacy itself since the Early Slavic dialect spoken by the Thessalonian brothers Constantine and Methodius, the creators of the oldest Slavic literary language, Old Church Slavic, can be labeled Macedonian and the writings in Old Church Slavic of the Ohrid School (late 9th-11th cc.) can very well be considered (and thus called) Old Macedonian. It is merely one of the injustices of history, so the saying goes, that the Macedonian people were not allowed to attain statehood before the formation of Federal Socialist Yugoslavia in 1945—except perhaps for a very brief period in the Middle Ages. The latter is true if we count, as some are inclined to do, the interlude of Macedonian independence under Tsar Samuil (late 10th - early 11th cc.), by others, however, considered merely a rump and successor state of the First Bulgarian Empire whose eastern half had succumbed to Byzantium in 972 while its western (or Macedonian) half had seceded shortly before that, in the 960s, and was not formally incorporated into the Byzantine Empire until 1018, four years after the death of Tsar Samuil.

In my own opinion, there is a small measure of truth in both of these sharply contradictory views, but essentially and on the whole they are both false, I would contend. Put succinctly, it is true, I suggest, that standard literary Macedonian is indeed a somewhat artificial, chiefly politically motivated creation of the 1940s (which has been further improved and perfected in the decades thereafter right up to the present but which has also its distinct prehistory going back to the 19th or even the last decades of the 18th century); by the same token, it is not true, of course, that this creation—artificial in one particular sense of the word though it may be—lacks all foundation in linguistic and ethnic reality. Let me elaborate.

The fact that a literary or standard language is created artifically, as it were, that is to say, for political and/or specific cultural reasons and frequently as a result of an individual, dedicated and highly motivated scholar's efforts, is by no means something altogether unusual. Largely, it may be argued, Old Church Slavic is the creation of one learned personality, Constantine (also known as St. Cyril), aided, to be sure, by his brother Methodius and, in all probability, by a small group of associates. The establishment of the currently used štokavian standard of Serbo-Croatian (in two variants) is the achievement primarily of one man, Vuk Karadžić and, for Croatian, to a considerable extent Ljudevit Gaj. Similarly, and going beyond the Slavic realm, the so-called New Norwegian language (*nynorsk*, now used in Norway along with the still more widely spread Dano-Norwegian language known as *bokmål*) is, again, the work of one man, Ivar Aasen.[22] The examples could easily be multiplied, of course. Often, when the creation of a literary standard is largely the accomplishment of one man, his own native dialect would be a decisive influence in the selection, from among competing features or items of a broader dialect area, of those to be elevated to the status of literary standard. In our century, personal preferences may play a smaller role than they did in the Middle Ages (when Old Church Slavic was devised) or even in the age of Romanticism when Vuk and Ivar Aasen were active. Yet even in our day and age subjective considerations ought not to be excluded and discarded altogether, and it might just be an interesting task—possibly even tackled already—to try to determine the share in what today is standard literary Macedonian of the personal linguistic usage of Blaže Koneski—the poet, writer, and scholar to be in particular credited with the establishment of the written language of Macedonia, though its crystallization has of course its prehistory and its standardization was the work of a special commission appointed for that purpose in 1944.[23] In some ways the emergence of literary Macedonian distinct from an independent of standard Bulgarian may be compared to that of Slovak as segregated from Czech in the 19th century and, more recently, of Moldavian (written in Cyrillic) as distinct from standard Romanian (Daco-Romanian), differences in international constellations, political pressures, and ethnic implications notwithstanding. The opposite process, politically motivated integration of a once separate language into another, predominant one, rather than segregation (as in the case of Macedonian, Slovak, or Moldavian), is also well known, of course. In our times, we can witness it, for example, in Poland where onetime distinct Kashubian now is in the course of being integrated into Polish (and relegated to the status of one of its more particular dialects or dialect groups).

If modern Macedonian in its grammatical structure (marked by a high degree of Balkanization) and lexical system is closest to contemporary Bulgarian, at least by comparison to other modern Slavic languages, its phonology clearly betrays the century-long impact of Serbian. To be sure, it would be a gross oversimplification to say that in its sound pattern Macedonian is Serbian (or even pseudo-Serbian) while in its grammar and vocabulary it is Bulgarian (or nearly Bulgarian); yet such a statement would probably come closer to reflecting the actual state of affairs than any other conceivable summary approximation. Clearly, however, contemporary standard Macedonian displays, in addition, a number of characteristics—phonological, morphosyntactic, and lexical—which it does not share with any of its neighboring Slavic standard languages; where this is the case, they are usually of local, dialectal origin or, in a few instances, established artificially and *ad hoc* for the very purpose of differentiating this young literary language from its older sister idioms in the area.

If, therefore, it can be agreed upon that Macedonian today is undoubtedly a full-fledged, separate standard language, there is no need, on the other hand, to look for a long independent history of that literary language which in fact does not exist or, at most, in rudimentary form can be traced back approximately two hundred years. To speak of Old or Middle Macedonian, even of a New Macedonian language amounts to an anachronism of sorts. There can be little doubt, I would argue, that the historical basis of contemporary literary Macedonian is a cluster of essentially West Bulgarian dialects—dialects which, owing to their geographic location, were exposed to a considerable degree of Serbianization, primarily in its phonology but to a lesser extent also in its lexicon. There is certainly no reason to exaggerate the linguistic differences which presumably existed and were reflected in the scribal habits of the early centers or "schools" of Old Church Slavic writing, Ohrid in the west and Preslav in the east, but both in the early phase of their flourishing within the borders of the First Bulgarian Empire (while subsequently part of Byzantium). Commenting on some of the specifics of the Preslav School, N. van Wijk, one of the most unbiased experts on Old Church Slavic, hastened to add:

> ... freilich darf man nicht den Osten und den Westen allzu streng
> voneinander trennen; es gab gegenseitige Beziehungen und Einflüsse,
> und zwischen den Maa. [Mundarten, H.B.] gab es kaum schroffe Gren-
> zen. Von gewissen Texten kann man kaum ausmachen, ob sie östlichen
> oder westlichen Ursprunges sind.[24]

If today scholars prefer the term Old Church Slav(on)ic or simply Old Slav(on)ic and their equivalents in other languages to the earlier common Old Bulgarian, this is certainly not primarily justified by the fact that some of the earliest texts in that language were written (or, rather, copied) in what today is Yugoslav Macedonia but what at the time of their being produced legitimately must be considered as having been western Bulgaria, at first (up to 1014/18) independent and subsequently Byzantine-ruled. Such historically unfounded sensitivities can possibly play some role in today's Yugoslavia but hardly elsewhere; here the broader and admittedly more vague term is usually preferred to allow for the inclusion of texts whose origin must obviously—on linguistic grounds—be sought outside the historical Bulgarian territory (e.g., *Kiev Leaflets, Freising Fragments*) and also to account for the Moravian-Pannonian period of Old Church Slavic writing from which no original texts seem to have come down to us.

To sum up, then, there is no reason, I believe, to assume the separate existence of an Old and subsequently Middle Macedonian language not allowed, for political reasons, to surface. Rather we should merely take into consideration the continued presence of a cluster of West Bulgarian dialects underlying present-day literary Macedonian and marked by specific features (at all levels of linguistic structure) which, even if labeled "Macedonian," would not however basically change their nature of originally forming part of the broader Bulgarian dialectal mosaic. It is another matter, of course, and chiefly one of terminology only that today when there exists a separate Socialist Republic of Macedonia as part of Yugoslavia as well as a Macedonian literary language, the dialects spoken on the territory of Macedonia can conveniently be labeled Macedonian. In essence I can thus only subscribe to the argument against the assumption of an Old and Middle Macedonian language as developed and substantiated in some detail a few years back by I. Talev in pertinent sections of his dissertation on the impact off Middle Bulgarian on the Russian literary language to the discussion of which I therefore herewith refer.[25]

THE SLAVIC VS. THE NON-SLAVIC LANGUAGES OF YUGOSLAVIA; LANGUAGE STANDARDIZATION AND LANGUAGE PLANNING IN YUGOSLAVIA

Yugoslavia is, as we all know, a multinational federal state not only in the sense that it is the home of several South Slavic peoples and languages (the exact number of which continues to be a matter of some controversy, cf. also below) but also that within its borders live several non-Slavic ethnic minorities. If the intra-Serbo-Croatian and, to some extent, the inter-Slavic ethnolinguistic relations in Yugoslavia and partly also between Yugoslavia and her neighbors, notably Bulgaria, have at times been strained and in many ways still are,[26] the federal goverment's and the individual republics' official policy vis-à-vis the country's non-Slavic minorities has been marked by an overall attitude of enlightened tolerance. This, in particular, applies to the sizable Albanian and Hungarian minorities of Yugoslavia.

According to the official statistics of the last nationwide census of 1971, the ethnolinguistic composition of the Yugoslav population is numerically as shown on p. 26 (also quoted for comparison are the figures of the 1953 and 1961 censuses).[27] While, obviously, it would lead us too far afield to comment here on, and analyze in detail, the figures cited there, at least a few general remarks are called for. Thus, clearly, in some instances major fluctuations noticeable in the results of the three censuses do not so much reflect actual increases or decreases in certain ethnic groups as they are a result of altered parameters in the statistic count. This, for example, applies to the near-duplication in the figure for "Moslems" in the 1971 census; to the uneven figures given for "Others"; and to the fact that the options not to state one's nationality or to claim merely regional affiliation (in lieu of any specific ethnic identity) were available only under the 1971 census while the option of declaring one's nationality as "Yugoslav" was not yet available under the 1953 census. The dramatic increase of the "Unknown" figure clearly also reflects a change in political climate.

Nationalities and Ethnic Affiliations of Yugoslav Population

	1953	1961	1971
Montenegrins	466,093	513,832	508,843
Croats	3,975,550	4,293,809	4,526,782
Macedonians	893,247	1,045,516	1,194,784
Moslems (in the sense of ethnic affiliation)	998,698	972,960	1,729,932
Slovenes	1,487,100	1,589,211	1,678,032
Serbs	7,065,923	7,806,152	8,143,246
Albanians	754,245	914,733	1,309,523
Bulgarians	61,708	62,624	58,627
Czechs	34,517	30,331	24,620
Italians	35,874	25,615	21,791
Hungarians	502,175	504,369	477,374
Romanians	60,364	60,862	58,570
Ruthenians	37,353	38,619	24,640
Slovaks	84,999	86,433	83,656
Turks	259,535	182,964	127,920
Others	212,803	89,945	166,641
Persons who did not state their nationality	—	—	32,774
"Yugoslavs" (according to art. 41 of the Constitution)	—	317,124	273,077
Regional affiliation	—	—	15,002
Unknown	6,389	14,192	67,138

As for the individual nationalities and ethnic affiliations, the following should further be noted. Montenegrins, although accorded the right of claiming their own, separate nationality (ethnicity), are usually considered speakers of Serbian. Moslems (in the sense of ethnic affiliation) applies to a large portion (*c.* 40 percent) of the population of the Socialist Republic of Bosnia and Hercegovina. In addition, a majority of the permanent residents of that republic identify themselves as either Serbs (*c.* 37 percent) or Croats (*c.* 20 percent). As for the standard variants of Serbo-Croatian used in Bosnia-Hercegovina, see above. Ruthenians (*Rusini* in Serbo-Croatian) does not merely refer to a Ukrainian minority but to an ethnic group of peasant settlers (mostly in Vojvodina and Croatian Slavonia) who migrated from the Carpatho-

Ukraine and East Slovakia across the Hungarian Plain to northern Yugoslavia. Their native tongue is a mixture of an East Slavic (dialectal Southwest Ukrainian) base, heavily overlayered with West Slavic (East Slovak) features and, more recently, affected also by the South Slavic (Serbo-Croatian) milieu in which the Ruthenians have settled.[28]

The most striking change that can be noted in the above statistics is of course the dramatic increase of the Albanians (Shqiptars), now constituting the majority of the population in the autonomous region of Kosovo. Second among the non-Slavic peoples of Yugoslavia are still the Hungarians, settled primarily in Vojvodina (Bačka and Banat). After a slight increase reflected in the 1961 census their figure is more recently slightly down. Next in size come the Turks (located primarily in Bosnia-Hercegovina, Macedonia, and certain areas in Serbia, especially on the Danube, including some islands in the river on the Yugoslav-Romanian border), the Slovaks, and, approximately equal in number, the Bulgarians and the Romanians (among the latter also the Aromanians in Macedonia and the rather few Istro-Romanians in Istria). The fact that the figure for the Bulgarians, after a slight increase in 1961, now is only insignificantly down certainly suggests that no undue pressure has been exerted on the members of that minority of Yugoslavia to declare themselves Macedonians or otherwise not to stand by their ethnic identity.

Albanian enjoys the status of national language (along with Serbo-Croatian) in Kosovo. As is well known, the main language of instruction at the University of Priština is now Albanian, and a great number of elementary and high schools, as well as the Yugoslav variety of junior colleges (the so-called *više škole*), not only offer instruction in Albanian but use that language as the chief vehicle of instruction. Similarly, in Vojvodina, where Serbian nationalistic sentiments traditionally have run high (the *Matica srpska* was after all transferred to Novi Sad—not to Belgrade!—from Hungary proper in 1864), elementary and high schools not only have Hungarian in their curriculum but a number even offer instruction of other subjects in the language of the sizable minority of that autonomous region. There is also a strong Hungarian department at the University of Novi Sad. It should be added that local newspapers and periodicals in Albanian, Hungarian, and in some of the other larger minorities' languages are not only tolerated but encouraged and supported by local, regional, and federal authorities.

Given the undeniable tension continuing to exist, if only under the surface, between some of the advocates of the Serbian and Croatian standard variants of Yugoslavia's predominant language, as well as the fully recognized and in part even particularly protected and cherished status of the two smaller South Slavic standard languages of Yugoslavia,

Slovenian and Macedonian, it is certainly worth ascertaining the fair and tolerant attitude of the present Yugoslav government and its executive organs vis-à-vis the country's many ethnic minorities. In this, the present situation undoubtedly represents an improvement as compared to the status of the non-Serbian nationalities in prewar Yugoslavia.

Contrary also to some of the pertinent practices of another multinational socialist federal state, the Soviet Union, whose official attitude to its many non-Russian nationalities is, to be sure, one of tolerance and recognition but where this attitude measured against the realities of the day has occasionally had more the character of paying lip service than actually and consistently upholding the rights of the smaller nations and ethnic groups united under Moscow's leadership, the Yugoslav authorities have, almost without exception, been at pains to practice what they have been preaching, and to live up to the letter of the law.

Whereas the standardization of the two variants of literary Serbo-Croatian has—as is well known—encountered certain unfortunate difficulties, at times with strong emotional and irrational overtones (briefly alluded to above), no quite comparable problems or difficulties are known when it comes either to the standardization of Slovenian (with its own well-established tradition) or the only relatively recently crystallized standard Macedonian language. That, of course, does not mean that internal discussions, conducted among writers, linguists, and other parties concerned, have not taken place or are not now in progress; on the contrary, an ongoing and continuous debate of the optimal normative rules for the use of the official languages in the various republics is characteristic for the situation throughout today's Yugoslavia.[29] When it comes to the languages of the more significant minorities—Albanian, Hungarian, Turkish, Romanian, Bulgarian, etc.—no attempts are, to my knowledge, being made in any way to set the linguistic usage of those minorities apart from the standards applicable in the respective national home countries of these languages—Albania, Hungary, Turkey, Romania, Bulgaria, and so forth. Particularly, when it comes to Albanian, this is insofar noteworthy as the Albanian-speaking population of Yugoslavia by now (1978) is said to numerically approach if not soon to outnumber that of Albania proper.

CONCLUDING REMARKS

Increasingly, after World War I and particularly after World War II, multinational states are becoming the exception rather than the rule among the countries of Europe and in other parts of the world. Where sizable national minorities persist within the framework of a particular state, they have more often than not aspired to independence or, at any rate, greater autonomy. The Basque region of Spain,

Brittany, or the province of Quebec provide but a few examples of as yet unfulfilled dreams and unsatisfied hopes. The obvious counterexample is Switzerland, where four nationalities coexist peacefully even though one may assume that the German and French majorities consider themselves in some respects privileged by comparison to the speakers of Italian and that the small population of native Rhaetic-Romance speakers probably do not feel their position as an ethnic group significantly preferable to that of their closest relatives living in Friuli-Venezia Giulia in northeastern Italy.

But what about Yugoslavia? Here, the focus of national—or rather nationalistic—tensions seems to be in the heart of the country, among Serbs and Croats, speakers of essentially one and the same language, rather than on the peripheries, among the smaller South Slavic nations of Slovenes and Macedonians or the non-Slavic minorities, as such generally well provided for. To be sure, Serbs and Croats claim a different historical and cultural legacy. But when animosities and hostilities go so far as to breed clearly separatist moods and movements as those which undoubtedly continue to glow in some quarters—in the embers of a bloody past—the concerned outside observer cannot help but ask himself, and his Yugoslav friends as well: In the face of the political realities, that is, considering Yugoslavia's precarious and, at the same time, stabilizing role in Southeastern Europe—now and potentially in the not-too-distant future, with a leadership less symbolically potent than that of the man who more than anybody else has shaped modern Yugoslavia—are not the values and the factors which could unite the country as a whole, among them the mosaic of its languages and the mutually enriching cultures they represent, more significant and precious than those other, bitter experiences which threaten to tear it apart?

Notes

1. For a fairly detailed discussion of the South Slavic dialectal continuum and the place of Serbo-Croatian within it, cf., e.g., P. Ivić, *Die serbokroatischen Dialekte, ihre Struktur und Entwicklung,* The Hague, 1958, 25–49, with further references. For some thoughts on defining 'language' vs. 'dialect,' exemplified with, among other things, South Slavic data, see, for example, H. Birnbaum, *Zeitschrift für slavische Philogie* 35 (1970), 1–5.

2. For further details, see H. Birnbaum, *Common Slavic: Progress and Problems in its Reconstruction,* Cambridge, Mass., 1975, 6, 11–13, and 307–8 (with reference to Trubačev's hypothesis about the secondary "occidentalization" of the West Slavic Sorbs). For some additional observations on and interpretations of the dialectal isoglosses of South Slavic and their complexities, including their prehistory (i.e., prior to the arrival of the Southern Slavs in the Balkans), see now also D. Brozović, "About the Characteristics of the Dialectal Isoglosses in the South-Slavic Language Territory," *Studia Linguistica A.V. . . . Issatschenko . . . oblata* (H. Birnbaum *et al.*, eds.), Lisse, 1978, 47–57, discussing, among other things, the possibility of two successive migratory waves of South Slavic settlers (the ethnic groups identified as *Serbs* and *Croats* in that case belonging to the second wave).

3. For more information on the migrations of the Southern Slavs, both before and after their landtaking in the Balkan Peninsula, see also P. Ivić, "Balkan Slavic Migrations in the Light of South Slavic Dialectology," *Aspects of the Balkans: Continuity and Change* (H. Birnbaum & S. Vryonis, Jr., eds.), The Hague & Paris, 1972, 66–86, with ample bibliography; cf. also the very erudite and original but in part controversial treatment in I. Popović, *Geschichte der serbokroatischen Sprache,* Wiesbaden, 1960, 1–47 (esp. 41–47, on the 'Pannonian Slavic' and 'Daco-Slavic' problems) and 104–346. On the gradual Balkanization of South Slavic and, specifically, the varying degree and spatial progress of this process in Serbo-Croatian, see H. Birnbaum, "Balkanslavisch und südslavisch: Zur Reichweite der Balkanismen im südslavischen Sprachraum," *Zeitschrift für Balkanologie* 3 (1965), 12–63, wap. 39–57 ("Das Randgebiet der Balkanismen im südslavischen Sprachraum: das Serbokroatische").

4. For a brief account of "Language and Nationalism in Yugoslavia" through early 1967, see T. F. Magner's somewhat personalized and casually worded article in *Canadian Slavic Studies* (1967), 333–47.

5. For a discussion of and historical commentary on the terms 'Serbo-Croatian' and 'Croato-Serbian' (with spelling variants), see R. L. Lencek, "A Few Remarks for [sic] the History of the Term 'Serbocroatian' Language," *Zbornik za filologiju i lingvistiku* 19 (1976), 45–53. Note here also, in particular, the opening statement of the author, himself a native Slovene and naturalized American: "The natural language of the

majority of speakers in the Yugoslav National Republics of Serbia, Croatia, Montenegro, Bosnia and Hercegovina, is one and the same, the Serbocroatian. Its
linguistic identity is defined in terms of its direct relation to the remaining three
South Slavic languages, Bulgarian, Macedonian, and Slovene, and to the Western
and Eastern Slavic languages." Though concerned with a different topic, the same
general concept underlies also, for example, the paper by S. Marković, "Šta je
zajedničko a šta posebno u varijantama srpskohrvatskog (hrvatskosrpskog) književ-
nog (standardnog) jezika?" *Zbornik za filologiju i lingvistiku* 14 (1971), 141–51.

6. R. Dunatov when quoting in English translation the relevant clause of that amend-
    ment at the beginning of his insightful paper "A Sociolinguistic Analysis of the
    Recent Controversy Concerning the Croatian/Serbian Standard Language(s),"
    American Contributions to the Eighth International Congress of Slavists, Volume I: *Linguis-
    tics and Poetics* (H. Birnbaum, ed.), Columbus, Ohio, 1978, 256–68, renders *narodni
    jezik* as "the *folk* language"; R. L. Lencek, *op. cit.,* 45, fn. 1, makes a point to justify his
    translation "*natural* language" for the same concept. To me, both renditions, though
    attempting to capture some of the overtones of SC *narodni,* seem a bit forced and
    therefore less felicitous than the more traditional "national," assuming that this latter
    is not overinterpreted and that it can presuppose two nations (peoples) or
    nationalities—here, the Serbs and the Croats—as well as one.

7. Cf. *Jezik* 21 (1973/4), 65–7.

8. Cf. R. Dunatov, *op. cit.,* 261–4.

9. Cf. R. Dunatov, *op. cit.,* 264–5.

10. Cf. P. Ivić, *Srpski narod i njegov jezik,* 139–42. Note there in particular also the
    reference (p. 141) to Rešetar who, sure enough, felt that one should not separate
    Serbian and Croatian "for they are one" but who also did not hesitate to explicitly
    state "whoever separates Serbian and Croatian must acknowledge that Dubrovnik, as
    regards its language, has always been Serbian" *(Godišnjak SKA* 50, 1940, 189). By the
    same token, Ivić, too, speaking of the present situation, concedes (p. 142): "Things
    are quite different today when the people of Dubrovnik form part of the Croatian
    nation which gives that nation the right to consider the literature of Dubrovnik its
    heritage. . . ." The—in my view, mistaken—hypothesis that there in fact did once
    exist a natural čakavian substratum in Dubrovnik has been elaborated especially in
    the mongraph by C. A. van den Berk, *Y a-t-il un substrat čakavien dans le dialecte de
    Dubrovnik? Contribution à l'histoire de la langue serbo-croate,* The Hague, [1957].

11. For a recent discussion, see, e.g., H. Birnbaum, "Der österreichische Jasomirgott und
    die frühere Verbreitung der Alpenslaven (Urslovenen)," *Anzeiger für slavische
    Philologie* 9 (1977), 33–48, esp. 37–40 and 43–8.

12. For a fairly detailed and objective account of the sensitive issue of the Slovenian
    minority in Carinthia today, with historical background, see D. I. Rusinow,
    "Nationalism Today: Carinthia's Slovenes, I: The Legacy of History; II: The Story of
    Article Seven," *Fieldstaff Reports, Southeast Europe Series* XXII: 4–5 (1977, The Ameri-
    can Universities Field Staff).

13. The quotation is from the English summary of Ivić's study "Prilozi poznavanju
    dijalekatske slike zapadne Hrvatske," *Godišnjak Filozofskog fakulteta u Novom Sadu* 6
    (1961), 21.

14. See *Aspects of the Balkans* (cf. n. 3), 71. On the relationship between Slovenian and Kajkavian and various scholars' relevant views, see also H. Birnbaum, *Anzeiger für slavische Philologie* 9 (1977), 39–43 (cf. n. 11 above; the specific phonological and grammatical agreements between Slovenian and Kajkavian, discussed by Ivić, are listed on p. 40 of my article).

15. Cf. Ivić, *Srpski narod i njegov jezik*, 36–7. In this context it should also be remembered that Kajkavian, after all, at one time did function as the *de facto* Croatian standard language.

16. See F. Sławski, *Zarys dialektologii południowosłowiańskiej*, Warsaw, 1962, 115.

17. Cf. N. van Wijk, *Les langues slaves: De l'unité à la pluralité*, The Hague, 1956, 104.

18. See *Književnost i jezik* 10 (1963), 28 (in his study "O klasifikaciji srpskohrvatskih dialekata").

19. Cf. P. Ivić, *Dijalektologija srpskohrvatskog jezika. Uvod i štokavsko narečje*, Novi Sad, 1956, 121. The English rendition of the two Serbo-Croatian passages is mine.

20. See P. Ivić, *Die serbokroatischen Dialekte*, 88–9, with further references.

21. Cf., e.g., H. Birnbaum, *Zeitschrift für Balkanologie* 3 (1965), 47–8. with additional references. For a brief survey of the discussion of the classification of Torlak (in the Serbo-Croatian dialectological framework), see also R. Alexander, *Torlak Accentuation*, Munich, 1975, 7–10. For a recent analysis of some morphological Balkanisms of Torlak (as well as some general information on these dialects), see further V. A. Friedman, "The Morphology of Case in Southeast Serbian Dialects," *Folia Slavica* 1 (: 1, 1977), 76–87, with ample references. In this context it should be noted, incidentally, that not all tendencies toward analytic language structure in South Slavic ought necessarily to be explained in terms of Balkanization. Thus, such tendencies can be observed also in the one South Slavic language not yet at all affected by Balkanization (but instead by much—here German-Slavic—bilingualism), Slovenian. For some observations on certain parallel developments, see H. Orzechowska, "Niektóre tendencje rozwojowe języka słoweńskiego a powstanie bałkanizmów słowiańskich," *Nahtigalov Zbornik* (F. Jakopin, ed.), Ljubljana, 1977, 357–73 (with English and Slovene abstracts).

22. For details, see E. Haugen, *The Scandinavian Languages: An Introduction to Their History,* Cambridge, Mass., 1976, 405–6.

23. For further information and some historical background, cf., e.g., H. G. Lunt, *Grammar of the Macedonian Literary Language*, Skopje, 1952, 1–7.

24. Cf. N. van Wijk, *Geschichte der altkirchenslavischen Sprache*, Berlin & Leipzig, 1931, 14–15.

25. See I. Talev, *Some Problems of the Second South Slavic Influence in Russia*, Munich, 1973, 151–61, with ample references. For the more or less official view in Yugoslav Macedonia itself on Macedonian and its evolution, see, e.g., relevant statements by B. Koneski in his *Istorija na makedonskiot jazik*, Skopje & Belgrade, 1965 (Serbo-Croatian version: *Istorija makedonskog jezika*, Belgrade & Skopje, 1966); cf. further also his pamphlet *Makedonskiot jazik vo razvojot na slovenskite literaturni jazici*, Skopje, 1968.

26. As regards Yugoslavia's relationship to Austria, the conditions of the Slovenian minority (mostly in Carinthia) and, to a lesser extent, those of the Croats in the province (*Land*) of Burgenland have been a cause for concern by the Yugoslav authorities (cf. also the report by D. I. Rusinow cited in n. 12, above). Earlier tensions relevant to the lot of the Slovenian population in border areas of Italy have since largely subsided.

27. Cf. *Statistički godišnjak Jugoslavije*, 1974. *Godina XXI*, Belgrade, 1974, 194.

28. For some comprehensive, and fairly up-to-date information on the Ruthenians (*Rusini*) of Yugoslavia and their background, the best reference known to me is, unfortunately, available in Swedish only: S. R. Gustavsson, *Rusinerna i Jugoslavien, deras kultur och språk*, Stockholm, 1975 (Stockholms Universitet, Institutionen för slaviska och baltiska språk, *Meddelanden*, Nr. 13). A more recent paper by the same author, "Rusinskij jazyk v Jugoslavii, diaxronija i sinxronija," including some further relevant references and listing a set of diagnostic criteria which suggest that the language of the Yugoslav Ruthenians now, in genetic terms, is predominantly West Slavic (East Slovak), is due to appear shortly.

29. For an excellent, unbiased, and insightful discussion of the particular problems of contemporary literary Slovenian viewed in a broad sociolinguistic context, see R. L. Lencek, "On Dilemmas and Compromises in the Evolution of Modern Slovene," in: T. F. Magner (ed.), *Slavic Linguistics and Language Teaching*, Cambridge, Mass. 1976, 112–52.

Addendum: Only after completion and presentation of this paper did the volume *Sociolinguistic Problems in Czechoslovakia, Hungary, Romania and Yugoslavia*, ed. by W. R. Schmalstieg & T. F. Magner, Columbus, Ohio: Slavica Publishers, 1978 (**h** *Folia Slavica* 1: 3), appear and was brought to my attention. In it, particularly the contributions by D. Kalogjera ("On Serbo-Croatian Prescriptivism," pp. 388–99) and K. E. Naylor ("The Eastern Variant of Serbo-Croatian as the *Lingua Communis* of Yugoslavia," pp. 456–68), commented on by C. E. Gribble (pp. 487–91), are of direct relevance to the topic treated in my essay and ought therefore to be consulted.

The Formation of Yugoslavia

Wayne Vucinich

IN NOVEMBER 1918, the South Slav lands of former Austria-Hungary were beset by grave external and internal problems. The National Council of the Slovenes, Croats and Serbs found itself in a serious crisis. The war was over and the groundwork had to be prepared for the Paris Peace Conference. Yet, the Allies had refused to recognize the State of the Slovenes, Croats and Serbs (SCS), whose borders were neither delineated nor recognized. The situation was paradoxical in that Serbia, Czechoslovakia, Austria, and Hungary, the four states most vitally concerned with the South Slavs, had recognized the State of the SCS, and that Austria-Hungary in her final moments of life had surrendered its fleet to it. The danger existed that at the Peace Conference the Yugoslav lands of former Austria-Hungary might be disposed of in a way detrimental to the South Slavs.

The most crucial task of the State of the SCS was to establish an effective government, an efficient police system and an adequate and loyal armed force to stop the Italian annexation of South Slav territory, and to secure international recognition. Moreover, the State of the SCS had to maintain peace and order in its domain and provide food for its population.

Lest large parts of territory would be taken by its neighbors, Austria, Hungary and Italy, the State of the SCS needed military support. The Italian army advanced toward Ljubljana in Slovenia and cast its eyes toward Karlovac in Croatia. The State of the SCS hastily organized an army of heterogeneous elements and a police force, but they proved inadequate to protect the State and maintain peace and order. The most reliable military formations were units made up of released Serbian prisoners of war. When an advance Italian unit approached Ljubljana, a battalion of Serbian troops (organized out of Serbian prisoners of war in Austria-Hungary), under the command of Lt. Col. Stevan Švabić, forced the Italians to withdraw by threatening to open fire. Likewise an Italian army stationed near Rijeka was initially stopped from taking the city by the Second Battalion of the Fiftieth Serbian Infantry Regiment, which entered the city first.[1]

In desperation, on November 4, 1918, the State of the SCS appealed for help to the Supreme Allied Command, which responded in the affirmative. The Serbian troops had already moved into Montenegro, Bosnia and Hercegovina, and Vojvodina. On November 8 *vojvoda* Bojović informed the National Council in Zagreb that he had issued orders for Serbian troops to move into Srem (Srijem) and Slavonia. Nine days later, on November 17, the commandant of Allied Armies issued orders to Serbian and French units to move into Rijeka, Dubrovnik, and Split. Thus, the Serbian, French, English and American units were stationed in Split placed under the Commandant of the French Eastern Army.

Not only did Italy plan to annex a substantial part of Yugoslav lands, but it backed the Albanian, Montenegrin and Macedonian armed bands whose purpose was to break up Yugoslavia. To achieve their objective, the Italians used military threat, supported disturbances and separatist movements inside Yugoslavia, and encouraged anti-Yugoslav activities by the countries bordering Yugoslavia.[2] Italy also kept the nationalistic passion of the small Italian minority in Yugoslavia inflamed.

The Italian plan against Yugoslavia was prepared by General Pietro Badoglio on December 3, 1918, and approved by foreign minister Sidney Sonnino on December 9.[3] In accordance with this plan, Italy backed the Montenegrin King Nikola and his followers financially and politically and assisted in the recruitment of volunteers for guerrilla warfare in Yugoslavia. With the help of the Italian army, the guerrillas or the *komiti*, as they were known, were transported to the Albanian and Yugoslav coast and from there sent into Yugoslavia. Italy also supported the activities of the Bulgarian-backed IMRO (Internal Macedonian Revolutionary Organization) in Macedonia. Some Croats, followers of Frank and Stjepan Radić, also appeared to have been in touch with the Italian officers, and later with Gabrielle D'Annunzio, the well-known Italian ultra-nationalist poet.[4]

One of the most acute crises in 1918 was the problem of land tenure in all the Yugoslav provinces with the exception of Serbia. According to the 1910 census, 91.15 percent of the landlords whose lands were tilled by Serbs were Muslims. The serfs were overwhelmingly Christians— Orthodox Serbs (73.92%) and Catholic Croats (21.49%).[5] The confessional disparity reflected in the land ownership gave the conflict between the landlord and the serf both a social and religious character. To peasants everywhere, not only in Bosnia and Hercegovina, the collapse of Austria-Hungary meant the end of the remnants of the feudal system of land tenure and the land-hungry peasant was determined to acquire legal rights to the land he tilled.

Class and political antagonisms in the village were sharpened when the new State emerged. In 1917 the population had begun to disregard the occupation authorities. To avoid Austro-Hungarian service, many fled to the woods and awaited the end of the war there. These deserters were called the "Green Cadre" (*Zeleni Kadar*).[6] The requisitions of food and the shortage of it, and the lack of consumer goods made the social conflict increasingly pronounced. Clashes between people and authorities became more frequent. No doubt the October Revolution contributed to the mounting social unrest.[7]

A conviction prevailed that the collapse of Austria-Hungary eliminated all obstacles in achieving national and social aspirations. In Vojvodina, the left socialists (*Pelagićevici*), immediately after the collapse of Austria-Hungary, appealed to the people to rise in opposition to the government. The peasantry was restless and demanded agrarian reform.[8] The situation was similar in Croatia, Slavonia and Slovenia. The exception was Dalmatia where, because of Italian occupation, the peasant movement had a predominately national character. Yet, there, too, the peasantry was determined to put an end to *colonate* and tenantry. The post-war situation in Dalmatia was aggravated by a shortage of bread and grain and by a dramatic fall in the price of local products such as wine and olive oil.[9] Everywhere, except in Macedonia where strong military control was established, the peasant movement posed a serious problem. The situation in the villages of Serbia and Montenegro was different. Here small peasant land holdings predominated and there was no particular clamor for redistribution of the land. The peasants were instead preoccupied with party and national politics.

To establish peace and order, the National Council proclaimed martial law and began in haste to organize a "national guard" for this purpose. The National Council in Zagreb, on November 2, 1918, ordered mobilization, but it was not successful. For insubordination, stealing, plunder and burning, the death sentence was prescribed. In some regions, committees of the National Council ordered martial law and court martial. In Banat, after proclaiming martial law and introducing court martial, it attempted to strengthen cooperation with former homeguard officers. Even the Social-Democratic spokesmen were disturbed, criticizing the masses for their excesses.[10] Disturbances in "Vojvodina" culminated in the creation of two "republics." The "Banat republic" was proclaimed in Timișoara, on October 31, 1918. The Hungarian leaders of the republic obviously sought to preserve Banat for Hungary. The socialists were for the autonomy of Banat and the Serbs wanted its union with Serbia.[11] The peasants of Kusić, near Bela Crkva, in the Banat, mostly Serbs, with some Romanians, rose in November 1918 and proclaimed a second republic. This movement was suppressed by Serbian troops.

The problem of national minorities proved insoluble from the very beginning. Backed by revisionist Bulgaria and fascist Italy, the bands of the Internal Macedonian Revolutionary Organization demanded continuous police action. The Macedonians protested against the new state which did not recognize their separate nationality. Re-visionist Hungary kept the Hungarian minority in Yugoslavia in a state of ferment. Romanian and Italian minorities desired union with their mother countries, as did the large Albanian minority. Only the German minority seemed passive until the ascendancy of Hitler in 1933.

Both the State of the SCS and the Kingdom of the Serbs, Croats and Slovenes faced the Muslim problem. For different reasons, the Muslims of Macedonia, Old Serbia, the Sanjak of Novi Pazar, and Bosnia and Hercegovina did not welcome the new Yugoslav state. Groups of Muslims in Old Serbia fled into the woods where they were organized into armed bands (*kačaks*) and for several years waged war against the established order. The government employed the police, the army, and Chetnik irregulars in running down the insurgents. The fighting was accompanied by many bloody and barbarous acts on both sides.

As the war neared its end, the pent-up animosity toward the Muslims in Bosnia and Hercegovina as feudal oppressors and foreign collaborators (fighting with the notorious *Schutzkorps*) burst into the open. The Serbian peasants attacked Muslims, their homes and families, especially in the districts bordering Serbia and Montenegro.[12] The peasants, particularly the Serbian Orthodox, saw in the end of the war the simultaneous end of the centuries-old Muslim feudal exploitation. They refused to meet their landlords, and claimed the land they worked as their own. The "National Guard," the hastily constituted police force, was unable to stop violence or to maintain order. At times, it perpetrated crimes against the Muslims itself.[13] The bureaucratic machinery that survived the previous regime was impotent. It lost its authority and the people lacked confidence in it.

The murder and plunder of the Muslims in eastern Bosnia and southeastern Hercegovina were aggravated by incursions of the armed *komiti* from Montenegro.[14] Neither the provincial government in Bosnia and Hercegovina nor the central government were able to stop the *komiti* activities, which lasted until the mid-twenties.

The State of the SCS was simply unable to cope with its many problems. It proved incapable of building an effective government, an army and a security force. Enormous wartime losses and general dislocation, coupled with limited material resources, made it impossible to resolve the deeply rooted economic difficulties, aggravated by the unstable international situation and activities of inimical neighbors. No other political system would have been any more successful in resolving the country's many problems.

National Council Discusses Union

The Serbian government was apprised of conditions in the State of the SCS by Lieutenant Colonel Dušan Simović, the representative of the Serbian Supreme Command in Zagreb.[15] On November 14,

Simović reported that all the Serbs and most of the Croats and Slovenes of what was formerly Austria-Hungary along with the majority of the National Council of the SCS supported the union with Serbia under the Karadjordjević dynasty. Simović found that only those groups which supported the Habsburg Dynasty (Frank's Party of the Right, Stjepan Radić's Popular Peasant Party, Ivan Lorković, and the people behind the journal *Obzor*) advocated a republic. He noted that one part of Starčević's Party of the Right was pro-Serb, while another advocated a separate state of Croatia in a federative Yugoslav republic.[16]

On the whole, Lieutenant Colonel Simović was a good observer who grasped the situation accurately. He learned that Pribićević was a strong advocate of the South Slav union and wished for immediate talks with the leaders of Serbia. Pribićević was apparently disturbed that Serbia had not responded to the National Council's note of October 31, which informed it and the Allied governments about the establishment of the State of the SCS and its readiness to enter into a union with Serbia and Montenegro. The National Council was anxious to secure recognition from the Serbian government in order to gain prestige at home and abroad.

On November 18, Simović reported that the National Council of the SCS had been having lengthy discussions on the future State of the Serbs, Croats, and Slovenes,[17] with particular emphasis on its form (monarchical, federal, centralized). Some were for quick decision while others cautioned against haste. Most of the National Council believed that a unified state would enable the South Slavs to protect their national borders from Italian invasion and bring them speedier recognition as one of the allied peoples. Considering the bleak domestic and foreign situation, many political spokesmen among the South Slavs felt that the union of the State of the Serbs, Croats and Slovenes with Serbia should be hastened. In a note from Paris, on November 10, 1918, Pašić recommended to Regent Alexander and the Serbian government the initiation of talks with the National Council in regard to the union. The Regent responded by urging Pribićević to take steps in this direction, a suggestion that was received enthusiastically in Zagreb.[18] This action was also urged by *vojvoda* Mišić and certain other Serbian military leaders.

The question of union was aired at the meetings of the Central Committee of the Council on November 23 and 24. The delegate of the Serbian government, Momčilo Ninčić, in the name of the Serbian government, invited the Central Committee of the National Council to begin disucssions with Serbia. Various proposals were made at the meeting on how to carry out the unification with Serbia and Montenegro and on the form of the future state.[19] The National Council was asked to send Valerijan Pribićević as its delegate to Belgrade to serve as contact man between Belgrade and Zagreb in connection with "the Serbian national movement in Vojvodina."[20] It appears that, if the

Croats became difficult bargainers concerning the union, the Serbian government was prepared to annex the Serbian territories of former Austria-Hungary to Serbia. In fact, Srem (Srijem) and Vojvodina had already indicated that they wished to be united.[21]

Sensitive to the Italian designs on Dalmatia and angered by the Italian behavior in the occupied territories, the Provincial Government for Dalmatia protested in Rome and planned direct union with Serbia if the National Council in Zagreb did not act first.[22] As early as November 16, 1918, the Provincial Government for Dalmatia proposed to the National Council that it immediately seek the union of the State of the SCS with Serbia and Montenegro, with a common government, parliament and regency. The government of the National Council of the SCS for Bosnia and Hercegovina endorsed the proposal.[23] Finally, on November 23, 1918, the Central Committee of the National Council decided to discuss the union with Serbia in earnest.

The various proposals for union, all of which were essentially for a centralized state, were opposed to Stjepan Radić, head of the Croatian People's Peasant Party. He wanted a loosely organized Yugoslav federation with a republican form of government. According to Radić's proposal, the government would be responsible to the federal legislative body and the provincial governments to their own provincial assemblies. He wanted the supreme authority vested in the three regents—the Serbian Regent, Croatian ban, and the president of the Croatian National Council (*Svet*). The principal task of the three regents would be to name a joint federal government made up of three ministers—the minister for foreign affairs, the minister for national resources, and the minister for national defense. Such would be responsible to the supreme council of the Slovenes, Croats and Serbs, made up of ten members each from the Serbian parliament, Croatian Diet and the Slovene National Council; four from the Bosnian Diet; two each from the Montenegrin parliament and Dalmatian Diet; and two representatives each from Vojvodina and Istria. There were to be four autonomous state governments (Slovenia, Croatia, Serbia, Montenegro), and three provincial governments (Bosnia and Hercegovina, Dalmatia and Vojvodina).[24]

The Slovene representative also urged immediate union with Serbia and Montenegro as a matter of self-preservation. The position of the Social-Democrats was similar, and so was that of the Trieste representative in the Central Committee, who said that his people "did not fear the Serbian people, but the Germans and Italians." All of them wanted an agreement between Zagreb and Belgrade as soon as possible.

A discussion at the next meeting of the Central Committee of the National Council, on November 24, 1918, was likewise interesting for the views expressed by the different political leaders.[25] A Committee of

Seven was chosen to examine all the proposals submitted before the Central Committee and on the basis of such to draft a joint proposal as quickly as possible for an immediate secret vote. At the evening meeting, held on November 24, 1918, the Committee of Seven presented its proposal before the Central Committee. The meeting was opened by President Pribićević, who read the proposal of the Committee of Seven and the "Instructions" (*naputak*, pl. *naputci*) by which the delegates would be guided in the discussions in Belgrade. In light of prior statements of the National Council and the Serbian government, the proposal called for the unification of the State of the Slovenes, Croats and Serbs with Serbia and Montenegro. The proposal further asked for selection of a Committee of 28 persons that would be entrusted with full powers to reach, without delay, an agreement with the government of the Kingdom of Serbia on the organization of a united state. Finally, the Committee of Seven proposed that the union agreement be ratified at the first meeting of the State Council, to be composed of the representatives of the Kingdom of Serbia and Montenegro, and all the members of the National Council of the SCS, enlarged by members of the Yugoslav Committee.[26]

Some members accepted the proposal of the Committee of Seven in its entirety, and others questioned particular points. Two members (or one, depending on sources) rejected it altogether. The first to talk was Stjepan Radić. He criticized the proposal and spoke for "democracy" and against "socialistic-bourgeois oligarchy," which in his words dominated the National Council. At a large meeting of his Croatian People's Peasant Party, in Zagreb, on November 25, 1918, Radić openly attacked the centralists, headed by Svetozar Pribićević, and demanded "a neutral peasant republic of Croatia." He repeatedly demanded recognition of full state rights of Croatia within a Yugoslav framework, in accordance with the principle of self-determination. Radić wanted Croatia organized as a state with its own diet.[27] There were also others who opposed the "Instructions." Dragutin Hrvoj spoke against the supporters of the federation and centralization and in favor of a "sovereign" and "independent" state of Croatia. Vilim Bukšeg, a Social-Democrat, objected to the "Instructions" which spoke of a State Regency because this prejudiced future discussions in favor of a monarchical organization of the state. Otherwise he accepted the proposal.[28] The National Council voted to send a delegation of 28 persons to Belgrade to initiate the discussion with the Serbian representatives, according to the given instructions.

The instructions given the Delegation intended that the final organization of the united state would be set by the Grand National Constituent Assembly of all Serbs, Croats and Slovenes, by a two-thirds majority vote. Such a Constituent Assembly had to meet, at the latest, six months after the conclusion of peace. The Constituent Assembly would have the power to adopt a Constitution, which would define the organization of the state, determine its form (monarchy or republic), list the fundamental laws of the citizens, and designate the state flag and the seat of the government.[29]

Until the Constituent Assembly met, the Delegation was instructed to see that legislative authority be exercised by a State Council to be made up of all members of the National Council (expanded by five members of the Yugoslav Committee), a proportional number of representatives from the Kingdom of Serbia, to be chosen by the Serbian National Assembly in agreement with the Serbian political parties, and a proportional number of Montenegrins, to be chosen by the Montenegrin National Assembly.[30] At its first meeting the State Council of Serbs, Croats and Slovenes would designate the provisional state and maritime flags.

Until the Constituent Assembly adopted a constitution, the ruler's authority would be exercised by the King of Serbia, that is, the heir-apparent Alexander, as Regent of the State of Serbs, Croats and Slovenes. The Regent would be responsible to the State Council and would take an oath before it.

In conformity with the principles of parliamentary rule, the Regent would name the government that would enjoy the confidence of the State Council. The Regent would have the power to initiate legislation. The State Council could not be dissolved prior to the meeting of the Constituent Assembly. The temporary seat of the government and State Council would be reached by an agreement between the Delegation and the Serbian representatives. The State Council's duties would be to hold elections and convoke the Constituent Assembly. The electoral system for the Constituent Assembly would be prepared by the State Council on the basis of universal, equal, proportional and secret right of vote.[31] The "Instructions" contained considerable details on the organization and powers of the central and provincial governments.

By adopting the decision for the union of the State of the Slovenes, Croats and Serbs with Serbia and Montenegro, and the accompanying "Instructimns," the National Council accomplished its principal task. At succeeding meetings, on November 25 and 26, the Central Committee of the National Council discussed such matters as when the Delegation should depart for Belgrade. On November 26, it decided to invite the Croatian People's Peasant Party to designate someone else in place of Stjepan Radić for the Delegation. The invitation was rejected. Few then realized that Radić had assumed a position that would be increasingly attractive to a very large segment of the Croatian electorate.[32]

Apparently the National Council thought that the "Instructions" which were given to the Delegation were sufficient to protect the autonomies of the provinces and their historical borders, to guarantee that the Constituent Assembly would determine the final form of the state by two-thirds of the vote, and to prevent the larger Serbian ethnic group from establishing hegemony over the numerically smaller peoples.

Trumbić was shocked when he heard about the Zagreb decision and knew at once that Croatia would not be able to preserve its individuality or secure equality in the unified state. He also felt that the Croatian diet had made a serious error for not having proclaimed, on October 29, 1918, only the liberation of South Slav lands from Austria-Hungary, and only later, after conditions settled, had undertaken through its representatives of the National Council the discussion of union with Serbia as mutually recognized and equal states. The Croatian diet also erred, Trumbić said, when it transferred its sovereign rights to the National Council in which the unitarist Croats and Slovenes and the Austro-Hungarian Serbs were dominant, and argued that the Croats and Serbs were one people who would rapidly become Yugoslavs.[33]

NATIONAL COUNCIL DELEGATION ARRIVES IN BELGRADE

While the discussions on the union were going on in Zagreb and the Delegation of the National Council was preparing for its all-important journey to Belgrade, Vojvodina (November 25) and Montenegro (November 26) declared their union with Serbia. Each of these events had deep repercussions in both Belgrade and Zagreb and made the urgency of the South Slav union even greater.

On the evening of November 27, the Delegation of the National Council (without Radić) arrived in Zemun, and on the following day it was transported by boat to Belgrade. There it was met by Ministers Momčilo Ninčić, Ljuba Jovanović, and Mayor Marjanović. The Mayor spoke about the historical significance of the occasion and of the great Serbian sacrifices and suffering in touching and patriotic words. His talk was followed by Ante Pavelić, vice president of the National Council of the SCS. He, too, spoke about the many centuries of suffering by the South Slavs whom he represented and added that his group had come to Belgrade to establish with the representatives of Serbia and Montenegro a united state in which every South Slav "tribe" would be guaranteed full equality and freedom.[34]

At the time of the Delegation's arrival, only Regent Alexander and three prominent members of the Radical Party (Stojan Protić, Ljuba Jovanović, Momčilo Ninčić) were in Belgrade. Later Regent Alexander received each delegate individually. On the Regent's request, the first delegate he received was Ante Tresić-Pavičić, a Croat known for his strong commitment to Serbia and her dynasty. He was followed by Pavelić, who told the Regent that the purpose of the Delegation was neither "Great Serbia nor Great Croatia, but a united state" which

would guarantee the individuality of each "tribe." Pribićević was received next, and his audience lasted more than an hour. Afterwards
Pribićević remarked that he could not comment about the details of his
discussion with the Regent.[35] One can assume, however, that Pribićević
promised the Regent that he would seek to expedite the procedures
toward an agreement.

In Belgrade, preparatory to the discussions with the Delegation,
the Regent and Pašić, each for reasons of his own, endeavored to keep
the government of Serbia and the Serbian national assembly (*skupština*)
out of the discussions with the delegation of the National Council. The
Regent and Pašić were also at odds with one another, and because of
this Pašić sent Protić to substitute for him in discussions with the
National Council.[36] Protić and the Regent, especially the latter, were
anxious to proceed with the discussions. Protić was the principal
negotiator with the Delegation of the National Council, but Regent
Alexander was the most important person with whom the delegation
had to deal. The Regent, in fact, in one way or another controlled the
discussions throughout the Belgrade meeting. The absence of Nikola
Pašić from Belgrade very much suited the Regent's purposes. This gave
him the opportunity to stand out as the leading figure in achieving the
national unification of the South Slavs. On more than one occasion the
Regent warned the Delegation that in two or three days he would have
to leave for Paris.[37]

The delegates of the National Council next entered into discussions with the Serbian government and the Serbian political parties.
Two questions had to be agreed upon—how to proclaim the union and
how to organize the first joint government. For this purpose it was
decided to organize a committee of six persons, each side contributing
three persons. The Serbian government was represented by Stojan
Protić, Ljuba Jovanović and Momčilo Ninčić, and the National Council
by Ante Pavelić, Svetozar Pribićević and Josip Smodlaka. The Committee of Six discussed how the act of proclamation of the union should be
done. Initially it was felt that the most just way to do this would be for
the Serbian national assembly to choose a delegation which would at a
joint meeting with the Delegation of the National Council proclaim the
act of union. But this was not possible because a large number of
deputies were abroad.[38]

Since it was felt that the act of unification could not be delayed, the
Committee of Six agreed that the act of unification should be carried
out by having the Delegation of the National Council direct an "Ad-
dress" to Regent Alexander, informing him of the decision of the
National Council which declared the union of the State of the SCS with
Serbia and Montenegro. After this the Regent would respond and in
his response proclaim the unification of Serbia with the State of the
SCS. The representatives of the National Council in the Committee of

Six informed the Delegation about this agreement, and the Delegation selected a Committee of Five to compose the "Address" to the Regent. As for the Regent's response, it was composed by members of the Serbian government (Protić, Jovanović, Ninčić), who met on December 1 with the Committee of Five and read both the "Address" and the Regent's response, making the final editing. They decided to have the ceremony for the proclamation of the union that very evening at 8:00 p.m.[39]

THE ADDRESS AND THE REGENT'S RESPONSE

During the deliberations of the Committee of Five the old differences between the two political groups in the National Council re-emerged. Pavelić, the representative of Starčević's Party of the Right, insisted that the position of the National Council be clearly stated in the "Address" and that it be in conformity with the decision and the instructions of November 24. He wanted the "Address" to emphasize the "state-right of the historical entities," the inviolability of historical borders, the autonomous rights of the provinces, and the ratification of the Regent's proclamation of the unification by the Croatian diet and the Serbian National Assembly. Finally, Pavelić proposed that Trumbić be designated foreign minister in the united government and several additional points.[40]

Svetozar Pribićević, Edo Lukinić, and certain others objected and asked that in order to delay the state union the question of state organization be left for a later discussion.[41] Pribićević sought quick unification because of the grave external threat to the State of the SCS, the necessity for the Yugoslav representatives to be present at the Peace Conference, and because the Regent had to leave for Paris. He did not attach the same importance to the instructions of the National Council that others did. For him they did not constitute "demands" but only the "wishes" of the National Council.

Here it should be added that unlike Pribićević, Pavelić also wanted to delay the drafting of the "Address" and the Regent's response until he consulted with Trumbić by an exchange of telegrams.[42] He dropped this request, however, when Rudolf Giunio, a delegate of the Yugoslav Committee (who had been invited to the meeting), explained that the Yugoslav Committee, and primarily Trumbić, considered an immediate proclamation of the South Slav union a national urgency, and that such a union should be based on the Corfu Declaration, the decision of the Croatian diet, and National Council in Zagreb.[43]

On November 30, a message from the National Council urged the Delegation to seek speedier action in Belgrade.[44] Also, a telegram from the Yugoslav Committee in Paris advised the same and said that Trumbić felt it important to remain in Paris in order to represent the "liberated people" and to press for recognition of the State of the SCS.

It should be noted that the South Slavs of Austria-Hungary were the only nationality not yet recognized by the victorious Allies, and there was real danger that the fate of the South Slavs of the former Habsburg Monarchy would be decided without their participation in the peace conference. The telegram from the Yugoslav Committee advised that the union with Serbia offered a great deal and that the Allied powers should be officially informed who would represent the South Slavs at the peace congress. Only through union would it be possible for the Yugoslavs to protect their interests. Needless to say, Trumbić's advice strengthened Pribićević's position.

To avoid deepening the chasm between Pavelić and Pribićević, Smodlaka proposed that the entire Delegation be involved in drafting the "Address," and the suggestion was adopted. All members of the Delegation, except Pribićević, insisted that the "Address" should cover all essential points of the "Instructions." No doubt the message from Trumbić and the pressure exerted by Protić and Pribićević hastened the agreement among the delegates of the National Council.[45] The final text of the "Address," edited by Pavelić, Pribićević and Smodlaka, represented a compromise between the views of the majority and the minority of the Delegation. The important points of the "Instructions," however, were included in the "Address."[46]

On December 1, 1918, surrounded by three ministers and the highest representatives of the Serbian army, the Regent received the delegates of the National Council. Pavelić read the "Address" which told about the decisions of the National Council on October 19 and November 24 in favor of a union with Serbia and Montenegro, and about the mission of the delegation of the National Council.[47] The "Address" demanded a responsible state government, in accordance with modern parliamentary principles, and a national representation made up of persons to be designated by the National Council and the representatives of the Kingdom of Serbia. It further asked that the national representation exercise legislative power until the meeting of the Constituent Assembly, that the autonomous provincial organs remain in force, but that they be responsible to their autonomous representative bodies (the diet of Croatia and Slavonia, and Dalmatia), and under the control of the central government. The "Address" asked that the permanent organization of the state be established by a Constituent Assembly that would be elected on the basis of a general, equal, and proportional vote. The Constituent Assembly was not to meet later than six months after the conclusion of peace. The "Address" noted that "large and precious" parts of South Slav lands were under Italian occupation, and that the South Slavs wanted to live in friendly relations with Italy. The "Address" also alluded to the fact that the South Slavs could not recognize the London Pact nor other agreements that might violate their national rights, the principle of self-determination, and place their lands under foreign rule.[48]

Special attention was drawn in the "Address" to the fact that the Italians had extended their occupation beyond the demarcation lines established by the armistice agreement, concluded after the South Slav lands of Austria-Hungary had already declared independence. The "Address" expressed hope that His Highness would see to it that the borders of the South Slav state would be drawn in conformity with ethnic lines and on the basis of national self-determination, the principle proclaimed by the Entente Powers.[49]

As a general reaction to the "Address," the Regent expressed his profound joy with the National Council's "historical decisions of November 24," and proceeded to say that he was convinced that he was fulfilling the aspirations of "the best sons of our blood, of all three religions, of all three names, on both sides of the Danube, the Sava and Drina." What has come to be, he said, was the work started by his grandfather Alexander I, and Prince Michael. Finally, in the name of his father, Regent Alexander proclaimed "the union of Serbia with the lands of the independent State of the Slovenes, Croats and Serbs into the united Kingdom of the Serbs, Croats and Slovenes."[50]

The Regent expressed gratitude to all those, including officers and men, who died for the cause of the union and for the Allied support to the South Slavs. He spoke touchingly about Serbia and his father, King Peter, promising the Delegation that he would conduct himself "with love of fraternal heart" toward all three peoples. He said that he fully accepted the wishas of the Delegation and said that his government would at once comply with all requests in regard to the transition period, including the election of the same. The Regent said that he would follow the example of his father and serve as the ruler of "free citizens," that he would always remain loyal to the constitutional, parliamentary and broadly democratic principles, based on the general right of the franchise. He promised to seek the help of the Delegation in the formation of the united government, that the government would be in constant contact first of all with the Delegation, and then with the national representation, and work with it and be responsible to it.[51]

The first task of the government would be, the Regent said, to see that the borders of the state coincided with the ethnic borders of the South Slav people. In this connection he expressed faith in the justice of the Allies. The Regent uttered a conviction that the work of liberation would not be impaired by leaving some Yugoslavs under foreign rule, and hoped that Italy would be guided by the same democratic principles and would find friendly neighborly relations better than the insistence on implementation of the London Pact, which the South Slavs neither signed nor recognized.[52]

SUPPORTERS AND CRITICS OF THE PROCLAMATION

Immediately after the proclamation of the union on December 1, 1918, disagreements surfaced over the manner in which the union was carried out, and the character of the state organization. While some individuals considered the Regent's proclamation inviolable, for others it was no more than a political manifesto. The Centralists considered it to have binding force on all legislators, including the future Constituent Assembly, but the federalists denied it such power.[53] The members of the Croat-Serbian Coalition who had agitated for a quick proclamation and union with Serbia hailed the unification as a great achievement. Since they contributed the most to the Act of December 1, the Coalitionists, headed by Pribićević, were now its staunchest supporters. For them the Proclamation Act had decided the form of government for the united state.[54]

The Starčević Party of the Right lauded the "Address," and the Regent's response. In a special declaration, issued on December 12, it commended the members of the Delegation, especially Ante Pavelić (not the same as the World War II fascist leader), the Party's president. The Party hailed the liberation and unification of the Croat, Serb and Slovene "people" into "a democratically formed state." It abandoned its erstwhile republicanism because that concept was shown to have been "a cover for anarchist, Bolshevik and separatist groups," and its ideas to have been detrimental to "our young freedom" and disastrous to the Croat and Slovene cause.[55] An increasing number of followers of the Starčević's Party, however, soon became disenchanted with what had been done in Belgrade and joined the ranks of Radić and Frank followers.

The most vocal critic of the act of December 1 was Stjepen Radić, head of the Croatian Republican Peasant Party;[56] he was not against Yugoslavia as a state but wanted its federalization.[57] For Radić, the Regent's Proclamation was not a legally binding act and the Kingdom of Croatia, Slavonia and Dalmatia had not ceased to exist.[58] He launched a war against the state centralization and Serbian hegemony. He rejected the monarchy, which the people did not choose, and at the meeting of February 2, 1919, changed the name of his party by including the word "Republican" in it.

The Frank Party of the Right, which had been on the verge of extinction when Austria-Hungary collapsed, came to life and gained supporters after the Proclamation Act. On December 2 the leaders of Frank's Party of the Right issued a declaration which was disseminated throughout Croatia. The declaration stated that the Party had decided for the union of the Slovenes, Croats and Serbs in expectation that it would be carried out on the basis of the free will of the entire people. This principle, the declaration stated, was included in the "Address" to the Regent, but the Regent ignored it in his response. Instead the

Croats lost their sovereignty when the rule in the new state was vested in the Serbian monarchy. The South Slavs were denied the right of self-determination and an opportunity to express their will.[59] The destiny of the Croatian nation, the declaration said, was decided without the participation of the Croatian diets of "Croatia, Dalmatia, Bosnia-Hercegovina, and Istria," and that this same participation was denied to the Slovene representative bodies and to the Serbian National Assembly.

Frank's Party of the Right complained that many of the 28 delegates of the National Council sent to Belgrade were not even elected deputies. The Frankovci, however, insisted that they were not against South Slaviunification. At least formally they stood for the union of all Croat lands into a republican state, that would be included in the "federation" of a free, independent and sovereign state of Slovenes, Croats and Serbs.

Other critics of the union were the Social-Democrats, who later turned Communists; they rejected the Proclamation Act for its "reactionary" character and for the "undemocratic" manner by which it was made. They saw the whole thing as a conspiracy of the middle class "oligarchic clique" that had close ties with Regent Alexander.[60]

The opposition to the established regime was formidable from the very beginning, and even led to violence. The most dramatic act of opposition occurred in Zagreb shortly after the Act of Proclamation, when, on December 5, 1918, a bloody clash occurred on Jelačić Square (Independence Square) between the units of former Austro-Hungarian army (25th Homeguard Regiment and 53rd Infantry Regiment), which had accepted the new government, and an armed unit of "Sokols" and sailors organized by the National Council at the end of October. The Serbian troops kept their distance and were not involved in the fray. According to the official figures 13 persons were killed and 17 wounded. The incident resulted in immediate repercussions throughout the country and was reported in the foreign press. The Italian papers interpreted it as a conflict between Serbian regulars and Croatian irregulars, and as a product of the Croat "Yugoslavs" against the "Serbian rule."[61] The Hungarian press saw it as a manifestation of the Croat dissatisfaction with the new political order.

The press reported that the soldiers shouted in favor of the republic and denounced the Serbian monarchy. Some blamed the clash on the "Bolsheviks" and still others on the "separatists." One newspaper reported that the soldiers were Bolshevik inspired and that those involved in the provocative action were bent on plunder.[62] Witnesses noted that the soldiers sought "Red Banners" to march with and that they had planned a putsch. Some described the soldiers as an "Austrophile" and an "anti-Serbian element."[63] What is definitely established is that the soldiers carried Croatian flags and shouted Croatian patriotic

slogans, and that there were among them some who were later identified with Croatian separatism. Members of the "Green Cadre" participated in the demonstration. Willfully or otherwise, some observers
had detected socialist and "Bolshevik" influence on the soldier demon-
strators. It would appear that both nationalist and socialist elements
figured in the abortive soldiers' movement.

Following this bloody clash, the National Council of the SCS established a military court to try the eleven leaders of the soldiers. Many
witnesses testified at the trial which lasted from December 27, 1918, to
January 6, 1919. On January 6, 1919, the Military Court meted out
varying sentences to twenty-three of the accused.

One consequence of the December 5 incident was the disbanding
of an unreliable army which the National Council had organized with
great difficulties. In agreement with the National Council, a military
mission was sent from Serbia which, together with the military section
of the National Council, reorganized the armed forces. A new army was
organized around the Yugoslav legions sent from Serbia. Although the
new army proved reliable, the disbanding of the old army became still
another source of discontent with and agitation against the state.[64]

FORMATION OF THE UNITED GOVERNMENT

In the meantime steps were taken to implement the provisions of
the Proclamation at once. Pribićević and Pavelić issued a statement
in Belgrade, on December 3, in the name of the Presidency of the
National Council. Pribićević was primarily responsible for the proclamation, signed by him, Pavelić and General Pešić.[65] The statement
reviewed the steps taken at the Belgrade discussions and summarized
the contents of the Regent's Proclamation and then declared that the
National Council, as the supreme sovereign authority of the State of
the SCS on the territory of former Austria-Hungary, had ceased to
exist. It further stated that until the united government was formed the
administrative function would be exercised by the presidency of the
National Council in agreement with the Serbian government.[66]

The Delegation continued for a time to function as a government
for the lands in the State of the SCS, although it had no legal power to
do so. When the State of the SCS had ceased to exist, the National
Council as supreme organ of authority in that State also ended.
Moreover, the Delegation was not entrusted with governmental power
either by the plenum or the Central Committee of the National
Council.

Trumbić proposed that the narrower cabinet—Pašić, Korošec,
Trumbić—be entrusted with questions of foreign affairs, that is, to
represent the new state at the Peace Conference. Only by the union of
the South Slavs of former Austria-Hungary with Serbia could the
Yugoslav cause be effectively presented at the Peace Conference. This

also was the reason why Trumbić wanted the foreign minister to be a person from former Austria-Hungary, agreeing in turn that Pašić serve as the head of the government.[67] Trumbić agreed to participate in the government until the conclusion of the peace. He urged the appointment of experts to various commissions such as military and naval commissions, and recommended that the *vojvoda* Mišić be designated as the head of the Military commission.[68]

The discussion on the composition of the united government was conducted between twelve members of the National Council and the representatives of the new Serbian government, recently formed with Pašić at the helm. Their first decision was that the united government should consist of ten persons from former Austria-Hungary, nine from Serbia and one from Montenegro, and be distributed by parties. It was agreed that the prime ministry should go to a member of the largest Serbian party.[69] The united government was formed on December 20, 1918, after nearly three weeks of wrangling and bargaining. Delay was also caused by the Regent's refusal to accept Pašić to head the government. Instead, Stojan Protić, a leading member of the Radical Party and friend of Pašić, was designated prime minister. Most of the political groups were represented in what was a coalition government. Only those groups, including Radić's Croatian People's Peasant Party, which did not accept the Corfu Declaration and the Proclamation of December 1 were left out of the government.

Two days after the formation of the government, the Ministerial Council of the new state extended the provisions of the Serbian 1903 constitution to the entire territory of the Kingdom of the SCS and created a separate commission (A. Kramer, M. Trifković, V. Korać) to draft a temporary constitution. When the constitution commission completed its job, the Ministerial Council, on January 30, 1919, adopted the temporary constitution it had proposed. The constitution was published ten days later under the title "Temporary Constitution of the Kingdom of the SCS." On the basis of the authority of the Regent, and in accordance with Article 130, the Constitution had to be submitted for "legal approval" to the National Representation, as soon as it met.

When Pribićević and Korošec informed Trumbić, then in Paris, about the Proclamation Act, he responded on December 7 that the Yugoslav Committee did not approve the move toward centralization, but in view of "the present situation," the Committee would give the delegates in Belgrade a free hand with full confidence that they would act responsibly. Should they fail to reach a satisfactory agreement with the Serbian representatives, Trumbić suggested that the National Council should then retain power. In any case, the arrangement proclaimed by the Regent should be provisional and exist only until the meeting of the Constituent Assembly.

Trumbić counselled the Delegation to proceed with caution, to make all agreements conditional, and to seek a government made up of the heads of parties, although able non-party leaders might also be included. By including the heads of the Serbian opposition parties into the government, he thought that the "Yugoslav" position in the government would be strengthened. Trumbić had hoped that despite the Serbian aspirations for hegemony, the Constituent Assembly would establish a rightful place in the new state for the Croats, Serbs and Slovenes. He recommended that a person from former Austria-Hungary be designated foreign minister because of the importance of the South Slav question. The Yugoslav Committee also requested that all diplomatic agents abroad be instantly presented to the foreign governments as representatives of the Serbs, Croats and Slovenes. Trumbić accepted the composition of the delegation to the peace conference (Pašić-Trumbić-Korošec) and agreed to join the government himself, insisting, however, that the foreign minister should be a person from the territory of former Austria-Hungary.[70]

Between December 20, 1918, and June 28, 1921, the provisional government of the Kingdom of the Serbs, Croats and Slovenes had as its main task the implementation of the Proclamation of December 1. By March 16, 1919, a temporary national representation (*Privremeno narodno predstavništvo*) was formed. Its function was to adopt the law for the election of deputies to the Constituent Assembly. The latter was elected on November 28, 1920, and after lengthy and often passionate deliberations, the Vidovdan Constitution was adopted on June 28, 1921.

CONCLUSION

The controversy over the Proclamation Act and the form of the Yugoslav state survived and was for years a source of the country's instability. It is understandable that many Croats and certain other ethnic groups should be disappointed in the way the Yugoslav unification was carried out and in the nature of the Yugoslav state. The reasons for this can be found in an unequal position of the negotiating parties.

The formal discussions that led to the proclamation of the Kingdom of the Serbs, Croats and Slovenes were conducted, in terms of politics, between two unequal partners. In 1918 Serbia was at the zenith of its prestige. Its government, armed forces and dynasty enjoyed unprecedented popularity. Its armies had scored one success after another in driving the enemy from their country. The Serbs everywhere rejoiced over their people's military and political successes. They knew that the Serbs sacrificed in human and material resources for union more than other South Slavs. The costly victory gave the Serbs a sense of pride and confidence that if Yugoslavia were not realized they were sure that a "Great Serbia" would be, through the acquisition of the South Slav provinces which were wholly or preponderantly Serbian. It is understandable that the Serbian representatives should be apprehensive about losing something they had (Serbia) for something tenuous and beset with deep-seated internal problems (Yugoslavia).

While the Serbs of former Austria-Hungary shared Serbia's successes with equal exuberance, and gloried in them, the other South Slavs, except those among them who were committed to the Serbs and fought in the Serbian army, could not share those sentiments with the same intensity. Moreover, the Yugoslav Committee, which operated abroad and which stood for a genuine Yugoslav program, lacked an organized popular following among their people in Austria-Hungary. As for the South Slav political leaders in Austria-Hungary, nearly all of them remained loyal to the Habsburg Crown until the final months of the war. The political parties and groups, in and outside of the representative institutions (e.g., Croatian diet, Austrian Parliament), did not take a firm stand for a completely independent South Slav State until the demise of Austria-Hungary. When the State of the SCS was proclaimed, it was a weak structure in the throes of religious and social unrest. While the Serbian representatives could speak from a position of strength, the representatives of the State of the SCS could not. In considering the union, the latter had much to gain and little to lose by demanding the union of the State of the SCS with Serbia on a democratic and egalitarian basis.

But whatever the complaints by those who objected to the Proclamation Act of December 1, the fact is in 1918 nearly everyone was for Yugoslavia. Even the Communists and the Croat nationalists who were powerful critics of the Yugoslav state did not reject the idea of Yugoslav unity. But they did not want the Kingdom of the Serbs, Croats and Slovenes and called it an artificial Versailles creation and the "Versailles Yugoslavia." The Communists were the first to employ these terms.[71] Actually, the independent state of Yugoslavia emerged before the Paris Peace Conference and the Versailles peace settlement,[72] and in accordance with the will of its people. The well-known Serbian geographer, Jovan Cvijić, observed that the Western Allies could do no more than to confirm the existence of the South Slav State and to recognize it.[73] The South Slavs were aware of their ethnic kinship[74] and wished to band together for common security.

The unification of the South Slavs was undeniably a development of momentous importance, a fulfillment of dreams of many of the best South Slav thinkers and writers. For the first time in their history the South Slavs were brought into a single state. To bring together a number of provinces and kingdoms with varying historical experiences, separate languages, religions, cultures and institutions posed many problems, some of which are still present. These problems were compounded by unfriendly neighbors which claimed parts of the new country.

Nonetheless, the first Yugoslavia gave the South Slav peoples an opportunity to learn to live together. Despite the powerful legacy of divisiveness, aggravated by new centrifugal tendencies, the Yugoslav solidarity grew steadily stronger. The Communist leaders of the Second World War recognized this when they announced that they would wage a struggle in the name of "brotherhood and unity" (*bratsvo i jedinstvo*) and chose the well-known Slav hymn (*Ej Sloveni*) as their anthem.[75]

Notes

1. For details, see Ferdo Čulinović, *Riječka država* (Zagreb, 1953), p. 42ff. Ferdo Čulinović, *Jugoslavija izmedju dva rata*, I (Zagreb, 1961), pp. 104–106. On the Italian threat in the period from October 29, 1918, to December 1, 1918, Ivo Banac, *The National Question in Yugoslavia's Formative Period: 1918–1921* (Ph.D. Dissertation, Stanford University, 1975), pp. 279–280. Bogdan Krizman, "Vanjskopolitički položaj Kraljevine Srba, Hrvata i Slovenaca godine 1919." *Časopis za suvremenu povijest*, II (Zagreb, 1970), pp. 23–28. The Italian occupation was checked by the establishment of the British, U.S., and French zones of occupation on the Adriatic littoral. Actually, the United States was the only power that undertook to curb the Italian territorial aggrandizement. See Dragan R. Živojinović, *America, Italy and the Birth of Yugoslavia (1917–1919)* (Boulder, Colorado: *East European Quarterly*, 1972), pp. 203–206, 245. For the reaction of the State of the Slovenes, Croats and Serbs and Zagreb's National Council to the Italian occupation, see: Bogdan Krizman, "'Narodno vijeće Slovenaca, Hrvata i Srba' u Zagrebu i talijanska okupacija na Jadranu 1918. Godine, Gradja o vanjskoj politici Predsjedništva Narodnog vijeća SHS od 29. X do 1. XII 1918," *Anali Jadranskog instituta JAZU* (Zagreb, 1956), pp. 83–116.

2. Andrej Mitrović, "Italija i stvaranje Jugoslavije 1918 god.," *Naučni skup u povodu 50-godišnjice raspada Austro-Ugarske monarhije i stvaranja Jugoslavenske države* (Zagreb, 1969), p. 269.

3. I.J. Lederer, *Yugoslavia at the Paris Peace Conference* (New Haven, 1963), pp. 71–75.

4. Bogdan Krizman (ed.), *Korespondencije Stjepana Radića*, 2 vols. (Zagreb, 1972), pp. 186–187, 256–257.

5. Atif Purivatra, "Formiranje Jugoslovenske Muslimanske organizacije," *Istorija XX veka: Zbornik radova IX* (Belgrade, 1968), pp. 393–394. *Rezultati popisa žiteljstva u BiH od 10. oktobra 1910.*, Sarajevo 1912., 58–60.

6. Bogdan Krizman, "O odjecima Oktobarske revolucije u zelenom kaderu," *Historijski zbornik* X, No. 1–4 (Zagreb, 1957), pp. 149–157. Ferdo Chulinovich, *Otkliki Oktiabria v iugoslavianskikh zemliakh* (Moscow, 1967). See Bogdan Krizman, "Gradja o nemirima u Hrvatskoj na kraju g. 1918.," *Historijski zbornik* X., No. 1–4 (Zagreb, 1957), pp. 11–129. Important collections of sources on "Green Cadre" have been published: See Josip I. Vidmar, "Prilozi gradji za povijest 1917–1918 s osobitim obzirom na razvoj radničkog pokreta i odjeka Oktobarske revolucije kod nas," *Arhivski vjesnik* I, No. 1 (Zagreb, 1958), pp. 11–173; "Prilozi gradji za historiju radničkog pokreta i KPJ 1919 god.," *Arhivski vjesnik* (Zagreb), II/1959, 2, 7–227; Josip Paver, *Zbornik gradje za povijest radničkog pokreta i KPJ 1919–1920: Dvor, Glina, Ivanić-Grad, Kostajnica, Jutina,*

Novska, Petrinja, Sisak (Sisak, 1970). Edmund Glaise-Horstenau, *Die Katastrophe-Zertrümmerung Österreich-Ungarn und des Werden* (Leipzig, 1939), p. 248 ff.

7. Milivoje Erić, *Agrarna Reforma u Jugoslaviji 1918–1941 god.* (Sarajevo, 1958), p. 143.

8. A Lebl, "Prilog istoriji agrarne reforme u Vojvodini 1781–1941," *Zadružni arhiv,* (Novi Sad, 1953), p. 60.

9. *Jugoslovenski ekonomista* (Zagreb), February 8, 1919.

10. *Socialistički pokret u Vojvodini 1890–1919* (Novi Sad, 1953), pp. 231–232. Erić, p. 146.

11. Bogumil Hrabak, "Zapisnik Temišvarskog narodnog veća," *Zbornik Matice Srpske,* No. 10 (1955).

12. Atif Purivatra, *Jugoslavenska muslimanska organizacija* (hereafter cited as *JMO*). (Sarajevo, 1974), p. 35.

13. Purivatra, *JMO,* p. 35.

14. Purivatra, *JMO,* p. 36.

15. Lieutenant Colonel Simović was later prominent as a General in the staging of the March 27, 1941 *Putsch* that led to the Axis invasion of Yugoslavia.

16. Dragoslav Janković and Bogdan Krizman, *Gradja o stvaranju jugoslovenske države,* II (Belgrade, 1964), p. 576. See also B. Krizman, "Izvještaji D. T. Simovića, delegata srpske Vrhovne komande kod vlade Narodnog vijeća SHS g. 1918," *Historijski zbornik,* VIII (1955), p. 123–124.

17. Janković and Krizman, *Gradja o stvaranju jugoslovenske države,* II, p. 430.

18. Svetozar Pribićević, *La Dictature du Roi Alexandre* (Paris, 1933), pp. 39–40.

19. Bogdan Krizman, "Zapisnici Središnjeg odbora Narodnóg vijeća Slovenaca, Hrvata i Srba u Zagrebu," *Starine JAZU,* Vol. 48, p. 107. Čulinović, I, pp. 106–107.

20. Ante Smith-Pavelić, *Dr. Ante Trumbić* (München, 1959), p. 203.

21. Ferdo Šišić, *Dokumenti o postanku Kraljevine SHS* (Zagreb, 1920), p. 267.

22. *Ibid.*

23. Smith-Pavelić, p. 200.

24. Čulinović, I, pp. 111–112. Šišić, *Dokumenti,* p. 271.

25. Janković and Krizman, *Gradja o stvaranju jugoslovenske države,* II, pp. 644–646.

26. Čulinović, I, p. 116. Šišić, *Dokumenti,* pp. 274–275.

27. Čulinović, pp. 159–160.

28. Janković and Krizman, *Gradja o stvaranju jugoslovenske država,* II, pp. 644–646. Srdjan Budisavljević, *Stvaranje država Srba, Hrvata i Slovenaca* (Zagreb, 1958), p. 159.

29. Budisavljević, p. 158. Čulinović, I, pp. 116–117. Šišić, *Dokumenti,* pp. 275–276.

30. Budisavljević, p. 158.

31. Budisavljević, p. 158. Čulinović, I, p. 117. Šišić, *Dokumenti,* pp. 275–276.

32. Čulinović, I, pp. 118–119. Šišić, *Dokumenti,* p. 279.

33. Smith-Pavelić, pp. 213, 223.

34. Čulinović, I, p. 151. Srdjan Budisavljević, *Stvaranje države Srba, Hrvata i Slovenaca,* p. 171. *Glas SHS,* No. 259, November 30, 1918.

35. Smith-Pavelić, p. 215.

36. Smith-Pavelić, p. 216.

37. Čulinović, I, pp. 141–142.

38. Budisavljević, *Stvaranje,* p. 171. Smith-Pavelić, p. 217. Čulinović, I, pp. 141–142.

39. Smith-Pavelić, p. 217.

40. Smith-Pavelić, p. 217.

41. Čulinović, I, p. 142.

42. Ante Smith-Pavelić, *Dr. Ante Trumbić,* p. 218.

43. Smith-Pavelić, p. 219.

44. Smith-Pavelić, p. 220. Krizman, "Narodno vijeće," pp. 112–113. Čulinović, I, pp. 142–143.

45. Čulinović, I, p. 143.

46. Smith-Pavelić, pp. 218–219.

47. Smith-Pavelić, p. 221.

48. Šišić, *Dokumenti,* pp. 280–282. Čulinović, I, p. 144. Budisavljević, pp. 172–173.

49. *Ibid.*

50. Čulinović, I, pp. 145–146. Šišić, *Dokumenti,* pp. 282–283.

51. *Ibid.*

52. *Ibid.*

53. Čulinović, I, p. 147.

54. Čulinović, I, p. 147.

55. Čulinović, I, p. 154. Šišić, *Dokumenti,* pp. 285–286.

56. Bogdan Krizman, "Hrvatske stranke prema ujedinjenju i stvaranju Jugoslavenske države," in Aleksandar Acković (ed.), *Politički život Jugoslavije, 1914–1945* (Belgrade, 1973), p. 124.

57. Čulinović, p. 40.

58. Čulinović, I, p. 148.

59. Čulinović, I, p. 157.

60. Čulinović, I, p. 148.

61. *Obzor*, December 11, 1918. *Bilancia* (Rijeka). Čulinović, I, p. 160.

62. *Obzor*, No. 277, December 7, 1918, No. 278, December 8, 1918, and following issues. Čulinović, I, p. 162.

63. Čulinović, I, pp. 166–167.

64. Čulinović, I, pp. 168–169.

65. Čulinović, I, pp. 151–153.

66. Čulinović, I, pp. 151–153. Momčilo Zečević, "Slovenačke političke stranke prema štvaranju jugoslavenske države," in Aleksandar Acković (ed.), *Politički život Jugoslavije, 1914–1945* (Belgrade, 1973), p. 167. Smith-Pavelić, p. 223. Krizman, "Zapisnici," p. 383.

67. Smith-Pavelić, pp. 224–225.

68. Čulinović, pp. 155–156. Smith-Pavelić, 244–245.

69. Smith-Pavelić, p. 225.

70. A. Smith-Pavelić, *Dr. Ante Trumbić*, pp. 224–225. Čulinović, I, pp. 155–156.

71. Jovan Marjanović, "Jugoslavija 1918 i socijalistička revolucija 1941–1945," *Naučni skup u povodu 50-godišnjice raspada Austro-Ugarske monarhije i stvaranja Jugoslavenske države* (Zagreb, 1969), pp. 101–108.

72. Marjanović, "Jugoslavija 1918 . . . ," pp. 101–108. Čulinović, "Raspad . . . ," p. 42.

73. Čubrilović, "Istorijski osnovi . . . ," p. 85.

74. Čubrilović, "Istorijski osnovi . . . ," pp. 61–62. Čulinović, "Raspad . . . ," pp. 56–57. Čulinović, "Raspad . . . ," p. 44.

75. Čubrilović, "Istorijski osnovi . . . ," pp. 61–62. Čulinović, I, p. 150.

The 1919–1920 Peace Conference in Paris and the Yugoslav State: An Historical Evaluation

Andrej Mitrović

THE LITERATURE CONCERNING Yugoslavia at the Paris Peace Conference is rather voluminous.[1] There are two general studies, most of the important sources are published, and specific and detailed research dealing with the problem of frontiers and the Montenegrin question exists. Some topics need further analysis, however, as for example the problem of war indemnity. In addition, we still lack a work which evaluates the significance of the Conference with regard to the Yugoslav state in general. I shall try and offer such an evaluation in a condensed form.

The Yugoslav state appeared for the first time at an international meeting during the 1919–1920 Peace Conference. This fact is by itself significant. Even more importantly the Conference dealt with legal stipulations which ended the first World War and laid the foundations for future political relations in Europe. The Kingdom of Serbs, Croats and Slovenes was internationally approved on that occasion and began participation in international politics. This recognition confirmed the Kingdom's first step in the world of international relations and made it the subject and object of international politics. At the same time the new state had to deal with international affairs exclusive of the conference itself, from 1919 to June 1920.

PROBLEMS OF THE YUGOSLAV STATE ON THE EVE OF THE CONFERENCE

Among the participants of the Peace Conference, Yugoslavia distinguished itself by the magnitude of problems and questions relating to its formation which had to be solved. This placed the new state in a most difficult situation.

At Paris, the Yugoslav state participated in the most important part of the peace negotiations only de facto. The presence of the Yugoslavs was tolerated by the other powers but de jure recognition was withheld. The majority of these powers and the Conference itself hesitated for a number of months before recognizing the new state. The reason for this policy stemmed from Italy's refusal to accept the situation created on the Eastern shores of the Adriatic and the obligations of France and

Great Britain towards Italy, resulting from the 1915 London Pact. The de facto participation of the Yugoslav state in the Conference was based on Serbia's war alliance with the coalition of victors. For that reason, the delegation of the new state worked during the first months in Paris as the Serbian contingent although it was made up of Serbo-Croatian-Slovenian representatives. The delegation nevertheless considered itself to be Yugoslav and presented itself as the representative of the new state.

To fully understand this situation one must realize that the majority of the powers were inclined towards recognition of Yugoslav unification. During the last months of the war, the United States had already declared itself in favor of unification and had de facto accepted the appearance of the new state. The United States finally internationally recognized it at the beginning of February 1919 (the first among the powers to do so). France and Great Britain took a more ambiguous position: obviously they did not deny the reality of Yugoslav existence. They did, however, delay recognition for some time. Although the considerations toward Italy played a significant role, the lack of detailed studies precludes a full understanding of the reasons for such an attitude. Japan was essentially interested, although its attitude deserves more profound study as well. The only power resolutely opposed to the recognition of Yugoslavia was Italy, which hoped to prevent Yugoslavia from acquiring the regions on the Eastern Adriatic which were in the domain of Italian territorial aspirations. It should be kept in mind, however, that Italy was the weakest and least influential among the big powers.

The result was a legally awkward situation in which official protocol listed the "delegation of Serbia" as participants while that same body labeled itself the "delegation of the Kingdom of Serbs, Croats and Slovenes." The Conference addressed itself to the "delegation of Serbia" and received answers from the "delegation of the Kingdom of Serbs, Croats and Slovenes." It was only at the end of May 1919 that the Conference officially mentioned the "delegation of SCS" in its documents. At the beginning of June, France and Great Britain recognized the Yugoslav state and the entire question was removed from the agenda with the signing of the Versailles Peace Treaty on June 28th. Reference to the "Delegation of the Kingdom of Serbs, Croats and Slovenes" appeared in the text of the treaty. Italy, however, still refused to acknowledge the new state.

The Yugoslav state, then, had to wait rather a long time to obtain recognition from the Peace Conference. This situation weakened substantially the Yugoslav position during the very important phases of negotiation. The Yugoslav delegation suffered an additional psychological burden and found it necessary to spend a great deal of time and energy obtaining international definition of its position. This fact lends credence to the idea that Yugoslavia was not an accidental formation of the victors. The Yugoslav state was the result of the process which was based on the Yugoslav movement and was developed indigenously. The powers accepted the situation which appeared as a fait accompli resulting from the war only after hesitation.

Subsequently, Yugoslavia shared the destiny of secondary or smaller powers and, in spite of the rank attributed to Serbia for her war participation, was essentially pushed out of those committees of the conference in which decisions were made. The Yugoslav delegation was not informed about the direction of negotiations concerning questions in which Yugoslavia was directly interested. Yugoslavia was the only country in permanent and acute conflict with one of the great powers. This conflict concerned territorial matters. Regardless of the fact that Italy was weak itself at that moment, it played a significant role by participating in solutions which affected Yugoslavia. Italy was able, therefore, to influence decisions concerning the Italo-Yugoslav dispute.

All the frontier questions with the exception of the frontiers with Greece remained open. Yugoslavia had pending disputes with six of the seven neighboring countries among which two were members of the coalition of the victors. Both of these countries possessed secret treaties from the war years. In these treaties they were promised territories settled by Yugoslavs (Italy through the London Pact of April 26, 1915; Romania through the Bucharest Treaty of August 17, 1916). Parallel to this, the question of the Montenegrin state remained open for some time and King Nicholas, supported by his followers, constantly tried to obtain a seat at the conference. These attempts were unsuccessful but added to the complexities of the situation. The payment of the war indemnity was of extreme importance for the economic stabilization upset by the war and still contending with a non-developed economy inherited from the past. At the same time, the question had a political meaning due to the decision that the former parts of the defunct Habsburg Monarchy pay indemnities directly to Serbia. Such a decision could only contribute to internal frictions in the Yugoslav state. Finally, provisions for protection of minorities, which became part of the Saint Germain Peace Treaty, were regarded by the leaders of the new Kingdom as a limitation of sovereignty. This was understandable as the country was in fact multinational, with certain specifics granted to Serbs, Croats and Slovenes only.

The delegation of the first Yugoslav state was faced with all of these problems, making its task even more difficult. This may explain the Yugoslav dissatisfaction with the conference's activity and decisions. In the spring of 1919 the Yugoslav delegates discussed the possibility of withdrawing from the Peace Conference. Yugoslavia hesitated for four months before signing the Saint Germain Peace Treaty.

TERRITORIAL DELIMITATION AS THE CENTRAL ISSUE

Territorial settlements were essential for the new country. There was a total of six such settlements which attracted the primary attention of the delegation in Paris and the government in Belgrade. These problems caused profound dissatisfaction among the Yugoslav delegates with the work and solutions of the conference. At the same time, the Yugoslavs were considered intransigent, even imperialistic, by the representatives of the great powers and by the French, Italian and British press. Of major importance was the territorial conflict with Italy. These territorial questions also provoked internal dissension in the delegation as well as some disagreements between the Yugoslav delegation in Paris and the government in Belgrade.

The Yugoslav representatives brought to Paris a project for territorial settlement, with detailed justification elaborated by the Serbian government. However, the delegates representing non-Serbian regions made serious objections to this project. In spite of this, at the beginning of 1919 the project served as a basis of new frontier demands elaborated in detail during the spring of 1919.

The concept espoused by the Yugoslav delegation was based on multifaceted principles. The principle of nationality was given priority, combined with the principle of ethnicity. In regard to the former, the accent was placed on the population conscious of its nationality. In regard to the latter the accent was placed on the population's ethnic origin and characteristics. Based on this ethnicity, the right to annex some peoples of Slavic although not Yugoslav origin was stressed (Ruthenians and Slovaks). Later, the strategic and geographic principles, two interrelated concepts, were applied. The strategic principle was based upon military and defensive criteria while the geographic principle dealt with the idea of natural frontier configurations. Special significance was attributed to the historical principle which dealt with the importance a certain region had for a particular Yugoslav nation in the past. The economic principle was applied by pointing to the economic interests of a region. All of the claims presented were supported by a combination of the above principles. The claims were also supported with the assertion that Yugoslav politics were guided by "justice and morals" and that Serbia deserved rewards for her role in the war and for the fact that she signed no secret treaties.

These principles were approached firstly in terms of the right of the victor. Secondly, it was argued that a strong and large Yugoslavia was necessary for the allies in order to prevent revisionistic disturbances on the part of the defeated nations. Thirdly, it was argued that the Yugoslav state was the only legitimate representative of the Yugoslavs as well as of all the Slavic populations dispersed throughout South-Eastern Europe. In this framework, Pašić followed the line that

Serbia was the only possible representative of all the Serbs, regardless of where they were settled in the Balkans.

The Yugoslav delegation was, however, divided with regard to priorities when applying these principles. For Pašić, the national principle was the most important one, because it was profitable and responsible to basic Yugoslav territorial claims. For Trumbić, as well as for Smodlaka, the application of this principle meant the best protection from Italian territorial pretensions and both, therefore, attempted to apply it with regard to other Yugoslav claims as well. Professor Cvijić thought that the national principle must be connected to the ethnical principle, but must also be supported by geographical and historical facts. General Pešić was in favor of the application of the strategic principle.

The first official Yugoslav demands concerning frontiers included territories behind the line which started from the former Serbo-Bulgarian-Greek frontier junction in the South and after crossing the river Struma followed the course of that river towards the North passing to the west of Sofia, somewhere between the Bulgarian capital and the former Serbian frontier, including the city of Vidin. After crossing the Danube, the frontier line proceeded through the Banat some 35 km from Bela Crkva and 40 km from Vršac. This line reached the river Tamiš at Arad, 65 km to the east of Temeşoara. From there the projected frontier turned at a right angle towards the West and, following the Tamiš and Mura rivers, stretched north of Subotica, omitting Segedin, Pečuj, Sigetvar, and Velika Kanjiža to Lendava. The line then turned north along the river Rab and reached the former Austrian and Hungarian border line. Turning further towards the south-west the line then descended to the Mura, thereby including Maribor, Celovec and Beljak. Finally, the line followed the former Austro-Italian frontier to the Adriatic, thereby including Trieste.

Later these demands were partially revised. By February 1919 Trieste and the entire area of Baranja were tacitly abandoned. The Croatian and Dalmatian Coast, and to some extent the Banat around Temeşoara, on the other hand, were stubbornly defended. In May 1919 some of the demands concerning Baranja were renewed. These demands were further enlarged in the fall to include Pečuj and the frontier on the river Meček. Simultaneously, the demands for Northern Bačka and Baja were presented.

The Peace Conference accepted some frontier rectification on behalf of the Kingdom of SCS towards Bulgaria. It divided the Banat along a diagonal line going from South-East to North-West, so that Bela Crkva, Vršac and Kikinda remained on the Yugoslav side while Temeşoara and Arad remained on the Romanian side. The Conference drew the frontier line south of the Tamiš river towards Hungary, leaving Subotica to the Kingdom of SCS but rejected Yugoslav claims to Baja. Baranja was divided in such a way that Mohač remained in Hungary; the middle course of the river Drava became the frontier. Prekomurje was added to the Kingdom of SCS, as was Maribor, while a plebiscite decided the fate of Koruška. Although the Peace Conference confirmed the 1913 Albanian frontier, the question of the Italo-Yugoslav frontier problems where the great powers were involved, with the exception of the territorial dispute with Italy, was solved. Related to this dispute, attempts were later made to compensate one or the other side to the detriment of Albania. As one can see, the Yugoslav territorial demands were not fully satisfied, but were completely rejected only in regard to Albania. They were partially accepted with regard to Bulgaria and Austria and the solution concerning the Banat of Temeşoara was reached only after Yugoslavia was pressured by the Supreme Council of the Conference.

There were also disagreements among the Yugoslav delegates concerning the frontiers. The primary conflicts were between the Serbian and Croatian groups. The first clash among them occurred in the second half of January 1919, when Trumbić and Smodlaka expressed the opinion that too much had been asked on the east, northeast and north, thus weakening the position of the demands on the West. A part of the Serb delegation, led by M. Boškovic, estimated that the stubborn attitude in protecting western frontiers weakened the eastern and northeastern side, which, according to this group, were of primary importance. New disputes and clashes occurred in the summer of 1919. Pašić was for a long time of the opinion that both directions, west and east, had to be defended with the same vigor. In January 1920, however, influenced by the British and French delegations, Pašić tried without the knowledge of his fellow delegates to obtain Scutari by sacrificing Rijeka.

THE FOUNDATION OF THE FOREIGN POLICY OF YUGOSLAVIA

The policy of Yugoslavia at the Paris Peace Conference determined its foreign affairs for some time to come. Conversely, the decisions of the conference determined Yugoslavia's international status.

a) *The establishment of the long-standing components of Yugoslav foreign policy.*

At the Peace Conference Yugoslavia presented itself as a national state and was internationally recognized as such. In the *Memorandum Concerning Claims*, Yugoslav delegates stated that "Serbs, Croats and Slovenes constitute one nation which possesses its own civilization and spiritual unity." Consequently, the state has "national foundations" and in territorial claims asks for only "what belongs to it." The delegates concluded that "the principle of nationality and the right of people for self-determination represent the basis of our State." Yugoslavia found strong arguments to support her rights, in spite of the soon revealed fact that the country's population was multinational. The lack of national homogeneity became the cause of weakness in further international politics. The idea of a Yugoslav community, however, contributed to the new state's appearance as a factor in international relationships.

The first Yugoslav state was included in the European bourgeois and capitalistic system, although the appearance of the USSR, born in the 1917 Revolution, had already offered a socialistic alternative, at least in historical terms. Yugoslavia was based on previous economic, social and political developments and, consequently, asked for support from the West European powers. The new state had economic, political and cultural ties with these Western nations. Relations with the USSR were insignificant until 1940. The Yugoslav state, therefore, based its foreign policy on the framework of middle-class liberalism. President Wilson and his position in the field of ideology played a large role in this regard. In spite of some waverings from 1935 to 1941, Yugoslavia went through the two interwar decades with this ideology.

At Paris, Yugoslavia considered itself to be a small state. The awareness of being "small" contributed to concerns dealing with guarding its independence. These concerns resulted in the conviction that it was necessary to obtain large frontiers and as many rich areas as possible at Paris. These same concerns also resulted in the conviction that it was necessary to find a strong ally among the great powers which would support and not jeopardize Yugoslav independence.

The slogan "the Balkans for the Balkan peoples" essentially developed out of this perceived weakness. Consequently the Yugoslav delegation at the conference stressed the desire that none of the great powers obtain territories in the Balkans. This policy was primarily directed against Italy and its endeavors to establish itself in the Balkans and to surround Yugoslavia with dissatisfied neighbors. Considering the fact that the influence of the great powers could not be completely removed from the peninsula due to their political, economic and cultural positions, these trends were transformed into a policy of promoting the pluralistic presence of the great powers, without simultaneously accepting great power territorial acquisitions in the Balkans. It aimed at cancelling or at least limiting great power influence. For this reason, Beograd continually attempted to find support in Paris and then in London, in spite of the crisis which this policy experienced on the eve of and at the beginning of World War Two.

Yugoslav policy was based upon the idea that since Yugoslavia had originated as a result of World War One, the peace treaties which brought the war to a close had to be protected. Yugoslavia, then, became a natural opponent to any restoration of the Habsburg dynasty and of any Danubian federation. Yugoslavia also opposed Magyar, Bulgarian, German as well as Italian revisionism. This orientation naturally led to an interest in close collaboration with France and Great Britain. Yugoslavia saw itself as a barrier to eventual attempts by the German Reich to reach the Middle East. The government made clear in the *Memorandum Concerning Claims* that "the peace must protect Western Europe from any future attack coming from Germany, which will try without a doubt to again fulfill her plans to push across the Balkans towards the Persian Gulf and India." It was further emphasized that "the Yugoslavs maintain the same ardent wish to oppose such a German invasion." The document made clear that "based on traditional, political and military factors, our people will certainly remain the most reliable opponents to German penetration towards the East and the Far East."

The basic premises of Yugoslavia's relations with her neighbors, which were to last until World War Two, were established at the Paris Peace Conference. Italy remained the most dangerous threat to the Yugoslav state throughout this period. Relations with Hungary and Bulgaria were rather cool. In spite of serious disputes over the Banat in 1919, relations with Romania remained relatively good. As early as February 1919 Pašić had stated that "the common interest and friendship existing between the Romanian and Serbian peoples is so important for the future that a solution must be found to satisfy both countries." In his *Memorandum* Pašić emphasized the wish to avoid anything "which could trouble the friendship which binds us to our Romanian neighbor." This explains the rapid improvement in Yugoslav-Romanian relations from the fall of 1919 and the beginning of their long alliance in the Little Entente. Relations with Greece were good during the conference and remained friendly. The opinion of General Pešić that the country should have asked for rectification of borders with Greece was not acted upon and did not influence relations. The 1919–1920 attitude towards Albania continued until 1939 and was marked by hegemonistic tendencies and territorial aspirations. All of the elements of Yugoslav foreign policy had existed before the war but were essentially confirmed at the Peace Conference. On that occasion these elements acquired new features which were to remain a part of Yugoslav foreign policy throughout the interwar period.

b) *Specifics of the geo-political situation.*

The Peace Conference confirmed the geo-political position of Yugoslavia. From the Karavanke mountains to the Kajmakčalan range, and from the Stara Planina to the Adriatic sea, Yugoslavia penetrated into Central Europe with its northern provinces, into the Aegean area with its southern regions and was connected with the Mediterranean by its long Adriatic Coast. The valleys of the six greatest South Eastern European rivers (Danube, Tisza, Drava, Sava, Morava, Vardar—only the Maritza was not included) are partially or totally within Yugoslav frontiers. Of special significance is the communication line along the Morava and Vardar (Axios) with the addition of the Morava-Nišava branch leading over the Maritza towards Istanbul. With this geographical position, Yugoslavia was directly connected to the historical crosscurrents between Europe, the Mediterranean and the Middle East. It must be kept in mind, therefore, that the Paris Peace Conference merely sanctioned the historical reality which had been established and carried out by the Yugoslavs themselves.

The Conference's decisions confirmed the fact that Yugoslavia was located in an area characterized as multinational. This consideration stamped the phases of Habsburg dissolution at the end of World War One. The area was filled with small to middle-sized states. This situation enabled the great powers to constantly renew their attempts to penetrate into the region.

The multilateral organization of the area resulted from its multinational composition. Each nation differed in regard to its distinct origin (Slav, Roman, Hungarian, Hellenistic). Throughout its long history, the area experienced a series of succeeding empires. History also left the mark of three basic religions which still exist today: Catholic, Orthodox and Muslim. All of these factors contributed to divisions, separatism and even animosity among the South-Eastern European states as they entered the modern period. The sources of conflict survived despite the fact that these states possessed similar historic traditions which they used in their attempts to achieve independence and fight against external centers of power. It was in this uneasy framework that Yugoslavia was confirmed at the Peace Conference as the second largest state in the Balkans.

Notes

1. The paper is based on primary sources which can be found in the files of the *Diplomatski arhiv Saveznog Sekretarijata za inostrane poslove u Beogradu,* fond Mirovne delegacije Kraljevine SHS no konferenciji mira 1919–1920 godine. (Diplomatic Archives of the Federal Secretariat for Foreign Affairs, The Peace Delegation of the Kingdom of Serbs, Croats and Slovenes at the Peace Conference 1919–1920). Important sources can be also found in: Vojna misija pri delegaciji Kraljevine SHS na konferenciji mira 1919–1920, in: *Arhiv Vojno-Istorijskog Instituta u Beogradu* (Archives of Military-History Institute) and the Papers of Ante Trumbić, in: *Arhiv Historijskog Instituta Jugoslavenske akadamije nauka i umjetnosti-Zagreb* (Archives of the Yugoslav Academy of Sciences and Arts in Zagreb).

The most important Yugoslav published sources and studies concerning the Peace conference are as follows (not included in the bibliography made by M. Gunzenhäuser, *Die Pariser Friedenskonferenz 1919 und die Friedens Verträge 1919–1920,* Frankfurt a.M. 1970):

a) *Publications of experts, members of the Delegation of the Kingdom SHS at the Peace Conference.* The experts for ethnography, ethnology and history among the Yugoslav delegates published numerous works containing significant documents to support territorial claims. These works made an interesting and very abundant collection of sources. (See: N. Radojčić, "Literatura o Vojvodini pisana za strance," (N. Radojčić, Literature about Vojvodina Written for Foreigners), in: *Letopis Matice srpske,* knj. 300, 473–475.

Questions related to Banat, Bačka and Baranja were dealt with in various studies by J. Cvijić, J. Radonjić, St. Stanojević, I. Zeremski, A. Belić and S. Mihaldžić. J. Cvijić, M. Brezigar, L. Erlich, I. Žolgar, N. Županić and M. Slavić were involved with studies concerning Mura (Prekomurje) and Koruška. Studies about Trieste, Istria, Rijeka and the Eastern Adriatic were written by F. Šišić, L. Vojnović, R. Lenac, N. Zic, G. Gregorin, I. Ribarić and A. Belić. Andrija Radović dealt with Scutari while B. Popović considered Bulgarian pretensions. Tihomir Djordjević opposed Rumanian assertions on national rights in Eastern Serbia on two occasions. Stanoje Stanojević and Jovan Radonić published two separate brochures concerning the history of the Serbs in Hungary. In this respect we would point especially to the extensive brochures such as those by J. Cvijić, *Frontière septentrionale des Yougoslaves,* Paris 1919, F. Šišić, *Aperçu de l'histoire du littoral orientale de l'Adriatique,* Paris 1919, and St. Stanojević, *Le problème Yougoslave,* Paris 1919. The later J. Cvijić study "Granice i sklop naše zemlje" (The Frontiers and the Structure of Our Land), in: *Srpski Književni Glasnik,* 1 and 16 December 1920, was not only a synthesis of Cvijić's views but also represented the views of the Yugoslav delegates at the Conference.

These works were published primarily in French, though some did appear in English. They were later translated into Serbo-Croatian.

b) *Memoirs.* One Yugoslav delegate published his memoirs: *Zapisi Dr Josipa Smodlake* (Notes of Dr Josip Smodlaka), Zagreb 1972. Dr Ante Trumbić expressed his views in a brief exposé: "O rešenju Jadranskog pitanja, Izveštaj dra Anta Trumbića u Opštinskom Kazalištu u Splitu dne 5 decembra 1920," (The Report of Dr Ante Trumbić at the Communal Theatre in Split on December 5, 1920), in: *Novo Doba,* 6 December 1920. The first to publish his reminiscences concerning territorial delimitation, however, was St. Stanojević, "Vojvodina na Konferenciji mira" (Vojvodina at the Peace Conference), in:

Letopis Matice Srpske, knj. 300, 81–91. He was followed by another expert, S. Mihaldžić, "Uspomene na rad i dogadjaje u Baranji i većim mestima Vojvodine" (Memoirs relating to the activity and the events concerning Baranja and larger cities in Vojvodina), in: *Spomenica oslobodjenja Vojvodine*, Novi Sad 1929, 81–91. Jovan Cvijić also published some of his personal reminiscences on Woodrow Wilson and the Peace Conference in the *Srpski Književni Glasnik*, 16 March 1924, 447–456 (The speech made at the solemn meeting of the Serbian Academy of Sciences). Mihailo Pupin in his *Od pašnjaka do naučnika* (From Pastures to Scholarship) only rarely touches on his activity at the conference.

c) *Official Documents*. The most important collection of sources is *Zapisnici sa sednica Delegacije Kraljevine SHS no Konferenciji mira u Parizu 1919–1920*, published by B. Krizman and B. Hrabak, Beograd 1960. Many important documents of special significance are included in the footnotes and annexes. There is a supplementary manuscript now prepared for publication: A. Mitrović-Lj. Tgrovčević, *Zapisnici sa sednica etnografsko-istorijske sekcije pri mirovnoj delegaciji Kraljevine SHS 1919 i druga akta za rad eksperata 1919–1920* (to be published by Istorijski Institut u Novom Sadu). The same could be said for the already published sources by B. Krizman, *Diplomatska prepiska predstavnika Kraljevine SHS na Pariškoj mirovnoj konferenciji (5 januar 1919–20 juni 1919)*, (Diplomatic Correspondence), in: *Glasnik Arhiva i Društva arhivista Bosne i Hercegovine*, II-2 (1962), 335–392. Ibid., *Zapisnici sednica Davidovićeve vlade od avgusta 1919 do februara 1920*, in: Arhivski vjesnik, XIII (1970), 7–92.

Most of the published sources dealing with the frontier question concentrate on the problem of Yugoslav-Italian delimitation. The first collection published by the Yugoslavs refers to this problem: Adriaticus, *La question adriatique, Recueil de documents officieles*, Paris 1920. It contains documents of importance concerning the work of the conference and was made public as early as 1919 and 1920. The collection had the obvious purpose to support Yugoslav politics in the question of delimitation on the Adriatic. Archival research shows that the pseudonym Adriaticus was used by O. Ribarž, who ranked seventh among Yugoslav political delegates. Also significant is F. Šišić's work *Jadransko pitanje na konferenciji mira, Zbirka akata i dokumenata* (The Adriatic Question at the Peace Conference, Collection of Acts and Documents), Zagreb 1920. The brochure Adriaticus, *Jadransko pitanje* (The Adriatic Question), Beograd 1925 written by Lujo Vojnović, is not significant except for some hitherto unknown documents (for example, the parts of the minutes of the meetings of the Yugoslav delegation at the conference). The brochure deals totally with political disputes between Pašić and Trumbić. Also of use is a manuscript which is a collection of documents by M. Antić, *O jadranskom pitanju* (about the Adriatic Question) now in the State Archives of Serbia (under sign. Varia-65).

Specific documents published by B. Krizman, Pisma Anta Trumbića I. Krstelju also belong in this general framework (Letters of A. Trumbić to I. Krstelj) in: *Historijski Pregled*, 1959, no. 4, 354–369, and 1960, no. 1, 59–68, then Zabilješka o razgovoru predsednika Wilsona s predstavnicima Slovenaca (Pariz 25 aprila 1919) (Note concerning the Conversation of President Wilson with the Slovenian Representatives) in: *Zgodovinaki Casopis*, XVII, 1963, 219–224, and Četiri pisma Ante Trumbića Ljubi Davidoviću o jadranskom pitanju (1919) (Four letters of Ante Trumbić to Lj. Davidović concerning the Adriatic Question), in *Mogućnosti*, 1968, no. 2, 222–233. Also of interest is the document which D. Zivojinović published under the title "General Pietro Badoglio's Political Instructions for the Occupied Territories," in: *East European Quarterly*, June 1968, 197–203.

Historiography: Studies published in Yugoslavia after World War Two concerning the Paris Peace Conference are registered in three retrospective bibliographies: *Dix années d'historiographie yougoslave, Beograd 1955; Historiographie yougoslave 1955–1965*, Beograd 1965; *The Historiography of Yougoslavia 1965–1975*, Beograd 1975. Further extensive literature can be found in two special studies dealing with the subject: Ivo J. Lederer, *Yugoslavia at the Paris Peace Conference*, New Haven 1963, and Andrej Mitrović, *Jugoslavija no konferenciji mira* (Yugoslavia at the Peace Conference), Beograd 1969.

Contributors

HENRIK BIRNBAUM is a professor in comparative Slavic linguistics, and medieval and renaissance Slavic literature at the University of California, Los Angeles, and was until 1978 the Director of the Center for Russian and East European Studies at that institution. He was awarded a Ph.D. in Slavic Languages and Literature by Stockholm University.

DIMITRIJE DJORDJEVIC is a professor in the history department at the University of California, Santa Barbara, where he teaches nineteenth- and twentieth-century Balkan history. He was until 1970 senior staff member of the Institute for Balkan Studies, Serbian Academy of Sciences and Arts in Beograd, Yugoslavia. He was awarded a Ph.D. in history by Beograd University.

DOMNA VISVIZI DONTAS is a collaborator of the Institute for Balkan Studies, Thessaloniki, Greece. She holds a London University Ph.D. in history. Dr. Dontas, the Director of the Greek Diplomatic Archives, is now Deputy Permanent Delegate of Greece to UNESCO.

ALEX N. DRAGNICH is professor emeritus at Vanderbilt University, Nashville, Tennessee, where he taught comparative politics. He was awarded his Ph.D. by the University of California, Berkeley.

MILORAD EKMEČIĆ is a professor of history at the Sarajevo University, Sarajevo, Yugoslavia, where he teaches modern European history. He is a member of the Academy of Sciences of Bosnia and Hercegovina. His Ph.D. was conferred by Beograd University.

FRITZ FELLNER is a professor of history, University of Salzburg, Austria. In 1978 he was the first Austrian guest professor holding the Austrian chair at Stanford University.

JOHN R. LAMPE is associate professor of history, University of Maryland, College Park, where he teaches European economic and modern Balkan history. His Ph.D. in history was granted by the University of Wisconsin.

ANDREJ MITROVIĆ is a professor of history at the University of Beograd, Yugoslavia, where he teaches twentieth century European history. His Ph.D. was conferred by the University of Beograd.

MICHAEL B. PETROVICH teaches Russian and Balkan history at the University of Wisconsin, where he is a professor of history. His Ph.D. was awarded by Columbia University.

GALE STOKES teaches modern Balkan history at Rice University, Houston, Texas, where he is an associate professor of history. His Ph.D. in history was conferred by the University of Indiana.

WAYNE VUCINICH is professor emeritus at Stanford University. Chairman of the Center for Russian and East European Studies and Robert and Florence McDonnell Professor of East European History at Stanford. He got his Ph.D. in history at the University of California, Berkeley.

Index

Adriatic, 28, 29, 31, 53, 54, 55–56, 57, 60, 65, 75, 84, 105, 211
Aegean Islands, 97–98, 102–103, 112, 117; *see also* Corfu
agrarian reform, postwar. *See* Kingdom of the Serbs, Croats and Slovenes
Albania, 26, 28–29, 96. 99. 101, 103, 117, 184, 212; Albanian Committee, 28
Alexander I (Karadjordević), Prince of Serbia, 37, 195
Alexander (Karadjordjević), Prince Regent of Serbia, 20, 39, 45, 46–48, 57, 59, 64, 65, 97, 111–112, 116, 187, 190–195, 199; *see also* Karadjordjević dynasty; Serbia
Allies, 19, 20, 23–24, 27, 29–31, 40–41, 43–44, 46, 51, 53, 55–56, 59–60, 63, 66, 75–77, 86–89, 100–117, 127, 194–195; defeated at Dardanelles, 110; secret negotiations, 126–127; Supreme Allied War Council, 62, 184; war aims, 87; *see also* France, Great Britain, Russia
Apis, Colonel Dragutin Dimitrijević-, 47, 57, 59; *see also* Serbia, army
Appearing Nation, The, 23
armed bands, postwar, 88, 184–186
Austria, 6, 7, 28, 38, 76, 100, 107
Austria-Hungary, 11, 12, 19, 23, 28–29, 39–40, 42, 43–44, 51–53, 56–57, 59, 63, 73–75, 86–89, 95, 97–98, 103–104, 183, 201; ultimatum to Serbia, 74; *see also* Habsburg empire

Bača, 40, 85
Balflour, British Foreign Minister, 63
Balkan Peninsula, The, 21
Balkans, 2, 7, 8–9, 12, 13, 22, 24, 27, 29, 30–31, 41, 53, 59, 74, 79, 81, 95–101, 127, 158–161, 215; Balkan

League, 95; "Balkans for the Balkan people," 212–213
Banat, the, 31, 40, 47, 77, 85, 211, 214
Bauer, Otto, 22
Belgrade (Beograd), 12, 45, 52, 65, 80, 88, 96, 104, 187, 191–192, 210
Belić, Aleksandar, 21–23, 55, 76, 80
Berlin, 20
Bissolati, 62, 127
Bolsheviks, 83, 87–89, 197–198; use of "Bolsheviki peril," 134, 197; *see also* communists
Bosnia, 8, 9, 11, 12, 26, 28, 31, 41, 55, 65, 163, 176, 184–186; *see also* Bosnia-Hercegovina
Bosnia-Hercegovina, 37, 39, 44, 45, 47, 76, 85, 87, 99, 163, 164, 175–176; *see also* South Slavs
Brest-Litovsk peace negotiations, 84, 86; *see also* Soviet Decree of Peace
Bucharest Peace Treaty. *See* treaties, Bucharest Treaty of 1913; Bucharest Treaty of 1916
Bulgaria, 20, 27–31, 54, 56, 57, 73, 77, 80–81, 85, 95–117, 160, 173–174, 185, 211, 213; Bulgars, 2, 8–9, 80 (language. *See* language, Bulgarian); Macedonians in, 28; revolution and defeat, 116; and Serbia; 107–111; wanted in World War I by Allies, 40
Buxton, Noel, 23

Cemović, Marko, 78
Central Powers, 39, 63, 86–88, 101, 103; *see also* Germany; Austria-Hungary
Charles, Emperor of Austria-Hungary, 59, 63; *see also* Habsburg empire, monarchy
class conflict, 88
Committee of Five. *See* proposals for union

DATE DUE

GAYLORD			PRINTED IN U.S.A.